MANAGERIAL PSYCHOLOGY

MANAGERIAL

PSYCHOLOGY

An Introduction to Individuals, Pairs, and Groups in Organizations

By Harold J. Leavitt

 THE UNIVERSITY OF CHICAGO PRESS

Library of Congress Catalog Number: 58-5679

THE UNIVERSITY OF CHICAGO PRESS, CHICAGO 37
Cambridge University Press, London, N.W. 1, England
The University of Toronto Press, Toronto 5, Canada

© *1958 by The University of Chicago. Published 1958*
Third Impression 1959. Composed and printed by THE
UNIVERSITY OF CHICAGO PRESS, *Chicago, Illinois, U.S.A.*

This book is intended both for people who already know something of managerial life and for those about to commit themselves to it. It is not so much a description of what happens to people in management as an attempt to account for some of the things that happen.

The title "Managerial Psychology" was chosen to indicate that the book is not chiefly about hourly workers or union-management relationships. It is mostly about human problems within the supervisory and management ranks. Applied social scientists have been focusing their interest on management more and more since the war, with correspondingly less emphasis on the organization and motivation of hourly workers. I do not wish to evaluate this shift of interest, only to point it out and to point out that this book goes along with it.

I have used the phrase "human relations" sparingly, being careful to keep it out of the title altogether. I have avoided it, not because I am against it, but because its boundaries are fuzzy, especially at the places where it touches important value areas like "democracy." If this book preaches any social values, democratic or otherwise, they have crept in unwittingly. My purpose here has been to describe and organize data and ideas.

The book begins with an examination of the individual and his behavior, i.e., with the way people tick. The second part is concerned with influence in face-to-face situations, with the problem of getting other people to tick differently. The third section covers committees and small groups and the special problems encountered by management people trying to tick effectively together. The fourth section is about the nature of business organizations and some of the problems that seem to arise only in large organizations. Some questions for discussion about each chapter are grouped in a body after Part IV. They are followed by a section of notes and references.

Dividing the material in this way appears reasonable both because it allows for systematic development from the single person on up to the large mass of people and because it covers the major categories of personal and social problems that modern managers are likely to meet. For the manager seems to be faced, first, with the problem of using himself to solve problems in a sea of industrial stresses; second, with the problem of coping with specific individuals who may or may not help him satisfy his needs and do his job; third, with the problem of utilizing groups of people in teams and committees, groups whom he must lead and stimulate; and, finally, with the problem of motivating and coordinating the efforts of large groups who work "under" him, but whom he seldom encounters face to face.

The decision to emphasize the theoretical, and thereby to allow only secondary emphasis on the "practical," was not taken lightly. My task was to try to design a book that would be useful to both actual and potential industrial people (i.e., a practical book) and that would also do reasonable justice to the social sciences. So I have chosen to emphasize theory but to present it in a way that is as simple, straightforward, and practical as I can make it. I have tried to do this by using illustrations, by working most points from the specific to the general, by sliding lightly over some areas that are too complicated to handle, by limiting footnotes, references, and sources of evidence (for which I beg my colleagues' indulgence), and by periodically devoting particular chapters to special industrial problems in order to illustrate the way theory can be used.

Several people who are entirely innocent of responsibility for this book have nevertheless influenced it considerably. The Massachusetts Institute of Technology team (now scattered) of Douglas McGregor, Irving Knickerbocker, Alex Bavelas, and Mason Haire will surely see much of their effect. My three years with Leo Nejelski in Nejelski and Company left their impression too. More recently I have been much impressed by developments in information theory and the model-building approaches to organizations developed at Carnegie Institute of Technology. Even though I am far from expert, I have tried to integrate some of these points of view into the book because I feel they are critically important.

I am grateful to the *Journal of Business* and *Personnel* for permission to use portions of my papers that originally appeared in those journals.

This book was written while I was on the faculty of the School of Business, University of Chicago. My thanks go to my former colleagues there for their stimulating criticisms of parts of the manuscript; to students in the University of

Chicago's Executive Program, on whom the manuscript was tried out as a text; to Miss Naomi Shoop and her staff (especially Walter Paichel) for their work on the preliminary manuscript; and to my wife, who really tore into the final version.

HAROLD J. LEAVITT

CONTENTS

CONTENTS

x

Contents

Part I

PEOPLE ONE AT A TIME
THE UNITS OF MANAGEMENT

In these next several chapters the reader will find a presentation of the concepts of human behavior that seem most relevant to managerial problems. Such consideration of people and their behavior seems a prerequisite to any conscious attempt to learn how better to "manage" people. "Conscious" is a key word, because many persons (including many businessmen), are extremely skilful managers even though they go about their activities more or less intuitively. Those of us who are not so gifted need to think out loud about human relations and about ourselves as mechanisms for solving business problems.

Although the book as a whole purports to deal with problems of management, this first section focuses almost entirely on the individual human being. The reasons for this "impractical" digression are several: First, the characteristics of people in general are a good base from which to build up to the characteristics of people in industry. Second, managers, unlike parents, must work with used, not new, human beings—human beings whom other people have gotten to first. Third, the manager is his own best management mechanism. An examination of his own makeup should therefore be useful to him.

Part I is designed as follows: It starts with some fundamental assumptions about what is "true" of all people everywhere. It moves then to a more detailed examination of the ways people differ from one another and some of the sources of those differences. Next, personality differences and their influence on the ways people see and deal with other things and other people are considered. Two chapters deal with the problem of *pressure*—the effects of frustration and conflict on behavior. One chapter is concerned with conscious problem solving, the everyday life of the manager. Finally one long chapter is given over to the practical problem of assessing people for particular assignments.

The goal of this section is both to simplify and complicate the reader's picture of people—to simplify by systematizing and interrelating some basic ideas (most of which are not new) and to complicate by pointing out the infinite shades of gray and the multitude of interacting variables that can occur in the behaving human organism.

Chapter 1

PEOPLE ARE ALIKE
SOME BASIC IDEAS

Businessmen's decisions, like other people's, are usually based on some combination of fact and theory. They are choices made by interpreting things observed in the light of things believed. And in most of their decisions businessmen are reasonably aware of the particular beliefs they are using in interpreting the facts they observe. They take supply and demand ideas into account in making marketing decisions, for example. And they often use high-level technical theory in attacking engineering and production problems.

Businessmen also use theory in dealing with human problems. But in the human area theorizing seems to be much more implicit or even unconscious. The theories of human behavior that businessmen hold seem also to be much more diverse than their economic and engineering theories, perhaps because they are much more the private property of individual executives. Here, for instance, are some pairs of theoretical assertions that have been made by business executives. Each of them necessarily reflects some basic assumptions about the nature of man:

People are basically lazy; or, People just want a chance to
show what they can do.

Always be careful of an executive who loses his temper;
or, Watch out for the man who never loses his temper.

A good salesman sells himself before his product; or, A
good product sells itself.

If you give people a finger they'll take the whole arm; or,
Kindness begets kindness.

Men need to know exactly what their jobs are; or, Men
will work best when they can make their own jobs.

Each of these statements (and the list is not at all exhaustive) is either an assumption about the nature of people or
a derivation from such an assumption. Each is a flat, unequivocal generalization, much like the statement, "Air is
lighter than water."

The fact that many of these generalizations contradict
one another suggests that they cannot all be right and therefore raises difficult questions of proof and consistency. This
section of this book does not aim to prove that some are
true and some are false. What it does aim to do is to provide a set of internally *consistent* generalizations; generalizations that should be *useful* in predicting human behavior,
whether they are fundamentally true or not.

All of us seem to make some kind of generalizations about
people, and this is important in deciding what is "practical"
and what is "only theoretical." Managers have a reputation
for practicality and hardheadedness, a reputation fledgling
managers may mistakenly equate with entirely concrete and
non-general thinking. Yet statements like those above are
extremely general, extremely theoretical. They may express
poor theory, but they point up the need for theoretical generalizations to serve as a foundation for practicality. Some

kind of psychological theory is just as necessary for the manager dealing with human problems as is electrical and mechanical theory for the engineer dealing with machine problems. Without theory the engineer has no way of diagnosing what might be wrong when the engine stops, no way of pre-estimating the effects of a proposed change in design. Without some kind of psychological theory, the manager cannot attach meaning to the red flags of human disturbance; nor can he predict the likely effects of changes in organization or personnel policy.

The particular theoretical position outlined in these early chapters will not be new to most readers. Most of us already accept it but often do not use it. If it is good theory it should lead to useful predictions. Incidentally, if it is good theory it may not necessarily be true theory. No one knows whether some of the things said here are true or false. The reader can decide for himself whether or not they are useful.

Three Basic Assumptions about People

Suppose we asked this question of many kinds of people: "What are the fundamental, unexceptionable truths of human behavior?" Suppose one asked it of college students, union members, top- and middle-level managers, foremen, salesmen, nurses, and housewives. The answers would include generalizations like these:

People are products of their environment.
People want security.
All people want is bread and butter.
People are fundamentally lazy.
People are fundamentally selfish.
People only do what they have to do.
People are creatures of habit.

People are products of their heredity.

Some of these answers, like the generalizations we talked about earlier, seem to contradict others, but at another level the contradictions disappear. If one organizes them, one comes out with essentially the same generalizations that many modern psychologists would offer. For three major ideas are implicit in that list:

The first is the idea of *causality*, the idea that human behavior is caused, just as the behavior of physical objects is caused by forces that act on those physical objects. Causality is implicit in the beliefs that environment and heredity affect behavior and that what is outside influences what is inside.

Second, there is the idea of *directedness*, the idea that human behavior is not only caused but is also pointed toward something, that behavior is goal directed, that people want things.

Third, the list includes the concept of *motivation*, that underlying behavior one finds a "push" or a "motive" or a "want" or a "need" or a "drive."

These three ideas can provide the beginning of a system for conceptualizing human behavior. With the help of these ideas, human behavior can be viewed as part of a double play from cause to motive to behavior-toward-a-goal. And it is also helpful to think of the three as generally forming a closed circuit. Arrival at a goal eliminates the cause, which eliminates the motive, which eliminates the behavior. Thus, for instance, a man's stomach is empty; the emptiness stimulates impulses interpreted as "feeling hungry"; the feeling of hunger stimulates action in the direction of food; he gets food. The food fills his stomach, causing cessation of the "feeling hungry" impulses, which in turn eliminates the behavior in search of food.

This closed circuit conception includes one major danger. Many "psychological" as distinct from "physical" goals are not finite and specific. One can consume a specific quantity of food and thereby temporarily stop feeling hungry for more. It is doubtful, however, that one can consume a specific quantity of prestige, for instance, and feel sated. Prestige and other "psychological" goals seem to be ephemeral and boundless; enough may never be obtained to inactivate the causes and hence the motive.

The Person

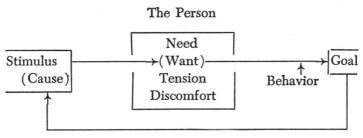

FIG. 1.—A basic model of behavior

These assumptions of causality, motivation, and direction are nevertheless useful assumptions if they are accepted as unexceptionable. Causality, motivation, and direction can be thought of as applying equally to all people, of all ages, in all cultures, at all times. When one makes such assumptions they should lead one, upon observing human behavior, always to seek motive and, behind motive, cause.

There are many different perspectives on these assumptions, but the basic assumptions remain intact. For example, one can say that behavior is an attempt to get rid of tension. Tension then equals motivation; and the objective of behavior is to eliminate the necessity for behaving. Words like "motives" or "needs" or "drives" are rough synonyms for each other as well as for words like "tensions" or "discomforts" or "disequilibriums." Behavior is thus seen as an effort to eliminate tensions by seeking goals that neutralize the causes of tensions.

Thinking about motivation in terms of tension and discomfort inside the person is useful in another way. It puts the emphasis on the *push* from inside the person rather than on the *pull* from outside. Managers, for instance, often encounter problems with subordinates who "don't know what they want." They feel restless and disturbed but can't seem to say what it is they are after. Most of us behave this way a good deal of the time, feeling the push of tension from inside but not being able to identify the precise goal that would eliminate the tension. We search vaguely, trying one job or another, one boss or another, one idea or another, until—if we are lucky—we hit on something that does the trick. Only then may we be able to tie up that particular feeling of tension with some specific goal, so that next time we can head directly for where we want to go. The baby, after all, doesn't start out saying, "I want a bottle." He starts out saying, "I feel discomfort somewhere inside." He then goes on to try all the different behaviors he can muster until he discovers that the bottle eliminates that particular discomfort. Only then can he identify this goal and narrow down his behavior so that he can get to his goal without exhausting himself.

But no matter how one views these concepts, they suggest that the ultimate condition of man can be thought of as an equilibrium condition in which he need not behave. This ultimate will be unattainable so long as one fly after another goes on landing on man's rump to stir up some new need and to force him to go on swishing his tail.

Of course the same landscape can be drawn from a brighter perspective. The tendency not to behave unless one has to can also account for man's capacity to learn. It can account for the baby's ability to become an increasingly efficient food finder. The diffuse kicking, squalling, and rolling give way over a few years to the simpler and more efficient behavior of learning to find and open the cookie jar. If people were not thus naturally stingy in their expenditures of energy, if they did not abhor unnecessary effort, if they were not lazy, then their factories would probably be no more efficient today than they were fifty years ago, if the factories existed at all.

This picture leaves no room for purely "self-starting" behavior. Something must always show up to stimulate needs. Nor does it allow for the idea of "habit," if habit means uncaused or undirected repetitive behavior. If the word "habit" is to fit here, it will have to mean something like "characteristic ways of trying to satisfy certain needs." The disorderly file clerk is not, then, just disorderly because he has disorderly habits. He is disorderly because he has learned to try to satisfy his needs by what we consider disorderly means. Nor is the inmate of the booby hatch just a different kind of human being from those on the outside. He is in there because his best methods for satisfying his needs have landed him there.

So these three assumptions (cause, motivation, direction) become theoretical starting points. Perhaps they are worth careful thought. For the reader should consider the implications of these ideas for such concepts as "free will," "habit," and "insane behavior." Accepting these assumptions will probably require some revision of the usual meaning of these ideas.

In Summary

This chapter has made three interrelated assumptions about human behavior:

1. Behavior is caused.
2. Behavior is motivated.
3. Behavior is goal directed.

In the process some alternative assumptions have been implicitly discarded. We have discarded the ideas that behavior is "self-starting" and that it is "random," i.e., that it is going nowhere, for no reason.

Moreover, the three assumptions are assumed to be interrelated in a circular sequence: from cause to motivation to goal direction. Arrival at the goal inactivates the cause, and hence eliminates the motive, and hence eliminates the goal-directed behavior; although some goals may not be finite.

Many different words can be used to deal with these three ideas. Words like "drive," "tension," "need," and "disequilibrium," for example, are all approximate synonyms for the word "motive."

Chapter 2

PEOPLE ARE DIFFERENT
THE GROWTH OF INDIVIDUALITY

While people are alike, they are also different. They are alike in that their behavior is caused, motivated, and goal directed and their physical equipment is roughly similar. They are different to the extent that they are subject to different kinds of stimulation, that they vary in kinds and degrees of motivation, that they behave in many different ways to achieve many different goals, and that they have different sizes and powers in their physical equipment. The purpose of this chapter is to try to account (only at the broadest level) for the range and kinds of differences that every manager has observed among those around him.

The Range of Motives

Consider the variety of motives which seem to occur in human behavior. Consider, for example, the class of behavior called "work." What are the motives for work; what are the tensions or discomforts that people try to eliminate through work? Why should people sacrifice so much of the good life to walk into the plant morning after morning, year after year? Clearly, different individuals will give different answers to such questions, and each answer may be perfectly true for each person. Clearly, too, any single individual may come up with a variety of motives to fit his particular case. Direct questioning of a random portion of the American population would certainly include such answers as these:

I work for money and the food, shelter, and goods money buys.

I work for status and recognition.

I work to belong; to be part of a group.

I work to get to the top.

I work because it's only right that people should work.

I work for knowledge and understanding.

I work for security.

I work for the feeling of accomplishment I get from a job well done.

This list is not exhaustive. Some of the statements are concrete and specific; others are vague and shadowy. Some seem to overlap one another in meaning. Perhaps the reader will, nevertheless, go along with the generalization that most people work for some variety of reasons like these and that most people would also be willing to do some work for almost any one of the reasons listed, even if the others did not exist. But perhaps before he will go along, the reader may want to add at least one qualification: these motives may be real only for *most people in America this year*. Although some of them may be universal, others may be specific to our culture or to certain subgroups within our culture. This would be a valid qualification.

The Classes of Needs

Looking back over the list of motives, one can classify them into at least two major groups. Some arise from needs that are essentially physical and "basic": needs for food, for water, for warmth. One could add others: needs to urinate, to defecate, to sleep, and so on. These are clear-cut, unambiguous needs; they are physiological; they are universal; they are present in infants as well as adults; they are even present in most other classes of animals. They seem unquestionably to be part of the person's original inborn equipment.

The second large class of needs, however, is less easily definable. Needs for achievement, status, and "belongingness" are much more "psychological," more clearly limited to human beings, and for the most part not immediately observable in the newborn. They also seem highly individualistic—much more so than the basic physical needs. They seem to be present to an extreme degree in some people and almost non-existent in others. We do not ordinarily characterize one another as "food seekers," but we do often characterize a person as a "power seeker" or a "prestige seeker." In fact, our judgment of the intensities of psychological needs in other people makes up a large part of our judgment of their personalities. Application blanks for industrial jobs seldom include questions about how much water a man drinks or how many sandwiches he eats for lunch. But they do include questions about his ambitions and his social interests.

It is in these so-called psychological needs that the bulk of industrially significant personality differences lies; we must try to account for the differential development of these needs in different individuals. This problem could lead us quickly into the question of the importance of heredity and environment, but that would be an unprofitable venture. If the reader prefers to believe that the psychological needs are acquired out of our environment, such a belief will not affect the position taken here. If he prefers to believe that the seeds of psychological needs lie in the genes and that environment only fertilizes and nurtures them, that position is also tenable.

Dependency and the Development of Personality

The most important issue seems to be this one: Can we, with as few assumptions as possible, account for the development of individually different adult personalities? For the back-slapping sales manager and the quick, methodical comptroller?

A theory, it has been said, is as good as its ratio of predictions to assumptions. To economize on assumptions, we may assume here that only the basic physical needs are inherited and then go on from there. It is then possible to account broadly for the elaborate complex of needs that exists in a twenty-year-old while assuming that all he had to begin with were (1) his basic physical needs and (2) his body. In his "body" we must include his sense organs, plus his memory—a mechanism for retaining information picked up by the sense organs—plus a decision-making mechanism, plus a tendency to be stingy in the expenditure of energy, plus a muscular system that allows the person to move and act upon his environment. If that is the person's original basic equipment, it is almost enough to account for the accessories he will have added by the time he is ten or twenty or forty. But he still needs one more characteristic, a characteristic that is not so much a part of the person as of the relationship between the person and the world. This additional characteristic is *dependency*—the dependency of the newborn infant on parents for the satisfaction of his needs; the dependency of the growing child on parents, teachers, and friends; of husband on wife; and of people in industry on their bosses; and vice versa.

If the human infant came into the world with almost complete physical development, like some other animal young, then we might have to devise quite a different theory to account for the adult personality. In fact, if the infant could fend for himself from the start, the adult personality would be noticeably different from what it is.

But any infant who survives to adulthood has necessarily passed through a period in which he was almost entirely dependent upon other people for the satisfaction of his basic physical needs. And this dependency, coupled with the presence of physical needs and a good but incomplete physical plant, may give us the leverage to account for the development of a great many secondary and tertiary mental needs. To see how this dependency lever might work, consider this entirely hypothetical illustration:

> Suppose that you suffer from a magical ailment. The major symptom of the ailment is paralysis—complete paralysis. But though you are paralyzed, your head is perfectly clear and your senses are perfectly keen. You can hear, you can see, you can feel, you can think—but you can't move.
>
> You have a brother who possesses a magical gift. Whenever his hand is on your shoulder you are cured; you can move as

well as anyone else. But when he takes his hand away the paralysis immediately returns.

Assume that your brother is a nice guy; he spends a good deal of his time with his hand on your shoulder, and he goes through considerable inconvenience to do this. Through his help you can lead something approximating a normal life. You have not had this disease very long, but by now you have gotten over the shock that it entailed, and you are trying to settle down to the best life you can work out.

This morning you awake, but of course you cannot move. You lie in bed until your brother comes in to put his hand on your shoulder. Whereupon you rise, dress, and wash. You have breakfast, chat, and read the morning paper. You do everything that you may have done before you had the disease.

Over breakfast your brother announces that he forgot to tell you he has a dentist's appointment this morning. He will have to leave the house about ten. He probably will not be back until noon. This is a matter of no great concern to you, since it's just a two-hour absence.

With his hand on your shoulder you arrange a comfortable place in which you can sit while your brother is gone. You set an easy chair by the window, put your feet on an ottoman, and tune in a radio to a program you particularly like. You open the window to let the warm air and sun in and to see what's going on outside. You settle down for the two-hour absence.

Your brother leaves.

For half an hour or so, as you expected, things are fine. You are perfectly comfortable; there's enough activity outdoors to keep you interested; and the radio program is good.

At ten-thirty the program changes to the thing you hate most—hillbilly music—but that's of no major concern. A fly manages to get through a hole in the screen and begins to buzz around your nose—but this is just one of those inconveniences you have now learned to bear.

By eleven o'clock there's a little itch from a rough place in the chair, but that's bearable, too. The fly is still around. The hillbilly music goes on. At eleven-thirty the sky clouds over. The air gets cold and windy. At a quarter to twelve it's raining hard. You're getting wet and cold. If you could shiver, you would. The itches increase. Your bladder begins to get a little too full for comfort.

But you reassure yourself: fifteen minutes more.

At noon you're waiting hopefully for your brother's step, but you don't hear it. He doesn't show at twelve-fifteen. The cold and the wet and the itches and the bladder and the fly and the radio become almost unbearable. By twelve-forty-five you're on the verge of explosion. One o'clock and no brother, but more rain, more discomfort.

At just about one-thirty you hear footfalls. Brother walks in, puts his hand on your shoulder, and says: "I was caught in a traffic jam. I'm sorry I'm late."

Now let the reader seriously ask himself these questions:

1. Just how would you *feel* about your brother at this moment?

2. What do you think you would *do* to your brother at this moment?

Your answers probably fall into one of these major categories: (1) I would feel angry and resentful. (2) I would feel extremely relieved; extremely grateful that he had finally arrived. (3) I would feel mixed up: angry and resentful, on the one hand, and relieved and grateful, on the other.

To the action question, answers range from: (1) I would sock him on the nose to (2) I would throw my arms around him and kiss him.

Each of these answers is appropriate and understandable. Together they represent the necessary conflict of feelings that derive from the complete dependency of one individual on another. The person who says he would feel angry and hostile will probably be ready to admit that those would be predominant but not exclusive feelings. While he feels angry, he may at the same time feel affectionate and grateful. The man who says he will feel grateful and relieved will probably admit that he is also angry and irritated. Some admixture of these almost polar feelings will probably be present in everyone. This is the peculiar phenomenon of *ambivalence,* of the simultaneous existence of opposite feelings in the same place at the same time.

Similarly, at the action level, the man who says, "I would sock my brother on the nose," might be willing to add, "But I might feel awfully sorry afterward." And the man who says, "I would throw my arms around him," might add that his embrace would include a touch of a bear hug.

Suppose further that this sort of incident happened often, for month after month. Might you then develop an increasing wish for independence from your brother? Might you also seek ways of controlling your brother, of "getting something on him," so that you would not have to count impotently on his good will? And suppose he was a particularly bad brother who didn't care much for you? Wouldn't that intensify your wishes for independence from him or power over him?

Extreme dependency thus serves as a lever for initiating other kinds of needs. To the extent that dependency yields ready satisfaction of existing needs that one cannot satisfy independently—to that extent one's feelings are likely to be positive, friendly, affectionate, protective, grateful, and one is likely to develop strong *social* needs. To the extent that dependency does not satisfy, but rather frustrates—to that extent one is likely to develop feelings of anger and hostility and to wish more strongly for independence and autonomy, to develop strong *egoistic* needs.

The infant suffers from this kind of magical paralysis. He is entirely dependent on adults for the satisfaction of his inborn physical needs. But because no parent can be entirely satisfying (or entirely frustrating), each child must necessarily develop some mixture of plus and minus feelings, first toward the parents and then, since the parents very often are the world, toward the world.

No parents can entirely satisfy or entirely frustrate an infant for these reasons: Infants who encounter only frustration in their very early attempts to satisfy their needs simply do not survive. Children who don't get fed die. At the other end of the scale, however, no infant can hope for perfect satisfaction. No parent has the prescience to foresee all the infant's wants before they arise or the patience to satisfy every want he does foresee. So no adult in the world grew up through complete frustration in infancy or through complete satisfaction.

The working range is the range between the extremes on the satisfaction-frustration scale. Parents can consciously or inadvertently work predominantly near one end of the scale or the other. And the extent to which the predominance actually is at one end or the other, together with the physiological givens, probably accounts for the *general* pattern of early personality development in any particular child. Teachers, bosses, and other people can perform in the same range later to finish off personality development.

To be more accurate, one can put it this way: Some infants face a world that is mostly non-satisfying, non-predictable, and non-controllable from the beginning. Some infants face a world that is more satisfying, more predictable, and more controllable. Children faced with an unpredictable and uncontrollable world are more likely to grow fearful and hostile early. They are more likely to wish strongly for independence. And they are more likely to be concerned with *egoistic* needs, with mechanisms by which independence may be gained, i.e., with power, ingratiation, acquisition of goods, and so on.

On the other hand, children whose early years are mostly satisfying are more likely to be secure and dependent. They are more likely to develop predominantly *social* needs, with only secondary concern (unless they learn it later) about autonomy and independence.

These acquired sets of feelings can now be thought of as two new classes of learned needs. One set is of essentially social needs, for dependency, for affiliation with people (because people satisfy needs), for affection, and the like. The other set is egoistic, i.e., concerned with the self in relation to other people rather than with other people per se. In this class belong the emerging needs for independence, for power (over other people), for prestige (as one kind of power over other people), for knowledge (another kind of power), and the like.

The Extent of Parental Control

Theoretically, the relative development of one of these sets of needs or the other in a child is partially controllable by an outsider, the parent. He can encourage social needs by satisfying physical needs, and he can encourage egoistic needs by frustrating physical needs. In practice, the problem is not quite so simple. For one thing, frustration of physical needs in infancy is likely to be accompanied by two by-products—hostility and fearfulness—as well as by a wish for independence. Moreover, if one were really to frustrate continuously, he would soon have to frustrate not only physical needs but the egoistic needs that begin to emerge from the early frustrations. So now the frustrating parent, having developed in his child a wish for independence, must withhold the right to independence. The next step then is the child who wants independence but cannot successfully get it. Nothing he does for himself is right or successful. Where then? Perhaps a retreat from the world, a kind of internal or fantasy independence. When he grows up a little this behavior may earn him a complicated psychiatric label.

There is another key factor in this picture. When a child, or an adult for that matter, is prevented from getting what he wants, he is apt to become angry and to attack the thing that blocks him. The child strikes out blindly at Mama, the adolescent uses his fists, the adult often attacks with words. Suppose our hypothetical parent frustrates the child so that he wants to attack the parent. He kicks and he bites and he howls. Does the parent now decide to satisfy or to frustrate this new behavior? Does he let himself be attacked successfully, or does he frustrate the attack by using his superior force to retaliate? If he does the first, what becomes of his dignity? If he does the second, what does he teach the child? Probably he teaches the child that he must suppress or repress his hostility. But the *suppression* of hostility is not the same as the *absence* of hostility. The child who is not allowed to kick still feels like kicking. Extend this behavior over time, day after day, incident after incident, and the pattern becomes one of internalized, non-expressed, "sat-upon" hatred and anger, sometimes with a cover of equanimity and calm.

This is not to say that the child is forever what he becomes in, say, his first year of life. On the contrary, the child is always something more than his history. And present needs plus dependency can account for the development of new needs in adults as well as in children. But the outgrowth of very early experiences (experiences in trying to satisfy one's physical needs through a wholly dependent relationship) is a foundation for the broad outlines of later personality. The first years have a good deal to do with determining whether or not the child feels essentially secure or insecure about his place in the world and essentially optimistic or pessimistic about other people.

Dependency in Industry

The things people learn in this first and most important dependency relationship probably also have a good deal to do with the way they face and deal with the less extreme dependency relationships of later life—like the relationship one has with his superiors in industrial organizations.

In fact, if we want to put this story in managerial terms, we need only to go over the last few pages and change a few labels. We can read "manager" for "parent," and "employee" for "child." And then we go on to tone down all the consequences a few notches. The employee, a "used" model of a child, enters a less extreme dependency relationship when he goes to work, and he enters with already existent social and egoistic as well as physical needs. If people in the company are "good brothers," the probability that the employee will learn to feel trustful and affiliative is pretty good—if he is already reasonably trustful of people with power. If people in the company are "bad brothers," his predominant local feelings (superimposed in a complicated way on the general feelings he brought in) are more likely to be hostile and competitive.

It is important to point out here that this view about early dependency may conflict with some widespread beliefs about training both children and employees. For example, this position suggests that strong discipline for the infant will probably lead to hostility and fear and to active power and independence seeking. It suggests further that a history of frustration probably makes later frustrations *more* difficult to take rather than easier. And, in a situation in which great psychological pressure is to be put on a man, holders of this position would place their money on the man who had *not* gone through an infantile school of hard psychological knocks. They would pick the man whose parental relationships and preferably his later ones had been comfortable and relatively free from psychological want. (Incidentally, the evidence from studies of successful executives is consonant with this view. Successful executives tend to come from harmonious, higher-income homes and to have liked their families and teachers.) For the first year or two, the best way to "spoil" a child would therefore seem to be to deny him what he wants. The best way not to "spoil" him is to help him get everything he wants. And, if one considers the new employee instead of the new baby, the same conclusions might hold. But more of this in later chapters.

In Summary

People are born with physical needs. They later either acquire or blossom out with a host of other social and egoistic needs. These new psychological needs can be thought of as outgrowths of (1) physical needs, (2) the nervous system of the physical body, plus (3) dependency on other people.

The child is dependent on adults. Adults can make that dependency predominantly satisfying or predominantly frustrating. Satisfaction builds security and social needs; frustration builds insecurity, hostility, and egoistic needs.

The dependency conditions of infancy recur in later life in industry and elsewhere. The same infantile learning formula may prevail at the adult level.

Chapter 3

PERCEPTION
FROM THE INSIDE LOOKING OUT

The two preceding chapters were about the world's influence on the development of the person; in this one the issue is the person's influence on the world. The major questions are these: How and why do people see things differently? How objective can people be? Do people see only what they want to see? or don't want to see? What part do people's personal views of the world play in the supervisory process?

The Perceptual World

Most of us recognize that the world-as-we-see-it is not necessarily the same as the world-as-it-"really"-is. Our answer depends on what we heard, not on what was really said. The housewife buys what she likes best, not what is best. Whether we feel hot or cold depends on us, not on the thermometer. The same job may look like a good job to one of us and a sloppy job to another.

To specify the problem, consider the line drawing in Figure 2. This is a picture of a woman. Here are some questions about it: (1) How old is the woman at the time of the picture? (2) Does she have any outstanding physical characteristics? (3) Is she "reasonably attractive" or "downright ugly"?

Show the picture to ten other people. Do they all see the same thing? If some think she looks between twenty and thirty, does anyone think she's over fifty? If some think she's over fifty, does anyone think she's between twenty and thirty? How does one account for the conflicts? Are the differences simply differences in taste? Or in standards of

Fig. 2.—Wife or mother-in-law?

beauty? Or is each person distorting the "real" world in a different way?

This old psychology-textbook picture is intentionally ambiguous. It can be seen either as an ugly old hag with a long and crooked nose and toothless mouth or as a reasonably attractive young girl with head turned away so that one can barely see one eyelash and part of a nose. More importantly, the picture will be based on the "facts" as they are seen by the viewer, which may be different from the "facts" seen by another viewer.

Incidentally, if the reader still sees only one of the two figures, he is getting a good feeling of what a "need" is. The tension or discomfort that one feels when he thinks he is missing somethings others can see or when he feels he hasn't quite closed a gap in his knowledge—that is a need. And it will probably be difficult to concentrate on reading further until he satisfies that unsatisfied need by finding the second face in the picture.

The Influence of Our Needs
on Our Perceptions

The hag picture is another demonstration of a commonplace observation, i.e., that people see things differently, that the world is what we make it, that everyone wears his own rose-colored glasses. But consider some additional questions: Whence the rose-colored glasses? Are the glasses always rose-colored? That is, does one always see what he wants to see, or does he see what he is afraid he will see, or both?

These questions are important because the primary issue of "human relations" is to consider ways in which individuals can affect the behavior of other individuals. If it is true that people behave on the basis of the perceived world, then changing behavior in a predetermined direction can be made easier by understanding the individual's present perception of the world. For if there is any common human-relations mistake made by industrial superiors in their relations with subordinates, it is the mistake of assuming that the "real" world is all that counts, that everyone works for the same goals, that the facts speak for themselves.

But if people do act on their perceptions, different people perceive things differently. How, then, is the manager, for example, to know what to expect? What determines how particular people will perceive particular things?

The answer has already been given in the preceding chapters. People's perceptions are determined by their needs. Like the mirrors at amusement parks, we distort the world in relation to our own tensions. Children from poorer homes, when asked to draw a quarter, draw a bigger than actual one. Industrial employees, when asked to describe the people they work with, talk more about their bosses (the people more important to their needs) than about their peers or subordinates, and so on.

But the problem is more complicated than that. People may perceive what is important to their needs, but does this mean people see what they want to see, or what they are afraid to see? Both wishes and fears are important to one's needs. The answer seems to be that we perceive both, but according to certain rules. We magnify a compliment from higher up in the organization but we also magnify a word of disapproval. We dream of blondes, but we also have nightmares. And sometimes we just don't pay attention at all to things that are quite relevant. We forget dentist's appointments; we oversleep when we have examinations coming up; we manage to forget to clean the basement or to call on this particular customer.

Selective Perception

What, then, are the rules of selective perception? The best answer we can give is this one: If one re-examines his memories of the past, he may find that his recall of positive, satisfying things is better than his recall of negative, unpleasant things. He may find it easier to wake early to go fishing than to get to a dentist's appointment. He may look forward, in fact, to doing pleasant, satisfying jobs but may evade mildly disturbing and unpleasant jobs. One senior executive recently commented to the author that the biggest problem he encounters with young management people is their tendency to avoid the little unpleasant decisions—like disciplining people or digging through boring and repetitive records or writing unpleasant letters. This executive felt that his younger men would be far more effective if they could learn to deal as promptly with these uncomfortable little decisions as they did with the big ones.

But we can see some sense in this selective remembering if we look for it. There are some advantages to a person in being blind to unpleasantness, even if such blindness cuts down his working effectiveness. Ignoring the unpleasant may represent more than "laziness." It may be a sensible defensive device, psychologically speaking. Thus, most people are able to ignore soft background conversation while working. In effect they are psychologically deaf to a potentially distracting part of the real world. And this defense helps them to concentrate on their work. Similarly, most people manage to ignore the threat of the hydrogen bomb and to go on eating and sleeping as though this dangerous part of the real world were not here. It can even be shown experimentally that words with unpleasant connotations tend to be recognized more slowly when exposed for very brief intervals than words with pleasant connotations.

The strange part of this defensive process, however, is that in order *not* to hear the distracting music or *not* to see the unpleasant words one must first hear and see them. One has to see the word, recognize that it is unpleasant, and reject it almost simultaneously, so that one can say, "No. I didn't see what that word was." Hence the label "defense" attached to this phenomenon—defense against the entry of preselected things mildly disturbing to one's equilibrium. So two of our rules of selective perception become: (1) see what promises to help satisfy needs, and (2) ignore mildly disturbing things.

Suppose, though, that while one is successfully ignoring background talk someone back there starts to shout; or, while one is successfully ignoring the H-bomb, an H-bomb falls on London. At those points, when the unpleasantness becomes intense and dangerous, people stop defending and begin attacking. They stop ignoring the irritation and start directing all their attention to it. This reversal seems to happen suddenly, at some specific threshold. The distant irritation increases to a point at which it becomes so real, so imminent, and so threatening that we reverse our course, discard the blindfold, and preoccupy ourselves completely with the thing previously ignored.

This is the third rule: Pay attention to things that are really dangerous. The whole picture now begins to look like this: *People perceive what they think will help satisfy needs; ignore what is disturbing; and again perceive disturbances that persist and increase.*

There is yet a fourth step in this process. What can happen when perceived threats become even more intense and imminent? When the soldier in combat watches his buddies die around him? That one we shall consider later, in the chapter on conflict.

This process may not seem entirely logical to an outside observer, but it is quite reasonable psychologically. For this kind of self-imposed psychological blindness helps the person to maintain his equilibrium while moving toward his objectives. An organism lacking this ability to fend off minor threats might well find itself torn apart in its attempt to deal simultaneously with all of them. Or, at least, an individual unable to ignore unpleasant realities might spend so much of his energy dealing with them that he would make little progress toward his major goals. For once a person has learned to perceive a multitude of threats and dangers in his world he needs a system of defense against them. One should add, however, that some individuals may see relatively few things as dangerous and therefore have little need for defense, while for others the world holds dangers at every turn.

In the preceding chapter we suggested that a person who has encountered a relatively helpful world is likely to perceive more of his environment as potentially helpful. If, however, the world has been mostly frustrating, then more of it, and especially new things in it, will be seen as potentially dangerous. Being dangerous, they must be fended off. But, paradoxically, to be fended off they must first be seen. So to protect himself from more insecurity, the insecure person must first see the things that will provoke insecurity and then manage to deny to himself that he has seen them.

Projections of the Perceived World

The basic point of this chapter, the point that the world as it is perceived is the world that is behaviorally important, underlies the development of the now generally familiar projective tests. Originally projectives were designed for the diagnosis of aberrations in personality, but the chapter on assessment will show how they are being used industrially. The same idea also underlies what market researchers now call "motivation research" into consumer attitudes, techniques for discovering people's personal views of the "facts" of advertising and product design. Consumer research in general can be thought of as an attempt to make a diagnosis of the relevant parts of the consumer's view of the world so that products can be designed to be seen as aids rather than obstacles.

For managerial purposes, the importance of the perceptual world is clear. If one's concern as a supervisor or counselor or committee member is to try to effect some change in the behavior of other people, and if in turn people's present behavior is determined largely by their perceptions of their environments, then it is critical that one seek to understand their perceptions if one is to understand the circumstances under which their behavior might change.

For example, managers assume almost universally that subordinates want promotions. And yet more than one subordinate has been driven into panic and disappointment because he felt psychologically forced to accept a promotion that no one (sometimes even himself) bothered to find out he did not want.

Often assumptions about the perceptions of others are wrong because they are incomplete. One may assume correctly that employees want more money, but he may fail to understand that more money is acceptable only within a certain framework of independence. This is the paternalism problem.

Sometimes the problem is simple lack of sensitivity for other people. Thus a foreman once complained to the writer about how odd people seemed. He said one of his employees had gotten terribly upset "for no reason at all." The foreman had said, "Hey, boy, go over there and pick that up!" The employee got angry. He had said, "Don't call me 'boy'; I have a name!" The foreman couldn't understand why the employee, a Negro, should get angry about a "perfectly reasonable" request like that.

Or again many parents argue for the importance of heredity over environment because their own children seem to be so different from one another. "Our second child," they will say, "was just a completely different person from the first, though we treated them both *exactly* alike." Parents may be truthful in feeling that they treated two children alike, but it is unwise to assume that the children were therefore treated alike. The first child's world did not include the second child; but the second's did include the first. Moreover, for the infant whose slate is relatively blank, the minor marks made by parents may be major marks for the child. Thus many parents pass lightly over the differences between feeding an infant now or ten minutes from now. But the child is not likely to pass over the same thing nearly so lightly. The manager is likely to pay little attention to his criticism of a subordinate's work. But for the subordinate it is a week's food for worry.

One more example. Sales managers often complain of the difficulties they encounter in getting salesmen to make cold calls. The salesman says he was too busy, or there were better prospects, or he had to catch up on some reports. Is he lazy? Or just defending himself—perhaps unconsciously—against a perceived threat? If it is a defensive process, there are two general ways in which the manager can try to shake the salesman loose. He can teach him to feel comfortable about cold calls, or he can change the mild threat to a major one so that it can no longer safely be ignored. But if he chooses the latter course he had better consider the by-products of frustration discussed in the next chapter.

In Summary

People see things differently. Even "facts" may be seen quite differently by different people. Relevance to one's needs is the most important determinant of one's personal view of the world. Things that seem to be aids to one's need satisfaction get seen quickly. But things that look like obstacles, if they are not critically threatening, may be seen quickly, only then to be denied so that they appear not to have been seen at all. By denying them, people "protect" themselves temporarily from them. If they really become dangerous, however, people drop the blindness and face them.

To ignore differences in perception is to ignore a major determinant of behavior. Yet it is easy to assume unwarrantedly that everyone views the world from the same perspective as the viewer and that time spent trying to reach a common view is wasted time.

Chapter 4

FRUSTRATION

THE ROADBLOCK

The hypothetical manager we have been talking about is now struggling continually to reach unattainable goals by a variety of means: first, by behaving in an attempt to satisfy his unsatisfied needs; second, by distorting his perceptions of the real world, i.e., by denying a multitude of minor obstacles in his environment that would push him into greater and greater disequilibrium and by spotlighting things that could be aids to the satisfaction of his needs; and, finally, by periodically stopping on his path toward some goals to deal with obstacles so significant he can no longer ignore them.

Another step is left in the development of this picture. It is the step of actually dealing with these serious obstacles between the person and his goals. The major questions are these: How do people behave under one special kind of pressure—the pressure created by a serious block between the person and what he wants? What kinds of people behave in what ways in the face of such blocks? Why do some people seem to run into more roadblocks than others? Why do some managers blow up so easily? Why don't some people seem to recognize what's good for them?

The Obstacle Course

Here is a hypothetical case that may illustrate some aspects of the problem:

> Let's go back, if we can, to the days when we were eighteen or so. We have met a girl and taken her out once, and we like her. Now the junior prom is coming up and we decide to invite her. We extend our invitation, and Mary accepts.
>
> This prom is important. It's the big event of the year. It will cost some money, and we don't have much, so we start saving our pennies. We take on extra odd jobs, washing cars, delivering groceries. We manage to borrow a car. We even work it so that a close friend and his girl will come with us and share the cost of the gas. We manage to scrounge up enough money so that by prom night we've rented a tux, gassed the car, and bought a corsage. Primped and combed and polished, we drive over to pick up our friend, and from there to Mary's house. We park at the gate and go up the walk with our corsage clutched in our little hot fist.
>
> We've never met Mary's parents. When we ring the doorbell and a man appears, we correctly assume it is Mary's father.
>
> We: "Is Mary home?"
>
> Mary's Dad, gruffly, newspaper in one hand, pipe in the other: "Why no, Mary's gone out for the evening."

End of scene. Two questions for the reader: (1) How would you feel? (2) How would you act?

People's reactions to this situation may be grouped into three major classes:

First, there are those whose predominant reaction is *anger* —at Mary.

Second, many people do not feel nearly so angry as they feel *ashamed* and *disappointed* in themselves.

Third—and very rarely—essentially rational rather than emotional feelings occur, i.e., "I wonder which one of us forgot the right date?"

The actions that may follow these feelings can, of course, be direct expressions of the feelings. The man who feels angry may express himself in action—in door slamming, cussing, or in seeking out Mary for verbal or physical attack. But there is another possibility. He may suppress his feelings and act as though he felt calm. Similarly, the man who feels ashamed and inadequate may act accordingly—with weeping and wailing. On the other hand he may act in many other ways. He may, for example, *act* angry as a face-saving device—though he doesn't feel angry.

The rare third man may feel neither angry nor ashamed. He may simply view the situation as a not-very-important problem to be solved. He thus has an infinite variety of actions open to him—to double check, or find another date, or go alone, or spend his money elsewhere—all without major emotional upset.

Two Kinds of Aggression and Who Shows Them

The third man is a rarity. Most people would feel like one of the other two. These two have one thing in common: intense emotional feelings of aggression. In one case the aggression is directed toward some outside object—toward Mary or toward her parents or toward women in general. In the other case it is directed toward one's self, one's lack of ability in these realms, one's unattractiveness for women, one's stupidity in getting involved with a girl like Mary.

Probably there is some admixture of these feelings in almost everyone, much as in the dependency relationship of infancy. But the sets of feelings that would predominate can be guessed at fairly accurately if we know just a little about the person in the situation.

For example, suppose man A is the Beau Brummel of the high school. Every girl in town would love to go out with him. He is perfectly self-confident about his ability to handle women. This is his area of major success, though in many other areas he is less sure of himself. Now he gets stood up by Mary.

Contrast him with B, the low man on the high-school totem pole. This boy has acne. He knows he is not very successful in his social relationships. The girls tease him but pay little serious attention to him. He didn't want to go to the prom in the first place, but you, one of his friends, urged him to. You almost had to force him ("for his own good") to call Mary.

What differences would one expect in the way that these two personalities would handle this situation?

Secure, self-confident A, moving toward an important goal and encountering an entirely unexpected and apparently insurmountable obstacle will probably want to attack the obstacle directly. He will be angry. He will want to fight.

B, who is pessimistic about his abilities but who nevertheless would like very much to be successful, might behave quite differently. When he encounters the sudden, insurmountable obstacle, his anger and hostility will probably be directed toward himself—at this further proof of his own inadequacy, at his stupidity in even venturing into this danger area. He will be just that much harder to entice into boy-girl relations in the future.

Frustration Is a Feeling

This area begins to look like this: When people meet serious obstacles between themselves and their important goals, they get aggressive. If they are optimistic about their ability to reach their goal, they get aggressive outwardly—they attack the obstacle. If they are pessimistic about their own ability, they get aggressive inwardly—they attack themselves.

Clearly a *series* of frustrations can begin to turn the secure optimist into an insecure pessimist. The Beau Brummel may lose his confidence if, having been stood up once, he bounces back only to find himself stood up again—and again and again and again. A point may be reached in the process at which he can no longer feel certain that the world has gone wrong. At this point he will begin unhappily to worry about himself. Similarly, a series of successes may turn the shy boy into a Beau Brummel.

The rare third man is still worth thinking about. He is the one who feels no emotional upset—no anger at Mary or at himself. He treats the incident the way most of us might treat running out of ink in the middle of a letter—troublesome, but not worth getting into a stew about.

An explanation of the third man requires us to go back to the chapter on perception. Different people perceive the world in different ways. What kind of world can the third man be perceiving that permits him to toss off this obstacle so lightly? His world probably includes, for one thing, a wide range of alternative behaviors to fall back on when he meets a roadblock, so that no single roadblock seems insurmountable. His is a bigger world. It is probably also a world in which most of his other egoistic needs have been successfully satisfied, so that being stood up is not so important.

But what distinguishes an important goal from an unimportant one? The word "important" here means something like personal, or where-the-hair-is-short, or dear-to-one's-self-esteem-or-survival. For what is the goal that is blocked for our frustrated subject? He is not upset because he cannot get to the dance. He is upset because his personal egoistic needs for status and self-esteem are challenged. Most of us will agree that being stood up on an important date might have been a major frustration when we were adolescents. But as older adults whose social relationships have jelled, whose range of interests has expanded, we are likely in this situation to be more like the third man. Just the experience of a few years may make the problem look much less important or even emotionally minor. Adult security and self-assurance usually hang on firmer threads, not so readily ruptured by a single social setback.

Incidentally, we usually save the word "frustration" for incidents that cause emotional reactions. For the third man, and for most "minor" obstacles, we talk about "deprivation."

The Explosive Businessman

Some odd implications evolve out of these generalizations about who reacts to frustration in one way and who reacts in another. The position taken here, in effect, is that the confident, secure person will be less likely to encounter serious (for him) obstacles, but that he will be more likely to blow up at such obstacles when he does encounter them.

Yet, although it is generally true that industry prefers secure, solid, optimistic people to shy, withdrawn, insecure people, it is also true that industry is likely to look askance at executives who have emotional outbursts. Emotional blowoff is seen as unbusinesslike behavior that earns the young executive only black marks on his boss's evaluation sheet. Hence we are likely to find in industry many cases of internal emotion and the external appearance of calm.

Thus it is possible for the secure optimist to avoid part of this problem—he can *feel* like blowing up but then stifle his corresponding actions so that what the boss sees is a controlled and rational façade. In fact, many executives in industry probably do just that, thereby perhaps contributing to the psychosomatic illnesses industrial executives are said to develop. For chronic failure to express intense emotion and through that expression to utilize the physiological products of emotion can lead to chronic physiological disturbance. Moreover, encountering an obstacle, then wanting to attack it, and then finding the avenue of attack is cut off by the disapproval of organizational superiors—such a series itself constitutes a secondary kind of frustration.

The occasional blowoff, therefore, ought to be viewed as an appropriate reaction by an imperfect but hard-working, highly motivated individual when he encounters, as he must at times, a difficult, unexpected, and apparently insurmountable obstacle.

It may be true that an executive would be an even better executive if he did not get frustrated to begin with; that is, if obstacles that were important for other people seemed minor to him, so that he did not even feel an emotional reaction. Most of us would consider it ideal if our model executive could be the rare third man, who would simply shrug his shoulders (both at himself and at the world) and start thinking about where to go from there. An ideal executive might then be one whose tolerance for things frustrating to other people would be so great, whose areas of personal security would be so broad, whose breadth of perception would be so wide, that only very, very few incidents in his lifetime would include insurmountable obstacles (because he would always have ways around them) or really important self-esteem needs (because his self-esteem would be so solid that few things could threaten it). His egoistic needs instead would be needs for accomplishment of organizational goals.

The problem is one of people's expectations about their ability to satisfy their needs; and expectations are, in turn, largely determined by past successes and failures. If through life one has come to expect failure, to feel unsure of his ability to satisfy his personal egoistic needs, then these needs loom larger in his perceptions than they do for the next man. The martini that is not dry enough stops being just a deprivation, i.e., *just* a martini that is not dry enough. It becomes instead a sign of disrespect from the bartender —a threat to one's self-esteem.

It follows that people whose self-esteem is easily threatened are less likely to be rational about their efforts to satisfy their needs. It follows, too, that if one can build up people's feelings of self-confidence, so that their expectations are optimistic, they will be able to deal with problems more rationally and objectively.

Frustration and Standards of Success

Perhaps the most important key to whether we encounter frequent frustration or not is our own individual standard of success. Two men may both want to make money, but "to make money" for one may mean $5,000 a year while for the other "to make money" means $50,000. If two such men are of about equal ability and have about equal opportunity, and if both actually achieve $15,000 a year, then one will be satisfied and the other frustrated. Both have achieved the same external level of success, but one may perceive himself a failure.

This problem has many facets: It is a question of the relationship between our aspirations and our ability to achieve our aspirations. If the two are close together, frustration is relatively unlikely. If our ability exceeds our level of aspiration—if we are much *better* than we need to be—then society probably suffers because we do not contribute as much as we can. If aspiration and ability are out of line in the other direction—if we want what we do not have the capacity to obtain—then we have a potential source of serious frustration.

It is useful to examine the ways in which people develop their individual ideas of how good is good and how high is high. Many of them seem to develop early in life. Even when quite young, some children seem always to need to win any game they play while others seem to want only to be "better than average." And occasionally we see still others who apparently can be perfectly happy as low man on the totem pole. Similarly, in industry some people seem consistently ready to accept the level at which they are working or only want to move ahead in small (but perhaps steady) steps. Others feel they are at the bottom unless they are at the top.

An illustration may show how such differences develop: Suppose someone puts a target on a wall and then leaves you alone with a set of darts and the target. Suppose you have never thrown darts before and have shown no particular interest in dart throwing. Do you set yourself a score to shoot for before you throw the darts for the first time? Probably not. But suppose you throw the five darts and score 75 out of a possible 250? Now what do you do? Before you throw the next dart do you set yourself a standard? Is the standard 250? Or is it anything better than 75? For most of us it would be the latter. In situations in which we are perfectly free to set our own standards, we are most likely to keep setting our goals just slightly ahead of our present abilities. Thereby, through learning and training and exercise, we can feel that we are continually moving ahead successfully.

Let us suppose, however, that instead of being alone in the room with the target and the darts, someone else is present—another man who has been a constant competitor of yours. The other man throws first and hits 100. Now what is your goal? And now how do you feel when you hit only 75?

Once other people enter into the goal-setting process the more or less "natural" tendency to set goals a little ahead of past achievement begins to give way. Goals may then, in fact, be set without any regard to ability. Thus one occasionally encounters a person who *must* become a great industrialist because his parents have hammered that notion into him since childhood. Failing to become a great industrialist constitutes failing to satisfy the people he wants most to satisfy and, hence, means frustration.

Take the case of a young engineer who was unhappy on his job. He had never wanted to be an engineer; he had always wanted to be a coach. But his father had been an engineer. His father, on his death bed, had extracted a promise from the student that he would become an engineer, and a good one. So the fellow was stuck first with a goal that had been imposed on him and, second, with abilities and interests that were not likely to allow him to reach that goal. He had no good solution to the problem except to continue through life jumping for the ring he would probably never reach—unless he could somehow change his attitude toward his now unreachable father.

It is a commonplace in industrial work situations to feel that one must set high standards for employees to "motivate" them. But may not standards beyond an individual's reach lead him into one of two other behaviors? They may lead him into a hopeless struggle to reach a goal that his abilities will not allow him to reach, and hence into a series of failures, and hence again into panic and insecurity. Or else overly high standards may lead a better-adjusted individual simply to remove himself physically or psychologically from the situation, to refuse to accept the standards that are set for him.

Perhaps one can argue that a person who is in a position to set standards for other people has a responsibility to set those standards neither so low as to provide inadequate opportunity for full expression nor so high as to guarantee feelings of failure.

In Summary

Frustration is a "feeling" rather than a "fact." It is a feeling that arises when one encounters certain kinds of blocks on paths to certain kinds of goals. These feelings arise when the block seems insurmountable and when failure to surmount it threatens one's personal well being—when the goal involves the self.

When people encounter such obstacles, they react with aggression; aggression mostly toward the obstacle when the person is sure of his own ability and aggression mostly toward one's self when the person is pessimistic about his ability, i.e., when he has had a history of failure.

Many obstacle situations are depriving rather than frustrating because the obstacles do not seem insurmountable or the goals are not central to the self. Some people may therefore meet fewer frustrations than others because they have more ways around more obstacles or because they are self-confident enough so that their self-esteem does not have to be proved again by every new problem they encounter.

Moreover, if a person's goals are in line with his abilities, then he may avoid another major source of frustration. If his objectives extend far beyond his abilities, he may consider himself a chronic failure because he cannot see that the carrot is really tied to his own nose.

Other people—parents, peers, managers—have a good deal to do with the development of self-confidence and hence with the ways people deal with obstacles. For self-confidence is tied to success, and success is in large part what other people may decide it is.

Chapter 5

PSYCHOLOGICAL CONFLICT
ROADBLOCKS ON THE INSIDE

Conflict may be thought of as a class of frustration, the class characterized by wanting to go in two directions at the same time. The obstacles one meets are not brick walls but drags that pull back as one goes forward. Conflict situations are frying-pan-and-fire situations, or donkey-between-the-bales-of-hay situations. They are choice situations, decision-making situations. And these, more than any other class of psychological situations, underlie major emotional upset and the irrational behavior that such upset usually entails.

Conflicts occur at all levels of personality and in all degrees of importance to the person. Some are minor. Few persons are likely to be psychologically crippled by trying to decide between two movies, though the presence of conflict is often visible in a tendency to vacillate before the choice is made. Nor is the donkey nearly so likely to be paralyzed between the bales of hay as the old story makes out. On the contrary, most of us encounter numberless conflicts in the course of everyday life, conflicts we manage to resolve in short order and without permanent scars.

Some of the same generalizations that apply to frustration also apply to conflict. Some conflict situations involve important central needs that appear to be inescapably opposed. Others involve relatively unimportant needs or offer so many substitute possibilities that we hardly recognize their existence. As with frustration, serious trouble arises from conflicts between intense central needs involving long-term critical goals, where no satisfactory alternatives are visible. Such conflicts can be a real threat to the personality.

In this chapter some extreme illustrations of more serious personality conflicts will be presented, in search both of better understanding of the process itself and of some ways in which the industrial environment can irritate or even create such conflicts. Then, after looking at some samples, alternative ways of handling and resolving them will be considered.

An Extreme Illustration

Here is a nightmarish illustration:

> Suppose I build a large cage and put you in it. Suppose you live in it for a long time and get used to it. This is home. Life is dull but not unbearable. You have a good bed and the food is good. But there is a peculiarity about the food. On the table in one corner of the cage is a box. The box has a cover. When you get hungry you lift the cover and inside you find an attractive meal. So whenever you get hungry, you just open the box, take a few things you like, and let

the cover close again. You eat and then you go over to your bed and take a nap.

One day something happens. When you get hungry, you go to the box as usual. You reach out to lift the lid, but when your fingers hit it you get a strong electric shock.

You draw back and rub your hand. You think about it for a while. You decide it must have been static electricity and reach out again. This time you get another shock, one that seems more intense than the first. This upsets you somewhat, so you begin to look around to see if there is something wrong. You look for a plug or a wire you can pull out. You look for some rubber gloves. But you can't find anything that will do the job. Of course, you're not very hungry—yet.

An hour later, you are hungrier, so you go over again. You say: "What the devil; so I'll get a little shock, so what?" You touch the cover, but the shock has now grown quite intense. It really hurts. You drop the lid in a hurry. You again sit down on your cot and think for a while. After twelve hours of this, with no food, you begin to get a little frantic. You begin to poke around the place, looking for the answer to the electrified box. You call for help. Nothing seems to work. You start looking seriously for a way out of the cage, something you haven't done since the first few days you were in it. You try to pull the bars apart, to break the lock, to crawl out. Nothing works.

You can smell the food in the box and your hunger begins to get desperate. You decide to risk it. You pull open the lid, get knocked back, but you still manage to reach in and

51

grab a bit before you let the lid drop. You eat your morsel and go back to your cot to think the thing over again.

The situation goes on. As you get hungrier, the shock seems to get stronger. As you approach the box, driven by your hunger, you can almost feel the pain of the shock you'll get when you touch it. You manage to get enough food to stay alive, but instead of adapting to the shock you seem to get more sensitive to it.

What do you do?

The Sanity in Insanity

The conflict here is an extreme one involving two basic, critical, physical needs: the need for food, and the need for the avoidance of pain. There is no physical escape, and the needs increase in intensity with time.

What, then, would happen?

Probably you would "go crazy." After some days of this, you would probably be huddled in a corner in a dazed and stuporous state. If we opened the cage and took you out, you would probably stay dazed and stuporous for a long time. If we tried to feed you, you probably wouldn't eat. If we tried to wake you, you probably wouldn't wake up. You're gone—even though you're alive and there's no specific physical defect.

If we sent you down to Florida and put you out to bask in the sun, if we held your hand and talked with you and reassured you, and if we used some of the methods that have been developed in psychiatry, we might be able to get back into contact with you. We might tease you into accepting food and into discovering thereby that things have changed and the world is no longer what it had been during those terrible days in the cage. We might, in other words, be able to cure you of the effects of this intense conflict. The cure might be complete, but most probably, no matter how many years passed, you would still get upset when you met up with cages or electric shocks.

Now suppose that we step inside your mind while you're in this stuporous state. What will we be likely to find? You may be off in some fantasy world. You may be the gourmet of gourmets, eating your way continuously through quantities of delicacies while in one fist you hold the only key to the master electric switch. You would be dealing with the conflict by escaping upward into unreality and fantasy. You cannot escape physically; you cannot handle the stresses as they exist; so you escape psychologically, through a "neurosis" or "psychosis."

Such behavior thus becomes, in a sense, reasonable behavior. It fits with the view that the organism defends itself from intolerable attack and seeks to keep itself together. Cutting off one's communication with the real world in favor of a world of fantasy is a desperation measure for meeting intolerable conflict. It is not necessarily a healthy way of meeting it, but to a person at a particular time it may be the best available way.

This illustration is extreme, of course. And it can only work because a cage exists. If we had not inclosed you in the cage, then you would have dealt with the conflict simply by walking away from it and looking for food elsewhere. In fact, one might say that the presence or absence of the cage makes the difference between conflicts that lead to extreme emotional reaction, especially withdrawal reaction, and conflicts that are handled more easily. But the cages one encounters in real life are usually built of social and cultural bars rather than steel ones.

Consider just one more illustration of major conflict before taking up the question of conflict in industrial situations. Consider two husbands, A and B, each married to an impossible shrew. Both have been married for a long time, both have children. A has a political job. He is in the public eye. He has no religious values of any significance. He is not interested in his children. He has no scruples about divorce. B loves his children, is intensely religious, and feels that divorce is sinful. Assume that the wives of A and B continue to make their lives miserable, and suppose further that the intensity of this misery increases continually. Suppose that A and B reach the same point at about the same time. Each decides he can stand it no longer and runs away.

Which one will be more successful in his attempt to escape? Which one will be able to settle down to life and work in a new community? The answer clearly is that A may be quite successful and B, quite unsuccessful.

The conflict for A is between his career and his desire to escape. Though much intensified in degree, this choice is not essentially different from the choice one must make in deciding between two radio programs broadcast at the same time. A's choice involves little guilt, little threat to his idealized picture of himself. The stimuli are largely external to his person. All he can lose is his career. But for B, leaving the field is no escape at all. His conflict resides entirely within himself. It involves his conscience, his self-esteem. No matter how far he may be from the physical location of the conflict tomorrow morning, his feelings of guilt and his loss of self-respect will be with him, for he has no easy way of cutting out communication within himself.

The troublesome conflicts, then, are those that involve needs "central" or "internal" to the personality. Usually these turn out to be conflicts between needs at different *levels* of the personality—between more or less basically impulsive needs and "conscience" needs.

Conflict in People in Industry

Much supervision is an attempt to control others through the use of conflict. For example, the threat of discipline to prevent some unwanted behavior is an attempt to introduce a conflict into another person's (B's) perceptual world. Where B had only one need, to get what he wanted, now he has a second and conflicting one, to avoid the punishment that getting what he wants now entails.

Such control, through conflict, cannot be classed glibly either as good or as bad. For the most part such measures do not introduce dangerous conflicts because they do not set up situations that involve feelings of guilt or threaten people's feelings of self-esteem. They are largely external to the personality. But insofar as some people may see rules as a challenge to their basic autonomy, the reaction may be intense.

Other uses of conflict as devices for controlling behavior can get more serious. Suppose, instead of the threat of discipline, we choose to try to develop "positive" feelings of loyalty and duty to the company—suppose we try to build a "company conscience" into our employees as we do into our children. If we succeed, we are setting up *internal* conflicts this time. Now it is not the boss that the employee must worry about, but his own feelings of guilt. People who thus begin to feel honor-bound can get themselves into a tense emotional tizzy. And the probabilities of an irrational emotional blowoff are consequently greater. Paternalism is that kind of problem. One simply showers employees with gifts or benefits and then makes it clear that they are expected to show their gratitude by submission. For those with strong needs for independence, the resulting conflict is essentially internal, and it includes the possibility of violent reaction.

There are many other places in industry where one may find serious long-term emotional conflicts. Many of these center in the same fundamental desires for independence and autonomy, on the one hand, versus one's desires for dependence and support, on the other. The whole pattern of industrial organization encourages this sort of conflict. Subordinates are by definition dependent on their superiors. Subordinates are therefore bound to feel ambivalent to some degree, i.e., to feel uncomfortably bound and yet pleasantly protected.

Sometimes one finds individuals who have managed to strike a balance between their needs for autonomy and for dependency, perhaps by finding a particular job at a particular level that satisfied both needs—like a job as assistant to a powerful superior. Or an executive may find himself a middle-level spot at which he fells both competent to do the jobs assigned to him and satisfied with his prestige and status. Often, however, higher management, blind to the subordinate's perception of the world, decides to "reward" him by promoting him. Promotion for one who has thus struck a satisfactory compromise between conflicting needs may result only in reinstating the old enervating conflict with greater intensity than ever. Now perhaps our subject begins to feel panicky about his ability to do this bigger job. It frightens him. However, he wants the status and the money it will bring, and he wants to conform to the social necessity of accepting a promotion. ("You'd be crazy to refuse an offer like that!") Shortly following such a promotion, one often sees beginning signs of active conflict: anxiety; "unpredictable" lashing out against subordinates; "inexplicable" refusal to delegate authority; self-isolation from peers and subordinates and, if possible, from superiors; and so on. In fact, many such cases end up in physical illness or alcoholic escapes or some other industrially unacceptable solution. Top management then usually decides it has misjudged the man—he wasn't as good as he looked.

This is not to suggest that fear of promotion should keep people from accepting promotion. Fears can be overcome by success in meeting them. But awareness of the existence of needs that drag against the rewards of promotion can help a promoter to plan the promotional process more wisely.

Sometimes a job demands of a man some activities that do not mesh with his conception of what is right or his conception of what is dignified or proper for him as a member of society. Salesmen seem to suffer from this conflict more than some other occupational groups. Sales managers beat the drums and wave the flag to get them to go out to sell Ajax iceboxes to Eskimos. But some Eskimos seem not to need iceboxes; or some other iceboxes look more useful than Ajax; or the salesman feels uneasy and uncomfortable about putting his foot in people's doors when he hasn't been invited.

Some sales managers try to resolve this job *vs.* moral-social conflict by "proving" to the salesman the social importance of selling. They point up the white man's burden of carrying the good life to the ignorant consumer. They try to resolve the conflict by building up the pressure on one side to such an extent that it overrides the other. The difficulties here are two: First comes the problem of the morning after. His enthusiasm drummed up by "inspirational" sales meetings, the salesman goes out and sells—temporarily satisfying his job needs and reducing them to zero. He then finds himself feeling depressed and guilty because the still unsatisfied moral-social needs are now naked and exposed. The second difficulty with this inspirational method is that it requires continual recharging. The sales manager must maintain the initiative by injecting periodic shots of enthusiasm, lest the salesman wake up one morning deciding his product and his job are really no damn good.

Finally, one can mention the role of conflict in consumer decisions. All the recent activity in motivational research centers in a conception of the human personality as a multi-storied structure. The occupants on each floor are at war with the others. Thus some people may deny that they buy a product for its snob value, because their self-respect requires such denial; but they may be able to buy the product for its snob value nevertheless, if the snobbery–self-respect conflict can be rationalized in terms of "good value," or "quality," or "utility."

Conscience

The conflict problem seems to be one of disorder in nature itself. If the development of human personality were entirely orderly, perhaps the need system of an individual would be so designed that there would never be two opposing simultaneous needs. But people do not grow up with any such well-integrated system of needs. On the contrary, they seem from the very beginning to develop more or less opposing needs which frequently demand simultaneous satisfaction. People get hungry and sleepy at the same time; they want to fight and to run at the same time; to love and to hate; to overpower and to submit.

Although the mere presence of opposing needs accounts for the existence of conflicts, it does not account for the intensity or the variety of reactions to conflict. What is required to account for these interpersonal differences in reactions to conflict is an additional dimension in the picture of the structure of human personality. We need to introduce the concept of conscience, of internal control by the person of his own behavior.

The development of conscience seems to pass through several phases, and you often can actually see them going on in a child. First, the child begins to avoid some things he wants to do because he fears reprisals from his parents or because he wants to please them by showing his self-restraint. When he finds he gets punished for throwing his milk at Mama, he may begin to think twice about throwing it. The next time the same impulse shows up, he may try to do it when Mama's not looking. But as he gets more socialized, as he begins to realize he can't outguess Mama, he begins to internalize and accept as his own the restrictions that originally came from Mama. At that point he begins to act, for himself, *like his parents.* He may throw his milk to satisfy the impulse, but then he will slap his own wrist to punish himself for what he has done. The final stage in this process is the child's refusal to throw the milk because *he* now feels it is a wrong act.

This is conscience. It is the difference between the person who is aware of the law but is afraid only of getting caught and the person who himself feels that the law is right and proper and that to break it is morally wrong. So learned conscience needs can be satisfied only by denying the satisfaction of other needs.

The conflicts that cause difficulty are long-term conflicts between increasingly strong action needs and severe conscience needs. Thus, in the military situation, one troublesome conflict may center in the soldier's duty and loyalty needs at the conscience level and his desire to avoid danger at a more basic level. In a husband-wife case, the conflict may be between the conscience notions of morality and propriety and the desires to escape physical and psychological harassment at the hands of a shrew. In industry the conflict may be between desires for psychological safety and the conscience wish to be what people expect one to be.

If, in early life, we develop an oversized conscience—if many things come to be seen as sinful or improper or dangerous—then we may encounter many serious conflicts. If one learns early that aggressiveness or sensuality or hostility are wrong and to be feared, and yet, in the course of living, one encounters situations that call for aggression or stir up sensual impulses or engender hostility, then one may be caught up in conflict much more than the next man. And if one's perceptual breadth is too limited to find ways around such problems, then the conflicts will be severe.

On the other hand, if a man develops an undersized conscience, if he can lie, or steal, or manipulate people without guilt, then he may suffer very little, although society may suffer a whole lot. Such people are usually labeled "psychopaths." They sit in a special psychiatric filing category because they are not exactly sick, except socially. They may make other people sick, but they themselves feel fine.

Unconsciousness

At this point we must add one more concept to the whole picture: the concept of unconsciousness. It has been pointed out that one extreme way to handle conscience-impulse conflicts is to deny the existence of one or both of the needs. Amnesias do this. This process of denying from memory something the conscience disapproves of is the process that is now called *repression*. It is another defense mechanism, another way of holding a personality together in the face of otherwise unsolvable problems. If there is no acceptable solution in reality, then the solution must somehow be found in unreality, and repression is a way of denying reality by literally forgetting about it. The conflict then no longer exists. Thus the soldier with combat fatigue is in a completely stuporous state and remembers nothing of what has happened. Except, of course, that he actually does remember. In fact, one might say he remembers too well, since his memories may be so threatening and so dangerous that he must deny them to himself. So unconsciousness is the burial ground for dangerous or guilt-provoking needs and experiences. Day dreaming and night dreaming are cues to such unconscious activity. Temporary voluntary escape into unconsciousness through alcohol, or hobbies, or movies are other less extreme ways of temporarily holding one's self together by forgetting the conflict. Psychosomatic (psychologically caused but physically manifested) illnesses are often unconscious ways of channeling off some of the tension that deep-seated conflicts may engender.

Handling Conflict

Obviously none of these many unconscious or semiconscious methods of handling conflict is particularly satisfactory from the point of view of mental health. Each of them is a last-ditch holding maneuver which itself requires a great deal of energy. So much energy, in fact, may be devoted to re-pressing what is feared that not much is left for the behavior required to satisfy the multitudes of other more mundane needs that most of us must satisfy in order to survive.

So we are left with this question: How can one *really* resolve emotional conflicts? Conflicts, like most other psy-chological phenomena, are conflicts only because they are perceived as such. They are not part of the real, but of the perceived, world. A conflict exists for a person because to him certain needs seem mutually exclusive. His conflict would be resolved if (1) he could find some new, previously unknown means to satisfy both needs fully, (2) he could change his mind about one of the needs so that he was no longer interested in it, or (3) he could reorganize, in one of a number of other ways, his view of the world so as to set the conflict in a new and less significant perspective.

For example, consider a husband caught between an im-possible wife and his social duty. Several alternative resolu-tions are *theoretically* available. First, he may come to feel differently about his notions of duty. If he decides it is, say, socially, religiously, and morally appropriate to leave his wife, then perhaps he can do so without trouble. Or he may somehow come to see his wife in a new light, so that instead of an ogress she becomes an unhappy human being in need of help. Still again, a man may be able to change his expec-tations about life, to reorient his standards and philosophy so that the sufferings he endures are not so much sufferings as the-things-one-must-expect-from-life.

This is not to say that one can resolve conflicts simply by asserting, "I feel differently about this." The problem is really to feel differently. The counselor and the psychiatrist offer to help people reorganize their perceptions of problems so that they can perhaps find new solutions.

One way to illustrate the idea of "reorganizing perceptions" is to ask the reader to compare himself today with himself as an adolescent. Consider what a skin rash might have meant in adolescence and what it would mean when he is thirty-five and settled down. The problem is simply not the same problem. As our worlds have grown, as new knowledge and new experience have been added, we have changed our perspectives, reorganized our perceptions.

Sometimes an adult conflict exists only because a person cuts off his channels of information from the world. The combat-fatigue victim, for example, may withdraw completely into himself, apparently seeking to avoid emotional repetition of arduous experiences. Unless he eventually opens his channels, he will never get an opportunity to learn that the world has changed and that he is surrounded by sunlight instead of explosions. Similarly, the process of repressing old conflicts so preoccupies many of us that we cannot observe our changing environments. We do not learn that elaborate defenses are unnecessary because now nothing needs defending. Thus, the poorly educated executive, after a series of perceived failures in coping with technical innovations, may go on avoiding technological change, never realizing that now he is—if he can bring himself to try it— perfectly capable of handling the situations that he is expected to handle. This tendency to narrow one's incoming communication channels in order to avoid psychological dangers is one major social cost of conflict. People avoid much of the world because they fear much of themselves. They "take leave of their senses," literally.

But though many reactions to emotional conflict are psychologically unhealthy and inefficient, they remain psychologically lawful reactions. They, like other behavior, can be thought of as attempts by the organism to bring itself into equilibrium.

In Summary

The development of personality allows for the coexistence of opposing needs. Conflict situations are those requiring decisions between such coexistent opposing needs.

When conflicts involve critical needs and seem to offer no ways out, reactions may be severe. Fantasy, delusions, and amnesia are such extreme ways out of conflicts.

Conflicts that require extreme solutions usually involve "conscience" needs, centering in morality and social propriety. Extreme solutions often require the person to push one of the needs into unconsciousness and thereby—by forgetting—to deny the conflict.

But such repressive defenses cost energy. Less enervating solutions call for reorganization of perceptions, finding new ways out of apparently dead-end situations.

Serious chronic conflicts may develop in the industrial organization. Conflicts between needs for dependence and for independence are especially prevalent because the industrial environment emphasizes dependency but values independence.

Chapter 6

LEARNING, THINKING, PROBLEM SOLVING
SOME REASONING PARTS OF PEOPLE

A first purpose of this chapter is to counterbalance the general impression of human irrationality and emotionality we have built up thus far. In the preceding chapter on conflict, we emphasized the emotional, unconscious, "illogical" aspects of human action. But even a cursory look at people's behavior will show that much of it represents quite reasonable and conscious efforts to satisfy conscious needs. Students learn to type and to solve arithmetic problems; workingmen search for ways to add to their incomes; architects try to improve the beauty and functionality of their plans; managers try to choose the most effective ways of budgeting their capital and of designing and marketing their products.

Just a decade ago, however, a chapter about these matters probably would not have been included in this book. Psychologists and social scientists were so deeply concerned with the emotional life of man that they ignored his conscious thinking life altogether.

This emotional emphasis was partly a reaction against still earlier, entirely rational approaches. Thirty or forty years ago, for instance, we assumed that workers worked only to earn money and that managers, in turn, sought only to maximize their profits. We built theories of economic behavior and industrial organization around these assumptions. Early industrial engineering grew up as a logical "scientific" process, unconcerned about irrational human quirks like hostility and resistance. Then, later, with the emergence of such odd bedfellows as Freud and the Western Electric studies, we bent in the opposite direction. Foggy conceptions of social and egoistic needs took precedence. Workers sought to satisfy ephemeral needs for "belongingness"; managers were not managing, they were unconsciously competing with childhood images of their fathers.

Only very recently have social scientists from many fields set about to integrate and modify these views; to deal with the undeniable whole man—the manager who may be unconsciously competitive but who also spends a fair share of his time trying to decide what materials to buy and what marketing strategies to follow. This chapter, then, is about those conscious efforts to learn, to think, and to solve problems—efforts that most managers work at a good many hours each day.

Earlier chapters have already said a good deal about learning. In effect they have said that people learn continuously; they learn their personalities; they learn many of their social and egoistic needs, their attitudes, and their habitual ways of behaving. At the same time they learn to speak, to walk, to read, to build model airplanes, and to make managerial decisions. They are learning whenever their behavior at time 2 is modified as a consequence of experience at time 1.

The question now before us is this one: Just how do people go about learning? If we set about to build a "thing" capable of learning, what would we have to build into it? And just how would the thing work?

This thing we are trying to build must demonstrate that it is a learning thing by behaving more effectively—perhaps more quickly and with fewer mistakes—the second or third time it tries to solve a problem than it did the first time. What characteristics do we have to build into it to permit it to pass such a test?

First, our thing will require some *intake channels* so that it can have "experiences" to learn from. It will need some means for getting information into itself from outside itself, something like human eyes or ears (maybe some photoelectric cells will do).

Second, it will need some *output devices,* some ways of acting and searching. It will have to be capable of moving through the world or of sending signals out into the world. It will need some equivalents to human muscles or the human voice, like wheels or a typewriter. For how can it modify its behavior if it cannot behave? How can it search for easier paths if it cannot explore?

Besides these external mechanisms it will need several inside gadgets. It will need some *selective device* to connect inputs with outputs. The device may be a simple one that makes only one choice—to connect or not to connect a given input with a given output. But without such a device the thing won't be able to close the circuit between what comes in and what goes out and hence will be unable to profit behaviorally from its experience.

Fourth, and again on the inside, we shall have to include some *rules about decisions* that will serve as instructions for the selective device; otherwise it can act only reflexively or randomly.

One of these rules ought to be a *stinginess rule*. If the selective device has a choice among outputs, it will have to be built either to select the most "efficient" output, the simplest and shortest one, or else the first output it comes across that will work (which may be easier in the long run).

It will also need a *motivation rule*. It cannot be allowed to sit still and ignore all inputs. It has to be built so that it is *on* when inputs are coming in and so that it stays on until it gets an answer. It needs, in other words, something vaguely like human needs.

We are not through yet. If this machine is to improve performance with experience, it needs to remember its experience. It needs a *memory device* for storing up its experiences as well as a way of using this stored up information when faced with new problems. Lacking such a storehouse, or lacking access to it, each experience will be a first experience.

One final requirement: the thing will need some way of getting *inputs about its own ouputs*. It has to know whether its own actions were right or wrong. If the archer could not see that he had missed the target, he could not know how to modify his aim. If the manager could never learn about the effects of his past changes in plant layout, he could not know by himself how to improve his layout.

Given all these characteristics, our learning thing begins to look like Figure 3.

Notice that the thing is full of closed loops, with the arrows completing full circles. It is also a relatively elaborate system; it is not a cellulose sponge. Notice, too, that it looks a little like some of the data-processing computers now showing up in industry that are designed with all these characteristics.

Theoretically, then, if we could build a thing like this, it could learn. If any of these characteristics were missing, it could not learn, nor, theoretically, could people. If we knock out all a person's input senses—his sight, hearing, touch, taste, smell—he can't improve his performance over time because he can't find out how he did the first time. If we knock out his memory, he can't learn because each new try is his first try. If we knock out his outputs—his voice and his muscles—he can't try at all. If he has no brain to make

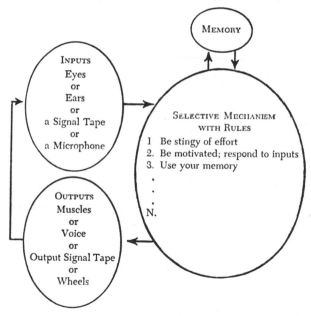

Fig. 3.—A learning mechanism

choices, he can't improve because he can't change; he can only repeat his behavior. If we knock out the stinginess principle or his needs, he won't improve because he doesn't give a damn—the hard way is as good for him as the easy way, and no behavior at all is as good as anything else. And if he can't see or feel his own hand—that is, if he can't determine the effects of his own outputs—he has no way of deciding how to change his outputs.

If we put all these requirements together, we come out with an essentially mechanical but nevertheless dynamic view of learning—learning as a process of doing things, finding out and evaluating what has happened, storing the experience, and trying again—using past experience as a jumping-off place. Psychologically speaking, one can say that we act, we perceive the effects of our actions, we reorganize and store our perceptions, and we act again on the basis of our reorganized perceptions.

Learning and Thinking Machines

Engineers, mathematicians, and others have been able to design machine equivalents for each of these requirements for learning in order to build machines that can learn. Such machines—specially programed high-speed computers are the best example—are capable not only of solving problems but of learning to solve similar problems faster after experience. Computers can be programed (e.g., supplied with choice rules) to learn to solve problems in symbolic logic in ways that are surprisingly human.

In such learning machines the inputs are usually tapes with information precoded on them in a language the machine can understand. The output is a tape on which the machine can "speak" in the same language. The memory can be a magnetic drum (there are better mechanisms now) that holds and stores electrical charges. There are several choice rules. They may be: "Take input No. 1 from the tape and put it at X. Then go to Y for instructions." At Y, the machine will be instructed, "Compare information at X with memory No. 1. If they match, punch Z on the output and store information from X in memory position 12. If they don't match, try No. 2." And so on. Instructions may be of several sorts: compare, describe, test, match, etc., each of which calls for specific actions by parts of the computer. "Stinginess" can be built into the machine by adding an effort counter, so that when a series of explorations along one line has reached a certain number of units of effort, the machine has had enough of that and sets out on an alternative tack. Another way of enforcing the stinginess rule is to design the machine so that it uses the *first* workable action it encounters while searching through a list of alternatives. The first workable action may not, of course, be the best one.

'These machines seem to simulate human learning and problem solving using other brick and mortar than that of the human nervous system. The simulation is not of neurons and synapses but of information processing.

They behave like people in the way they go about attacking difficult, non-routinized problems. They do *not*, for example (just as you do not), consider all *possible* attacks. They pick an alternative that "looks" plausible—perhaps an alternative that worked on a similar, earlier problem. Like humans too, they may sometimes be fooled. They may try a plausible-looking short-cut method, only to find that they would have been better off starting from scratch.

Several questions about the man-machine analogy have

stirred up considerable heat. It seems clear that by usual definitions of learning, machines really can learn to solve difficult, non-routine problems. They can do much more than arithmetic. It is not clear that machines are necessarily going to end up smarter or dumber or more important than people, though many observers, including this one, are convinced that some present middle-management jobs may ultimately be filled by programed problem-solving machines, after an intervening period of programed problem-solving people. And certainly it is not perfectly clear that people do, in fact, learn in the same way as machines. Nevertheless, experimental models of learning and problem solving made possible by the high-speed computer seem extremely promising, with implications and applications of tremendous scope.

Some Complicating Factors in Human Learning and Problem Solving

No matter how one views the capacities of machines, it is clear that currently people show more complicated behavior than machines. Some of these complexities enhance people's capacities, but some interfere with conscious problem solving.

For one thing, people's decision rules about what is relevant are rather broad, reflecting the complexity of memories and needs that exist within us at any one moment. As a result, we are likely to learn more from an experience than is intended. The new management trainee not only learns about the company's finances, he also learns that the financial vice-president likes to push people around. He learns attitudes and feelings as well as facts. A person learns the whole show; not only geometry but the geometry teacher and attitudes toward geometry. He perceives all these as parts of the problem-to-be-solved because his need satisfactions are tied up with all of them. Learning to solve the geometry problem is only one of several potential satisfactions to be gained from the learning situation; learning to please the teacher is another; learning that geometry is something to stay near, or to escape from, is another. Certainly one major and difficult task of a teacher who sets out to teach geometry (or management, for that matter) is to be sure that it is geometry and not himself that the students see as the major problem-to-be-solved.

Another complexity stems from people's limited (in one sense only) storage capacity. We can not hold many raw bits of information in our memories unless we classify and categorize them. It is as though we had a limited number of file folders to work with but could label them any way we chose. If we insist on putting just one piece of information in one folder, we soon run out of space. But if we can find useful ways of grouping information, the same set of folders can hold an almost limitless quantity of information.

One problem in human learning then becomes the problem of appropriate categories—appropriate to the class of problems with which one must work. The manager who insists on separately classifying each bit of information about his operation will soon be overwhelmed by detail, as some managers are. But if he can set up an efficient system of categories, he can handle all he needs to remember.

Unfortunately, categorizing systems, once set up, are difficult to break down. The clerk has difficulty giving up his clerical categories even though he is now in a managerial job. He goes on "thinking like a clerk." As a later chapter on management development will point out, one weakness in up-through-the-ranks and job rotational training is that it demands frequent and difficult recategorization at each step on the ladder. Why, one may ask, teach a man to think like a clerk if we later want him to act like a manager?

A third source of complexity in human learning lies in the fact that mistakes in problem solving are both costly and valuable. We often (being stingy) want to learn only the "right" way of doing things. But learning only what is right means that all the other possibilities are unknown, uncharted, and unstored and, hence, cannot be categorized for dealing with similar but not identical problems in the future.

Suppose, for instance, that you are in a hotel in a strange city. You want to drive to plant X. The hotel clerk gives you directions, and you follow and memorize them. What have you learned?

Suppose, instead, that you just got into your car and started out, stopping to ask, noticing landmarks, and finally, after many mistakes, getting to X. Then you try again the next day, and the next, until you end up on the same route the clerk would have given you anyhow. Now what have you learned?

By the first method you learned one efficient path through an otherwise unknown jungle. By the second you learned a lot about the jungle and alternative ways of getting through it. You have a list of alternatives against which to apply your decision rules—but at the cost of time and energy.

Now suppose the clerk's route gets dug up for road repairs one day; so you have a detour. The advantage of earlier explorations becomes obvious. You can "feel" your way through the city; the list of mistakes you have stored up will help you solve this new problem.

Insofar, then, as the world of the manager is a world of

new problems, one must worry about balancing the fledgling manager's profitable exploration against the costliness of those explorations. If management were a series of repeatable routines, the choice would be easy. But if every problem in management is a new problem, why teach routines?

Still another complexity in human problem solving is brought about by the peculiarities of interaction between human goals and the stinginess principle. What, after all, constitutes a "satisfactory" solution to a problem? What is a "satisfactory" level of performance? Do we need to search until we find the best machine for a job? Or just until we find one that will work? We used to assume, especially in economic theory, that only the best would do, that people rationally select the one very best alternative from an array of all possible alternatives laid out before them.

There are two things wrong with this assumption. The first is that we do not usually have anything like a complete array of alternatives laid out before us. The manager does not know all the machines on the market or all possible marketing strategies, and *it would cost him a great deal to find out*. The second thing wrong is the idea that only the best is satisfactory. In practice, people often save themselves a great deal of time and effort by searching only until they find something that works, by their own private standards of satisfaction, and then using it. In fact (as the chapter on frustration pointed out), it is precisely when people feel impelled to find the very best, when their levels of aspiration are set by others far above their abilities, that they are likely to be inefficient problem solvers, unable to decide and act because every available decision and action is less than perfect. All of us have encountered people who "block" in problem solving, who never can get themselves past the searching stage into action, because there *may* be something they have not taken into account. Most managers, if forced to choose between these extremes, would probably prefer people who behave in the opposite direction, who rush precipitously into the first alternative that comes along.

Learning and problem solving, as we have been looking at them, are *active* rather than *passive* processes. People don't absorb things, they *work* at learning. They search for information, they make decisions, they act upon their decisions, they remember, and they modify their decisions after observing the effects of their actions. People do learn from exposure to experience, but, in this context, experience means doing things to the world as well as letting the world do things to you.

This distinction between active and passive learning is important in management. If we take the passive view, it follows that the trainee should be pumped full of knowledge and experience. So we probably invest heavily in classrooms, lectures, and job-rotation schemes. If we take the active view, we invest in projects, problems, coaching staffs, and the like.

If we take the passive view, we go on to count heavily on the wisdom and experience of superiors, that wisdom and experience to be communicated to the youngsters through advice, written and verbal. We encourage juniors to learn from authoritative seniors. If we take the active view, the wisdom and experience of seniors goes into a secondary, supportive category, available when juniors need it. We encourage juniors to learn first from the problems they are trying to solve and only supportively from seniors.

If we take the passive view, we assume that learning

should precede action—that we should first learn potentially useful things and *then* try to apply them. If we take the active view, we in effect encourage the learner to get himself stymied and only then to search for useful tools.

Moreover, if we generalize a little, the passive view would probably support the sequence of school first and job practice afterward. It would suggest that the business school ought to come before the business job. The active view would support a back-and-forth sequence, one that started with the job, then went *back* to school, and so on—back and forth as, and if, required by the problems encountered on the job.

In defense of schools of business, however, even the most assiduous activist must face up to one dilemma. If we start with active problem solving, how does the problem solver know *where* to search for solutions? How can he know what better tools may be available?

One answer might be that the motivated business problem solver is probably highly accessible to new tools and ideas, because he has competitors and because his level of aspiration doesn't ever quite settle down. But to get to those new tools, he, or their inventors, had better open up channels of communication. This is to say that industry, with its host of opportunities for trying to solve problems, is an ideal active learning ground for management—a better one, in many ways, than any university can hope to be—if it can maintain communication with universities and other research groups.

Learning and Motivation

Active learning occurs, we said earlier, when people are motivated; and people are motivated, by definition, when they are *not* satisfied. So we come up against another curiosity. On the one hand, psychologists, this one included, have been arguing that stability, security, objectivity, and many other fine things emerge when needs are satisfied. But now we discover that effective problem solving, which is what business is all about, emerges when needs are *not* satisfied. What's the escape from that paradox?

One answer is that there need be no escape. If the purpose of business is to get things done at a profit, and if things get done by discontented people, then let's keep people discontented, whether they are stable, secure, and objective or not.

But even if we argue that people's stability and security are not the business of the businessman, objectivity is. We would like problems to be solved "reasonably," "rationally," "sensibly," and unstable people may not be objective ones. So we are still in a box.

Another way out can be pulled from the distinction made, in the chapter on frustration, between the words "frustration" and "deprivation." People could be dissatisfied, it was pointed out, without being frustrated. They could want to solve problems without being in an emotional uproar, if they felt reasonably confident that they could satisfy their central emotional needs. So the trick—if that's a fair word—would be to keep them dissatisfied about job problems—about making the sale or designing the package—but comfortable about themselves—about being competent, appreciated salesmen or package designers. Then they can concentrate their energies on the job to be done and do it with some degree of objectivity.

If we learn through dissatisfaction, repetition need have little to do with learning. Repetition of experience in itself, without appropriate motivation, may yield little learning. Pulling dollar bills out of our pockets for years has not taught most of us much about dollar bills as such. We have learned a good deal about their use, but whose picture is on them? How many signatures? Whose? How many times does the number 1 appear? Where?

Repetition of an act may indeed help people to perform the act more skilfully, but not *because* of the repetition; rather, because the repetition provides opportunity for trying out different behaviors and seeing the results, for differentiating and mapping out the act. So let's not assume that frequent exposure to selling situations has necessarily taught the veteran to be a better salesman than the novice. It has only given him the opportunity to learn. Whether he took the opportunity and what he learned—these are quite separate questions.

In Summary

People are not perfectly rational, but neither are they incapable of thinking and learning reasonably and consciously. They are endowed with all the equipment they need: input senses, output muscles, memory apparatus, motivation, and a decision or choice mechanism. Only recently have we come even close to equipping machines with like endowments, so that they can perform a few intellectual acts as well as competent people.

On the other hand, people seem to use their endowments with considerable inefficiency. Partly because their equipment is too good, they can and do "learn too much." They learn feelings and attitudes that often interfere with other learning.

People's capacities for learning are in one sense limited,

in another, almost unlimited. By devising categories—systems by which they can classify and remember things that are appropriate to the levels of problems they are dealing with—they can store and use huge amounts of information.

If capable people are not lured by the rest of the world into seeking "perfect" solutions for their problems but limit their searches instead to finding satisfactory solutions, they can operate with considerable savings in effort. For to find a *good* product design costs far less, in both money and psychic energy, than to find *the best* product design.

It is useful to consider thinking and learning to be active processes that begin with motivation. All the activities of searching the world and the memory, of making choices, of trying out new behaviors—all get actively underway when people feel dissatisfied.

Chapter 7

THE ASSESSMENT OF PEOPLE
ONE APPLICATION OF PERSONALITY THEORY

Two equally appropriate subtitles might have been attached to this chapter. One could have been: "How not to be snowed by test salesmen." The other might have been: "How not to be snowed by anti-test salesmen." For management people are under attack from two fronts: from those who offer tests as a solution to selection problems and from those who attack tests as unethical, unscientific, and anti-individualistic.

This last chapter in Part I, then, is devoted to a practical problem: the problem of assessment. Its function is to show how the material in the preceding chapters can be applied to a large and real area of managerial decision making.

The Scope of the Assessment Problem

People in industry continually need to forecast the behavior not only of the economy, of competition, of prices, but also of one another. "Assessment," "selection," and "evaluation" are all varieties of people-forecasting.

Both professionals and laymen have frequently failed miserably in forecasting how people will behave in specified jobs. One reason is the difficulty of the job. If our earlier chapters were right, what has to be predicted is the result-ant of a complex maze of hard-to-specify interrelated forces. Forecasting the behavior of one individual is much like trying to predict exactly what pattern of cracks will result when a particular thrower throws a particular ball against a particular pane of glass. We can be fairly certain that the glass will crack. But we seldom know enough about the ball, the air currents, the thrower, and the particular pane to be sure about the directions and lengths of the cracks that will result.

Nevertheless, we cannot escape in industry from the problem of having to assess people for tasks. Every job as-signment that a manager makes includes the requirement that he assess the people available against the job he has in mind. Every contact with a customer, with a new member of his own organization, with every individual who is rele-vant to the manager's work, includes some need for assess-ment—some evaluation of how this person will behave when faced with this kind of suggestion, or that kind of job, or this other kind of person.

So assessment is not limited to "formal" problems like selecting new employees or rating the qualifications of old ones, nor is it limited to the assessment of personality. It must necessarily involve assessment of knowledge, experi-ence, education, and many other aspects of the person.

For the formal phases, like personnel selection and merit rating, a good deal of research and experience is available. Every executive in industry these days is aware of person-ality tests, patterned interviews, personnel-rating forms, and the like. Underlying each of these is a large (but not large enough) body of theory and empirical research. Unfortunately no comparable amount of work has been done on the day-to-day problems of assessment to help the business executive make increasingly accurate spot judgments about other people. Even so, some useful things are coming to be known. So, when the boss asks, "well, what did you think of him?" the executive can honestly say something more than, "He's a nice guy" or "I don't like him."

Formal Methods of Selection and Evaluation

One can single out at least three more or less separate formal approaches to the selection and evaluation of personnel for industry. Looked at right now, the separations among the three are indistinct, for they have been growing together. But historically, each has made its way over a different route.

PENCIL AND PAPER TESTS AND THE EMPIRICAL METHOD

The first approach, one largely American in origin, can be roughly labeled the "pencil and paper test approach." The great bulk of short intelligence tests, aptitude tests, etc., belong under this heading. So too, for the most part, do standard interview forms, most merit-rating scales, fitness reports, and the like. Until recently, they were mostly tests of specific skills or abilities, like numerical ability, finger dexterity, and so on.

These are typically American products in the sense that they derive from American behaviorism, with its emphasis on quantification and measurement and on empirical data gathering and with its corresponding de-emphasis on unquantified, introspective, judgmental data. As a conse-

quence, the pencil and paper approach has been characterized by efforts to improve the empirical reliability and validity of the procedures more than by efforts to improve the
rationale or depth of the material being sought. It is considerably harder to apply to over-all personality than to
specific aptitudes or abilities.

The pencil and paper position is this: The task of selecting people for jobs is a task of predicting in advance how
people will behave. Clearly, then, what is required are some
measurable advance predictions and some corresponding
measurements, taken at some later time, of how people actually performed. If the task is to select salesmen, these are
the appropriate procedural steps:

1. We gather—in a standard way—information about people who come to look for jobs as salesmen. We can do this
by setting up standard questions about, for example, education, asking them of job applicants, and coding the answers
into several categories. We can do the same with questions
about home ownership and applicants' preferences for one
kind of occupation or another, and we can measure the time
required by applicants to solve certain arithmetic problems,
and so on.

2. Ideally, we next lock up the test answers in the nearest
safe and allow *all* the applicants to go to work as salesmen.

3. Now we wait a predetermined time, perhaps a year.

4. During that year, or before it, we set up some standards about what constitutes success in selling. What is
needed is an unequivocal, quantifiable criterion of success.
In selling, a theoretically ideal approach would be to permit
all test subjects to work in the same territory or exactly
comparable ones, with precisely the same amount of training
and precisely the same selling tools. One might then use

dollar sales at the end of the year, or number of sales, or percentage of returns, or some combination of them all as the criterion of successful behavior.

5. The tester now has available (*a*) the scores of test-subject Jones on the tests he took a year ago, showing his rank on the test in relation to the other applicants, and (*b*) a measure of his subsequent actual job performance in relation to the other applicants. The next move is statistical: to measure the relationship between predictions and performance; to estimate the reliability of this relationship (i.e., to guess how frequently we could expect the relationship to be about like this in the future); and then to decide if any of the tests are worth keeping.

We may discover that a test of intelligence actually predicted sales performance somewhat better than chance. The tester would then consider his intelligence test useful for selection. And, logically, it would not matter what direction the test-performance relationship might take. That is, it would not matter if more successful salesmen were significantly more intelligent, or significantly less intelligent, than the less successful ones. For the method is rigorous here. The problem is not whether the predictions make sense, but whether they predict. If they predict, they are useful; if they do not predict, they are not useful.

The only connection between this kind of rigorous pencil and paper approach and any theory of personality lies in the manner in which particular tests are selected and constructed. For the pencil and paper approach is itself a method of measurement rather than a theory of man's behavior. Any theorist of any persuasion may use it. Some test items may be based on a theory of physiognomy, some on Freudian psychodynamics, some on the color of a man's shoes. In actual practice, the current pencil and paper personality tests used in business derive largely from a semi-behavioristic theory of personality. They have been, until recently, notable for their failure to include "deep" areas of personality.

This pencil and paper method has a great many advantages and some practical disadvantages. It has the huge advantage of quantification and empiricism. It also has dollar advantages. Pencil and paper tests, once standardized, are easy to manufacture, administer, and score. Professional testers are often needed only in the developmental stages because administration can usually be turned over to trained, but not professional, technicians. Such devices are not very time consuming, so that large numbers of people can be tested, frequently in groups of indefinite size, at reasonable costs.

Perhaps the greatest disadvantage of such procedures is that they are designed for statistical, rather than individual, prediction. That is, they are most useful in making predictions about the behavior of large numbers of people rather than about particular individuals. Thus, a pencil and paper tester may be able truthfully to tell management that, if his tests are adopted, "Of every fifty applicants whom my tests pass, you can expect an adequate job performance from forty. Under your present selection methods, you can expect adequate job performance from only twenty-five." The tester could not go on, however, to say whether or not Joe Doaks, subject No. 23, who received adequate test scores, would be among the successful forty or the unsuccessful ten. Further, the tester would also have to admit that some rejected applicants would be "false positives"—people who would have been successful but whom the tests nevertheless rejected. He could not predict who those individuals would be.

This tendency of pencil and paper methods to predict en masse rather than individually raises two questions. The first is an ethical question and perhaps a specious one. Is it "right" to turn any job applicant away, even if he is only one in a hundred, who would have been perfectly competent if he had been hired? Is it "fair" to the applicant to so depersonalize him that he becomes simply a score among hundreds of scores, his fate inexorably tied to a numerical system? Perhaps these are valid questions, and perhaps it is somehow more fair to tie an applicant's fate to the rose-colored perceptions of a non-quantitative interviewer. It would seem, however, that the ethical issue properly attaches to the whole selection problem itself, not to the issue of selection by tests.

The second question that can be asked is about the utility of pencil and paper devices at higher organizational levels, where the number of applicants for particular positions may be small. The usual statistical indexes of validity do not apply to very small samples. So if the task is to select assistant general managers rather than typists, the utility of the method is sharply reduced. It is even more sharply reduced when the task is to decide which of two applicants ought to be selected for a particular key post in, let us say, the research and development division of an electronics corporation. At this level so much depends on the correctness of a specific prediction, and similar testing experience is usually so rare, that the pencil and paper *method* becomes inapplicable.

PROJECTIVE TESTS AND THE CLINICAL METHOD

A second approach to formal selection lays much more emphasis on the dynamics of personality, much less on empirical validity. The approach may be labeled, somewhat unfairly, the projective approach. Projectives are much more "head doctor" techniques than pencil and paper tests. They are European in origin, springing theoretically from Freud and technically from the Swiss psychiatrist Rorschach. They build on the internal, perceptual frame of reference talked about in chapter 3, assuming that one can get a valid picture of a person quickly by assessing the way he projects his personality onto some standard, ambiguous parts of the world. All projectives contain these elements of standardization and ambiguity. The "questions" on the Rorschach test are some standardized ink blots that the subject is asked to describe. The tester then interprets the number, quality, and variety of the subject's responses against the tester's theory of personality and against his and others' experience with the responses of other people to the same blots.

Similarly, in the Thematic Apperception Test, the subject is asked to tell stories about a standard series of pictures. The tester records the stories and the subject's behavior. He then interprets the subject's personality in the light of the themes used in his stories.

The end result of a battery of projective tests, then, is not a numerical score comparing subject X with other subjects. It is a verbal report assessing the subject's dominant needs and ambitions, his tolerance of frustrations, his attitudes toward authority, the major conflicts that seem to be operating in his personality, and so on. Given such a report, a manager clearly must decide for himself whether the tester's judgment deserves heavy weighting in the final decision.

One important industrial advantage of projectives is also their scientific weakness. They are essentially individualistic, and they cannot be easily "proved" right or wrong, even by their proponents. Projectives, therefore, push decision making back to where it belongs anyway, into the hands of management. The projective tester says to the manager, in effect, "Here is my expert judgment of John Jones. You have your judgment of him to which you can now add mine. I have tried to add information to your fund of relevant information, but I cannot guarantee that my judgment will be right. You make the decision."

When one considers the history of projective tests, it is reasonable that they should be used in this way. Projectives have their origin in clinical psychology, in the atmosphere of psychiatry and pathology, rather than in education or industry. It is only in the last few years that these tests have even appeared on the industrial scene. In the clinic and the hospital, their primary function has been to help the physician seeking to diagnose the meaning of the psychological pains of a new patient. Perhaps, if the physician had known his new patient intimately for five or ten years, he would have no need for the projective tester. But the patient is an individual, and it is his individuality that accounts for his illness; so the physician needs a highly individualized, relatively detailed and speedy picture of this personality. This is what the projective tester tries to give him.

Unlike the pencil and paper tests, projectives seldom get to the stage at which they can be scored by technicians because the interpretation always remains individual. The judgment of the tester is a large factor. When management buys pencil and paper tests, it buys a quantitative tool from which most subjective elements of interpretation have been eliminated. Any honest technician counting up the yeses and noes on an interest inventory will come up with the same score as any other honest technician. Not so with honest projective testers. The professional judgment of the test administrator plays a far more important part than the projective tests themselves in determining what comes out. In effect, then, when management buys projective tests, it buys the tester, just as when one buys a chest X-ray, one buys the judgment and experience of the interpreting physician rather than the plate itself.

Projectives are expensive. Although efforts are being made to standardize and simplify them for mass administration, they remain largely one-at-a-time tests. A professional tester may spend eight hours or more testing and interpreting a single subject. Consequently, projectives have entered industry at the level at which they are most likely to be both useful and worth the money—at the executive level where pencil and paper tests are relatively useless.

Management's only bases for determining whether projectives are worth the investment are, first, its own opinion of the tester it has hired, and, second, *its experience over time in relating the actual behavior of applicants with the predictions that testers have made.*

In the face of these difficulties, one wonders how projectives have made their way into supposedly hardheaded business circles at all. One reason may be that projective reports seem to catch the subtle realities of executive behavior better than most pencil and paper tests. The reports are complicated and qualified, full of ifs and buts, somewhat like managerial life itself.

Here is a typical excerpt taken from a test report on an applicant for an executive position:

Mr. X is of superior intelligence. Problem situations, even those for which he is momentarily unprepared, do not throw him. He usually does not become emotionally involved when he has to work on a problem but adheres to, as he says, a strict formula which forces him into an intellectual and rational approach. . . . The problem is uppermost and feelings are disregarded. More specifically the feelings of others are disregarded for when his own personal satisfaction is involved then his approach to problems is somewhat less systematic. For example, he wants others to think that he is a very capable individual and tries hard to maintain this impression because of the satisfaction that this gives him. However, because of this attitude he is apt to become too self-confident, or "cocky," and thus makes errors in very simple situations or problems that he usually would not make under such circumstances. The amount of effort he puts forth on a problem varies with how difficult he thinks the problem is. The more complicated the problem the more interested he becomes —and in turn more systematic, planful and analytical in his approach. In a sense, he feels that he is "on the spot" under the circumstances described above, and he puts forth all his energy to demonstrate to others his capabilities through the solution of the problem. . . .

Mr. X is an overly-controlled individual in the sense that feelings play a minor role in the execution of a job. The job is paramount in his mind and he believes that he and others should subjugate themselves to it. Consequently, he is highly critical of the performance of others who work for him—but he demands as much of them as he demands of himself. Furthermore, because the job is so important to him, he does not take sufficient time out to realize the nature of the personalities working with him. He does not accomplish a job by the "human approach" but by insisting that there is a job to be done and all must do it regardless of their personal needs. The only personal needs he does become aware of are his own. *He* feels the sense of accomplishment and *he* feels that *he* has done well. In this sense he is an egocentric individual. He realizes this attitude full well. It should be pointed out that if he could realize that other people may have the same needs as he and that they, too, may want the satisfactions that he wants and that by giving them these satisfactions they will in no way threaten his position, then he may become more effective on the job than he is now. . . .

Being a competitive individual with a high level of aspiration, Mr. X may be a member of a group with whom he is associated but he will not feel as part of them sharing with them all that he knows, etc. To some extent he feels superior to those with whom he is associated, he feels that he could direct and lead them. But he does not win their confidence since he is too forward in this regard and they may resent his attempts to be in the limelight. When working with his subordinates, his status is well-defined; but with colleagues, when he has to win the status he desires, he is somewhat uncomfortable. This lack of comfort makes him put forth even more effort to demonstrate his brilliance and ability which in turn is definitely resented by the group. He is apt to be impatient with those with whom he is working because they do not see things as quickly as he. Although he tries to control himself under such circumstances, his impatience is obvious. Others would work more effectively with him and he would become more successful if he could pay more attention to and accept more of what others have to say.

Managers sometimes react against these qualifications, wishing for more "practical," black and white decisions. Realistically, though, selecting an executive is not a black and white problem. It is *not* usually true that people simply succeed or fail. They succeed or fail "if," or they would have succeeded or failed "but." They might have succeeded if they had worked for another kind of superior; or if management had given them a little looser or a little tighter rein; or if they had been provided with a high-powered assistant; or if the job description had been rewritten so that the new man was given more responsibility in area A and less in area B. For success on a job, especially a decision-making managerial job, is not a function of personality alone but of a personality in an environment. Any testing procedure that tends to describe the complications of a personality, rather than to contract and simplify it, provides extra data for relating the person to the environment. If the person is relatively unmodifiable, perhaps the environment is not.

If a projective tester, therefore, can start management

worrying about whether to put a new employee to work for systematic department-head Smith or for loose, easy-going department-head Jones, that in itself may be a considerable service to the company.

SOCIOMETRIC METHODS

Sociometrically, people are not assessed by tests or by testers but by other people: peers or subordinates or superiors. The "buddy rating" system used by the military in the Second World War is a typical sociometric device. A platoon of potential officer candidates, for example, trains together for several weeks. Then each member is asked to nominate the three men he thinks would make the best combat officers and the three he thinks would make the worst combat officers. They might be asked, too, to rate their buddies on honesty or intelligence or sense of humor or any of a number of other characteristics. Positive and negative votes received by each man are totaled and a score assigned to that man. The score represents his peers' joint estimate of his aptitude for a particular job.

Sociometric techniques do not require the judge to give a rationale for his judgment. No explanation is demanded. Individuals are simply asked to express their over-all feelings about other individuals. The sociometric method thereby short-cuts across an area of great difficulty, since both our language and our communicable knowledge about men are usually inadequate. Moreover, what we do know about personality, however inadequate, suggests that personality is not a thing to be torn apart and dealt with as a set of separable elements but is more susceptible to a kind of all-at-once, whole-man evaluation. For, as the first five chapters of this book tried to show, personality—if it can be thought of as an entity at all—is an elaborately interacting and dynamic kind of entity. When, sociometrically, one simply asks men to make an over-all judgment of one another, one is, in a way, automatically taking the wholeness of personality into account.

This coin has another side. When our data consist of the general feelings of some people about some other people, the dangers of distortion are many. Such distortions may be partially eliminated by using large numbers of judgments. Although the judgment made by one platoon member may be far off base, the judgments of fifty platoon members are reasonably valid—at least more valid, as World War II experience showed, than many paper and pencil tests, rating scales, and even military-school grades.

Sociometric methods have been used in a variety of ways for a variety of purposes. Sometimes one asks several judges to observe and listen to a group of applicants talking to one another. The judges sit on the periphery and observe the applicants. They then decide which one of the applicants would best perform a particular job. A number of variations of this "leaderless group" method are in current use.

In general, though, the sociometric methods are slow runners in the industrial race, despite their validity. A partial explanation for their lagging development may be the indirect organizational implications of their use. Sociometric methods, especially buddy ratings, are something like the voting process. Voting democracy in industry carries many dangers for traditional managerial "prerogatives" and for the whole power balance within an organization. If operators are allowed to select their own foremen, managers will argue, political plots and fixed "elections" may not be far behind. Selection by "popularity," they add, will replace selection by ability, despite the fact that research to date has shown that such ratings are *not* popularity contests.

If such methods came into widespread use without accompanying changes in the organizational context, these dangers could be real. Nevertheless, the sociometric approach fits with principles of "participative" management that are currently popular in American industry. Moreover, with tailor-made modifications to fit the needs of particular organizations, it is being used in industry today.

Day-to-Day Assessment of People

People directing an organized human effort must necessarily spend some of their time making judgments about the fitness of certain members for certain tasks. Some judgments can be formalized, but it is at an informal, day-to-day level that most assessment goes on. Top management informally, gradually, imperceptibly, perhaps even unconsciously, decides that Jones looks like presidential timber and that Smith is never likely to go anywhere.

The professional psychologist has surprisingly little to offer the industrial manager in this area. The social scientist has offered industry tests and measurements and forms and systems to help with the massive formal job of screening and selecting and record keeping. But he has helped comparatively little with the job of improving the manager's personal skill in making judgments about the people he encounters in his business life. Of course the capacity to judge other people is not one that can be easily handed from one person to another. It is a skill requiring effort and practice and also requiring the absence of certain personality blocks. Parental and other early environmental influences probably have more to do with this skill than anything else. A man's capacity to judge probably correlates positively with the extent to which he can view the outside world undistortedly, i.e., it correlates with his own security and self-knowledge. For judging is one kind of problem solving. It can be reduced to three phases: determining what information is necessary to make a judgment; obtaining that information, usually through communication with other persons; evaluating that information into a judgment. Each of these processes is likely to be as good as the judge's own internal information-processing system.

The first, deciding what information is relevant, requires also that we ask: "Relevant for what?" Is he being considered for a specific job? What kind of a job? Working with whom? And so on. If we can get a good psychological picture of the task, we may be able to isolate the kinds of psychological information that would be relevant in a personality.

But even with a clear objective, how shall we go about ordering the information we can hope to get? Many schemes are possible. The one that follows is a crude one, but perhaps it will be useful. It is made up of three categories: first, the "givens" in a personality; second, the goals of a personality; and third, the methods by which a personality uses its givens to achieve its goals. Put another way, we can say that the accuracy of our predictions of a person's behavior would increase if we could adequately answer this question: How does this person use what he has to get what he wants? This question asked in conjunction with the question "What are we judging him for?" constitutes a reasonable starting point for the assessment process.

THE GIVENS IN A PERSONALITY

By the time we have become adults, all of us show some relatively unchanging characteristics. Some of these characteristics are givens in the sense that they were inherited, some in the sense that they were learned early and intensely and aren't given up easily. Intelligence is such an aspect of a person; so is the general energy level of his personality— almost his biological metabolic rate; so are his skills and knowledge, his educational background, the things he can do well; so, too, probably, are his sensitivity to others, the level of concreteness or abstractness with which he thinks; and certainly his physical makeup and appearance. We can find out something about these things indirectly. When we know them and when we know what we are judging for, we begin to have some basis for making comparative judgments.

THE GOALS OF A PERSONALITY

To a considerable extent people are known by their needs. We can communicate something to a third person if we can describe the dominant pattern of needs in a personality. Something imprecise, but nevertheless meaningful, is achieved by saying of another person that he has an uncommon need for orderliness, or that he is unusually affiliative, or that he has a strong need for autonomy or independence and tends to react against restrictions. Long lists of such needs can be set down, and, though they are likely to be poorly and overlappingly defined, communication about the pattern of a particular personality's needs contributes toward defining it, at least temporarily.

One can also seek information about a person's "habits," his manners of behaving. If personality is a dynamic but goal-directed system, then these characteristic methods of behaving must represent the personality's characteristic ways of trying to achieve what it wants. Like the computer, we can expect people to use methods that have worked for them before. At this level one is asking: How does X perceive other people? What is the nature of his social relationships? What are his relevant attitudes toward relevant issues? To what extent does he satisfy his needs through methods that conform to the culture of the organization in which he must work? To what extent does he use methods which do not conform? How does he control his moods and his areas of insecurity? Are his methods consistent or variable?

It is possible to follow out each of these three categories in some detail: to provide a list of givens, a list of needs, and a list of methods for using givens to satisfy needs. But the usefulness of such a process for this book is doubtful. Perhaps what is most useful here is to suggest that a judge order the information that he can obtain about another personality into categories like these and then compare what he finds with the purpose for which he is judging.

Getting Information about a Person

A good deal of information about A can be obtained by talking to B or C. A good deal more can be gotten from talking to A. If the judge has lived closely and intimately with his subject, the process of gathering additional information to make a new judgment is minimal. He probably knows all he needs to know, and his task is to order it against the problem for which the judgment is being made and to try to extricate himself from his prejudices. If one is dealing with a relative stranger, however (and it is in this category that most problems of assessment reside), then gathering information is a major part of the problem. Historical sources provide the assessor with one kind of information. He can use records, biographical information, recommendations from other people, etc., and try to infer future behavior from this secondhand knowledge of past behavior. But he will have to form some large part of his judgment in the here and now by talking with the person being judged. The conversations may be one or more formal interviews or several brief informal discussions of business problems, or they may take a social form, a cocktail party or an evening at home. In all cases, the personal evaluation process goes on, even if there is no particular job about which an evaluation needs to be made.

Such personal, face-to-face evaluation always means that information about the other person filters through the screen of the judge's own needs and prejudices. Nevertheless, the wise judge may not always try to discard his own feelings and prejudices entirely in favor of an "objective system." Discarding such feelings might be desirable if it were possible. But it is doubtful whether it is possible. The alternative for the judge is to recognize the characteristics of his own filters and then to pay attention to what comes through these filters.

For whether one tries to or not, he listens to another person at two levels: at the level of the speaker's words and the information they carry, and at the level of the listener's own feelings about the speaker's words and the feelings these words convey. For example, most people can decide quickly whether or not another person seems to be afraid of them, or angry at them, or comfortable or uncomfortable with them, whether he talks too much for their liking, whether he has what they consider a good sense of humor, etc. And yet, in most formal evaluation situations, we often try consciously to block out and ignore this fundamental source of information, preferring to deal with what we like to think of as "the facts."

This tendency to discard our own semiconscious but nevertheless valuable insights probably derives from our justifiable doubt about our own ability to make judgments. Certainly such self-doubt is warranted. Most of us would like to have something more solid to lean on than our own amorphous judgment. We prefer to draw inferences from grades in school, test scores, number of jobs the applicant has held, and any piece of objective, "factual" information we can find. Yet, paradoxically, especially outside the office, only the most insensitive of us would try to estimate another's friendliness by asking whether he has read Dale Carnegie. Instead, data about friendliness are obtained by talking and socializing and then filtering the results through our own conception of what "friendly" means. In effect, we listen with our "third ear." Of course, the third ear is only as good as the person using it is objective about himself. But the same can be said about the first and second ears.

In industry "subjective" personal assessment may lead an organization always to find new people like the old ones. "Good" people may become people that today's management likes. And the people today's management likes may well be people like today's management. Subjective, personalized assessment, with little reference to the question of assessment-for-what, may indeed ultimately yield an in-group of "all-alike" people. But since all-alike people may be able to work together better than all-different people, an organization may, under certain conditions, profit from just such prejudice. For example, one can argue that in a period of growth and youth an all-alike team has many advantages; later in an organization's life the same subjective prejudices may be stifling to the birth of new ideas.

There is another side to this picture. When people are being assessed and know it, they behave in ways they think will evoke the best assessment. If a personnel interviewer asks Mr. X, "How do you get along with people?" his answer might be, "Oh, just fine. I like people etc., etc., etc." But if a psychiatrist for whose services Mr. X was paying asked him the same question an hour later, his answer might be different: "Well, Doc, that's just the problem. Some people don't seem to pay any attention to me etc., etc., etc." This truism, that people play to their audiences, is frequently overlooked in industrial interviewing.

One method for dealing with it is to evaluate in disguised situations. This alternative immediately introduces procedural as well as ethical questions. A second alternative is to make the evaluator an ink blot. Thus the interviewer does not ask, "How do you get on with people?" but instead asks, "What are the kinds of people you like best?" By opening up his questions, by modifying them so that the "right" answers are not at all obvious, the interviewer at least provides a situation in which the subject's answers are his own and not the interviewer's. Even so, people being assessed through interviews will make some guesses about the "right" answers; but, as long as they remain guesses, they represent a valid projection of the personality being interviewed. The major assumption underlying what has come to be called "non-directive" interviewing is just that one. It is the idea that an ambiguous stimulus (an uncommitted interviewer) requires the interviewee to "project" his own attitudes into the interview. An unambiguous interviewer, for whom the "right" answers are obvious, yields only a reflection of himself.

The idea is simple and sensible. The purpose of an interview is to gather information about another person, not about the interviewer. It is appropriate also that the interviewer provide a situation free enough so that the interviewee can talk about himself and be himself. In practice, the application of this principle suggests that an information-gathering interview should be designed like a series of inverted triangles. The interviewer opens each area of information he is seeking with big, broadside queries so that the interviewee can talk at length about his perceptions of the question, raising points in the order that seems significant to him and with the intensity that he thinks is appropriate to them. If the interviewer is still unsatisfied because he wants specific areas of information in more detail, he can then proceed to narrow his questions down to greater and greater specificity. Then he is ready to open up a new area with a new broad and ambiguous question.

These thoughts about day-to-day evaluations of other people are general and incomplete. Ultimately, after all, an evaluation of one person by another is a judgment and nothing more. A good judge needs all the information he can get from all the sources he can find. To an extent, scales, forms, and categories can be helpful. But no "system" provides a means for escaping from one's own lack of sensitivity or understanding in making such judgments. There are no formulas that can rule the judge out of the judging equation.

*Assessment and the Atmosphere of the
Organization*

Drawing from earlier chapters, we can predict that people in an organization will try to evoke the best assessment they can get. They will (and should) try to stack the cards in their own favor. More than that, however, we can predict that they will have mixed feelings about assessment, both resenting it and seeking it out. We should expect resentment because assessment is a threat to independence and autonomy. But we should also expect people to "want to know where they stand," to want to know whether they are loved and thought well of by those on whom they depend.

From the managerial point of view, then, the problem of assessment is more than a problem of technique. The tests, the interviews, the other ritualistic paraphernalia of assessment, are only a small part of the problem. The bigger parts raise questions like these: Shall we consciously assess our people? Shall we formalize the process? Shall we report back results? All results? Or only "good" ones? Who shall assess? Superiors only? Or peers? Or subordinates? What is to be assessed? Personality or performance? Shall we build a work environment permeated with an atmosphere of assessment?

This book can offer no pat answers to such questions. There are none. But the chapters that follow are devoted, in large part, to examining such problems of human relationships and to considering the implications of some alternative courses of action.

In Summary

Three general approaches to formal assessment have been described: pencil and paper tests, projectives, and sociometric methods. Each has its own advantages and costs. Pencil and paper devices are relatively cheap and relatively standardized, but their use is largely limited to mass-selection situations. Projectives go deep and are rich in the material they dredge up, but subjective, individualistic, expensive, and poorly validated. Sociometrics are easy and relatively valid but carry serious implications for the power relationships in an organization.

Day-to-day assessing of people is a more difficult problem. It can be helped by a set of categories for thinking about personality, by utilizing modern interviewing techniques, and by increasing one's insight into one's self.

The larger questions of assessment are not "how" questions but questions of "why" and "how much."

Part II

PEOPLE TWO AT A TIME
PROBLEMS OF INFLUENCE AND AUTHORITY

The focus of this second section shifts from the singular to the plural, from one person to relationships between people and especially to the efforts of one person to influence and change the behavior of others.

Influence is not a small problem. It is not only a problem that pervades business and industry, where people must continually devote much of their energy to trying to change other people. It is also a central problem in the family, in education, in psychiatry, in international relations, in politics, and in every other phase of human interaction.

To some extent, one can say that the behavior-change problem is growing more and more complex in America. Our technological, specialized culture has made people increasingly dependent on one another for physical need satisfaction. And some as yet undefined psychological characteristics of our culture seem to be making people increasingly interdependent for social and egoistic need satisfactions too. One observer has called us an increasingly "other-directed" people—people who need others not only for bread and warmth but for justifying our presence and for providing us with standards to live by. The young executive finds it hard to separate good work from his boss's approval of it.

The author cannot feel sure he has written a good book until the critics laud it. The housewife's new sofa is successful only if the neighbors want one too.

The behavior-change question is such a universal one that it cannot be tossed off lightly with a few clichés about hand shaking and open office doors. Another thing is clear, too. No adequate answers will be found in this book. The most we can hope for is to try to isolate some of the dimensions of the problem as it seems to exist in industry and to look at some ways that people outside industry have tried to tackle it.

This section puts a good deal of emphasis on the idea of communication because communication is the most important prerequisite to any attempt to change human behavior. Many of these pages therefore do not have their origins in psychology or sociology but in the physical and engineering sciences. I have also tried to interweave some other ideas that evolve mostly from social psychology. And I have tried to treat the whole in the light of the picture of man that was drawn in Part I.

Part II begins with a brief consideration of relationships in our society in order to set the background and to show how Part I, on individuals, is related to Part II, on influence. Then we consider some ideas about communication, the basic mechanism of influence. The next chapter hits the problem head-on, describing some dimensions of influence and their implications. Then one chapter is devoted to the possibilities and limitations of authority as a tool for influence, and the next to alternative tools. The last chapter of this part, like the last chapter in the first part, picks one major applied problem of influence, the problem of money incentives, and examines it from a psychological perspective.

Chapter 8

RELATIONSHIPS
THE FOREST AND THE TREES

Back in chapter 2, in the discussion of dependency and the paralyzed brother, one important item was omitted. We treated the case as though *only* the paralyzed brother were dependent. The big brother was free of dependency. But is that ever really true? Isn't big brother dependent too? Clearly the child is dependent on the parents, but aren't the parents also dependent on the child? The employee is dependent on the boss, but why does the boss put ads in the paper asking, literally, for "help"?

What was omitted, then, in the first section was the emphasis on *inter*dependency; on the idea of the *relationship*. We can define relationships as situations in which individuals or groups seek mutually to satisfy needs. In this section, we try to broaden the spotlight to include a bit of the forest of relationships as well as the individual trees.

Interdependency

In modern American industry everyone is, to a degree, the paralyzed brother, and everyone is also, to a degree, the big brother. Modern industry is complicated, socially and technologically, so complicated that everyone from the chairman of the board on down requires the help of other people for the satisfaction of his needs.

If that assertion is true, then the next step should be the same one talked about in chapter 2—ambivalence. Anyone who lives in an organization is living in an atmosphere of dependency. He should therefore feel some love and some hate toward the organization. The intensity and direction of feelings should, in turn, vary with the ups and downs of organizational life.

The morals of this tale are simple and important ones. Don't look for psychological equilibrium in organizations (or in marriage or any other relationship, for that matter). Look for variation and change. Don't look for statics; look for dynamics. Don't look for a permanently "happy" organization; look for one that is self-corrective, that doesn't build up unexpressed grudges.

Big brother (the organization) must always be frustrating as well as satisfying. He fools himself if he thinks he can be otherwise. But what he and the paralyzed brother can do is to limit the duration and build-up of frustration by providing mechanisms for expressing and acting upon it. Big brother had better also be satisfying as well as frustrating, because the dependency is mutual.

Some Categories of Relationships

If relationships are cases of mutual dependency, it follows that each member is trying to satisfy his needs through the other. Each is trying to influence and modify the behavior of the other to satisfy his own needs.

Influence or efforts to change behavior, then, become the

property not only of ethically questionable "manipulators," politicians, advertisers, and hard-selling salesmen. Influence is also the property of husbands, children, staff people, schoolteachers, managers, and just about everyone else in our society. So much so that it is nonsense for any of us to be "against" influence.

Let us consider here several categories of relationships to see what limits they put on influence techniques and what ethical questions they raise.

The first category, the *one-shot* versus the *long-term* relationship, provides some serious, ethical-technical questions. In a long-term relationship, when A knows he must go on living or working with B *after* he has tried to change B's behavior, he may proceed with caution no matter what his personal ethics. His own dependency on the others in the relationship serves as a built-in governor on his influence techniques, even if his conscience doesn't. But in short-term, one-shot relationships, when A never expects to see B again —after the door-to-door sale or after A has talked B out of giving him the traffic ticket—then the range of influence techniques A may use is limited only by his own conscience and his fear of the law. Incidentally, except for selling (and most of the time even there), relationships in industry are *not* of the one-shot variety. That may be why some observers see salesmen as the last stronghold of individualism and independence in industry (and why other observers see salesmen as the last stronghold of amorality).

Besides variation in duration, relationships vary along a *power* dimension, too. Big brother may need little brother, but little brother needs big brother more, or at least he may think he does. If that is so, the constraints imposed by the relationship on big brother's behavior are fewer than those on little brother's. Big brother may feel free to use influence methods that outsiders might feel are exploitive and harsh, if he uses his power directly, or manipulative and paternalistic, if he clothes his power in silk.

Relationships also vary in the extent to which *rules of interpersonal behavior* and *escape clauses* are clearly specified. There are legal and religious constraints, for instance, surrounding the marital relationship, making escape from it rather difficult. The union contract, similarly, is often the umpire of union-management relationships; and the law sets other limits on the use of managerial power over employees.

The rules need not be written, however. Unwritten ones are often equally significant in controlling behavior. A death in the immediate family of an employee evokes a clause in an unwritten contract that says that he shall have time off and shall be free of undue pressure for a while. Any superior who breaks that unwritten rule may find himself facing the disapproval of his peers and superiors, as well as of his subordinates. Such unwritten social rules exist for a society as a whole, but they also differ from company to company. In some companies executives expect to have to work overtime, to call the boss "Mister," to wear white shirts, to have a cocktail at lunch, and so on. People who break such unwritten rules are punished as much as people who break written ones. But it is possible for people to break off relationships with a company. A self-selection process in organizations with numerous and well-established social rules can, therefore, eventually yield a homogeneous, "think-alike" group of personnel simply by driving out or modifying those people who are not initially willing to accept the rules.

The currently popular and important debate on individualism versus conformity centers on this problem of the depth
and extent of social sanctions on individual behavior. Strong
sanctions encourage homogeneity of interests and outlook,
which some companies feel is good, but thereby discourage
individuality and peculiarity, which many observers feel are
even better. At least one question is appropriate here: Are
there some stages in an organization's life at which it needs
conformity and homogeneity to make for orderliness and
efficiency in its operations? Are there other stages when it
needs heterogeneity and interpersonal conflict, and the creativity and re-examination of assumptions that may accompany heterogeneity? Using the terminology of chapter 6,
are there some unprogramed classes of problems that need
individuality? And some programed, semiroutinized problems that need conformity?

One last category of relationships is worth mentioning
here. Some relationships center on the satisfaction of *personal* needs, others center on *impersonal* needs. Salesmen,
for example, usually set up customer relationships which,
from the salesman's standpoint at least, are largely impersonal. The purpose of the relationship for him is to sell the
goods, not to make friends per se. Occasionally, however,
salesmen's relationships with customers deepen in subtle,
inadvertent ways so that the salesman finds himself on
"intimate" terms with a customer. Personal, social, and egoistic needs enter the scene. The relationship becomes valuable to both parties *in its own right*. Often if that happens
the salesman finds himself in a trap. He can no longer use
the influence tactics ordinarily drawn from his regular arma-

mentarium. He begins to feel stirrings of guilt and conscience about goals and methods he normally uses without concern. He wants to maintain the friendship as much as he wants to sell the product.

Similarly, within the organization, managers often discover that the relationships they see as primarily impersonal and problem-oriented are seen by subordinates as *personal* relationships, involving central social and egoistic needs. The boss says something about changing the method of promotion in a merchandising problem, and the subordinate feels his personal competence has been criticized or that his boss has stopped liking him.

These variations in the kinds and intensities of relationships lead one immediately to expect, quite rightly, that the problem of influencing behavior is a complicated one, varying with the internal nature of the relationship and with the nature of the external social, legal, and economic environment. Simple magical rules of thumb will have no very useful place in such a complex and dynamic set of situations.

The Place of Communication

The next chapter discusses communication in relationships. It is an appropriate next step in a consideration of behavior change for these reasons: First, it is by communication that people try to modify others' behavior in order to satisfy their own needs. Second, it is by communication that the needs and perceptions of others become known. So A influences B by talking to him, and he learns about B by listening to him.

We come back then to the closed-loop notion of active learning discussed in chapter 6. Only now A is not learning to solve arithmetic problems, he is learning to solve B.

Our chapter 6 conception of learning looked something like this:

A acts upon a target problem and receives information back from the target about the effects of his actions. Then he tries again. In this chapter we have replaced the word "target" with the words "person B." *But when we do this we can see that the diagram describes not only how A acts upon B, but also how B acts upon A.* The *mutuality* of the relationship, and therefore of the influence process, begins to show up. It suggests that A's don't just change B's. If the loop is a closed one, A and B always change one another.

In Summary

Our new unit of discussion is the relationship between A and B, rather than A or B alone.

Relationships are defined as multiperson efforts to satisfy needs through one another. Members of relationships are therefore *interdependent.* They can then be expected to hold mutually ambivalent feelings toward one another. Hence we should not expect organizations, which are structures built of relationships, to reach any lasting psychological equilibrium.

Relationships vary in duration, power distribution, environmentally determined rules of behavior, and in degree of "personalness." Each of these aspects raises questions about the ethics and the techniques of influence to be used by one member to satisfy his needs through others.

Communication is the basic tool of relationships. In most relationships it is simultaneously a tool for information gathering and for influence by *all* members of the relationship.

Chapter 9

COMMUNICATION

GETTING INFORMATION FROM A INTO B

People begin, modify, and end relationships by communicating with one another. Communication is their channel of influence, their mechanism of change. In industrial organizations it has become popular recently to communicate about communication—to talk and write about the importance of communication in problem solving. The talk about communication is appropriate because communication is indeed a critical dimension of organization.

Unfortunately, though, much of the talk has been either nonsensical or unusable. For one thing, the word "communication" has been used to mean everything from public speaking to mass merchandising. For another, most of the talk has been hortatory rather than explanatory. Managers are urged to use "two-way" communication, because it is "better" (what does "better" mean?) than one-way communication. The fad has extended to "three-way" communication, again without evidence or precise definition.

The purpose of this chapter is to describe some major dimensions of the communication process, to examine what can be meant by "better" or "worse" communication, and to relate the idea of communication to the ideas of inter-personal influence and behavior change.

Some Dimensions of Communication

Sometimes there are advantages to asking simple-minded questions. They can help to strip away some of the confusing gingerbread surrounding an idea so that we can see it more objectively.

Suppose we ask, simple-mindedly, what are the things that can happen when A talks to B? What is involved in two people's talking to one another?

First, A usually talks to B *about something*. The process has a content. They talk baseball or they talk business or they talk sex. The content is what usually hits us first when we tune in on a conversation. Content of communication, in fact, is what psychologists and businessmen alike are usually thinking about when they think about human relations.

We can see subclasses within content too. We can differentiate categories of content like, for example, *fact* and *feeling*.

Other things, quite independent of what is said, take place when A talks to B. Some conversations take place in the presence of a great deal of *noise;* others are relatively noiseless. In this context "noise" means things that interfere with transmission. We can encounter channel noise like the static on a telephone line that makes it hard for B to hear what A is saying. We can also usefully think of psychological noises, like B's thinking about something else, so that again it is hard for him to hear what A is saying; or like B's being so afraid of A that it is hard for him to hear what A is saying. Language or code noise may make it hard for B to hear: he doesn't understand the words A is using in the way A understands them.

All sorts of noise can occur independently of content. We can find noisy or noiseless communications about *any* content. We also can usually observe that A, in the presence of noise, is likely to communicate more *redundantly*—to repeat his message in the hope that B will be able to hear it better the second time or to say the same thing in a different way. Redundancy is one of the most common weapons for combating noise. It is "inefficient" in the sense that repetition is wasteful of time and energy. It is "efficient" in the sense that, so long as noise exists, it helps to push the content through.

Besides the content and noise dimensions of conversation between A and B, a third dimension is the *communication net*. Usually we think of A to B conversation as a direct one; but many such conversations, especially in organizations, are mediated through other people. One thing an organization chart is supposed to tell us is that A can speak to B only through C or D. As a later chapter will show, the structure of the net a particular organization uses can have a lot to do with the speed and accuracy of members' talkings to one another.

One more dimension of the process is worth noting, especially since it has been ridden so hard in recent managerial literature. It is the *direction* of communication—its one-wayness or two-wayness. Again it is an independent dimension. No matter what A and B may be talking about, no matter how much static may be involved, no matter what the network, A may talk to B this way: A → B; or this way: A ⇆ B. A can talk and B can only listen, i.e., one-way communication; or A can talk and B can talk back, i.e., two-way communication.

This last aspect of the process, one-wayness versus two-

wayness, gets special attention in the remainder of this chapter. Is two-way communication really better? What does
"better" mean? Better for what and for whom? When?

One-Way versus Two-Way
Communication

In its simplest essentials our problem is to clarify the differences between these two situations: (1) One person, A,
talking to another, B, *without* return talk from B to A; versus (2) conversation from A to B *with* return conversation
from B to A. The differences can be clarified best by testing
one method against the other. Here is such a test situation:

The pattern of rectangles shown here is an idea you
would like to tell some B's about. Suppose you try to communicate it *in words* to a half-dozen of your friends who
are sitting around your living room:

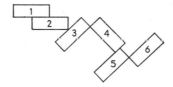

Assume that the rectangles touch each other at "sensible"
places—at corners or at midpoints along the line. There are
no touch points at any unusual places. All the angles are
either 90° or 45° angles; there are no odd ones. This pattern
of rectangles is an idea comparable perhaps to a complicated
set of instructions you may have to give to a subordinate or
to the definition of a policy that you would like to pass
along or to the task of explaining statistical quality control
to a sales manager. This idea can be communicated to others
under (1) one-way or (2) two-way conditions.

If you are the communicator, these are your *one-way* instructions:

1. Turn your back on your audience so that you cannot get visual communication back.

2. Give the audience blank sheets of paper, so that they can listen and draw exactly what you are communicating. Ask them to try to draw as accurate a picture of the pattern of rectangles as possible.

3. Describe the pattern of rectangles to them *in words* as fast as you can. The audience is not permitted to ask questions, or laugh, or sigh, or in any other way to communicate back to you any information about what it is receiving.

This game is a good parlor game, if you can find some people to try it on. Try it, time it, and then check the accuracy of your communication by determining whether or not your audience has drawn what you have described. If they received what you tried to send, so their pictures match the test picture, then you have communicated. To the extent that their pictures do not match the one in the drawing, you have not communicated.

Two-way communication can be tested for contrast in the same way. The same rules apply, and here is a similar test pattern:

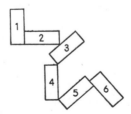

This time the basic job is the same, to describe the pattern verbally so that the people who are listening can draw it. But here are the differences:

1. This time you may face your audience.
2. They are allowed to interrupt and ask you any questions they want to at any time they want to.

Try it this way and time it. The differences between what happened the first time and what happened the second time are the differences between one- and two-way communication. (The order in which the two methods are used does not matter.)

Under experimental conditions these findings have emerged from this game: (1) One-way communication is considerably *faster* than two-way communication. (2) Two-way communication is *more accurate* than one-way, i.e., more people in the audience correctly reproduce the drawing under two-way conditions. (3) The receivers are more sure of themselves and make more correct judgments of how right or wrong they are in the two-way system. (4) The sender finds himself feeling psychologically under attack in the two-way system, because his receivers pick up his mistakes and oversights and *let him know about them.* The receivers may make snide remarks about the sender's intelligence and skill, and, if the receivers are trying very hard and taking the task seriously, they may actually get angry at the sender, and he at them. (5) The two-way method is relatively noisy and disorderly—with people interrupting the sender and one another, with the slowest man holding up the rest, and so on. The one-way method, on the other hand, appears neat and efficient to an outside observer, but the communication is less accurate.

Such a demonstration points out both the advantages and the costs of one-way and of two-way communication. If *speed* alone is what is important, then one-way communication has the edge. If *appearance* is of prime importance, if one wishes to look orderly and business-like, then the one-way method again is preferable. *If one doesn't want one's mistakes to be recognized,* then again one-way communication is preferable. Then the sender will not have to hear people implying or saying that he is stupid or that there is an easier way to say what he is trying to say. Of course, such comments may be made about him whether he uses one-way or two-way communication, but under one-way conditions he will not have to listen to what is said, and it will be harder for anyone to prove that mistakes were made by A rather than B. *If one wants to protect one's power,* so that the sender can blame the receiver instead of taking blame himself, then one-way communication is again preferable. The sender can say: "I told you what to do; you just weren't bright enough to get the word." If he uses two-way communication, the sender will have to accept much of what blame there is, and it will be apparent to all that he deserves some of it; *but he will also get his message across.*

Those are the major differences between one- and two-way communication. They are differences that most people are aware of implicitly. If a person gets a chance to ask questions, to double check what he might have missed, then he can make sure he has gotten exactly what he is expected to get. On the other hand, if he must only sit and listen, he may or may not get the word, and he is likely to feel frustrated and uncertain about what he does get. Moreover, that bit of frustration and uncertainty is likely to grow because he has no way of making sure of things he isn't sure of.

To put it another way, one-way communication is not

likely to be communication at all. It is more likely to be talk. One can talk by passing words out into the air. Those words don't become communication until they enter meaningfully into somebody else's head.

Of course, it is simple for a communicator to claim that his responsibility is only to pass a message along, that the receiver's responsibility is to make sure that he understands it. But this is not a very adequate claim. If one really were to argue through the question of who is responsible for the success of communication, one would certainly conclude that communication is largely the communicator's responsibility. For if the communicator's job is to communicate—and if to communicate he must get his message into the receiver —then his responsibility cannot end until the receiver has received. And he cannot be sure that the receiver has received until he gets confirming feedback from the receiver. On the other hand, the location of responsibility becomes a far less significant issue when one perceives communication as a two-party process to begin with.

A partial definition of communication is now possible. First, to communicate is to shoot information *and* to hit a target with it. Shooting alone is not communicating. Second, to have more than chance probability of hitting a target requires that the sender get feedback from the target about the accuracy of his shots.

If an artilleryman had to fire over a hill at an invisible target, he would have to fire blind and hope that by luck one of his shells would land on the target. He would spray the area with shells and go away, never being certain whether he had or had not destroyed his objective. But by the simple addition of a spotter standing on the hilltop, the likelihood of accurate shooting can be greatly increased. The spotter can feed back to the gunner information about the effects of the gunner's own shots. "Your last shot was a hundred yards short. The second was fifty yards over." And so on. The advantage is obvious, and it is precisely the advantage of two-way over one-way communication—the communicator can learn the effects of his attempts to communicate and can adjust his behavior accordingly. Like the learning machine we discussed in chapter 6, the decision maker needs inputs as well as outputs to correct his own behavior.

With our definition of communication, the issue of one- and two-way communication in industry can be cast somewhat differently than is usual. For now one encounters apparent conflict between the short-run efficiency of two-way communication and the long-run need to maintain power and authority at various levels of the hierarchy. Two-way communication makes for more valid communication, and it appears now that more valid communication results not only in more accurate transmission of facts but also in reorganized perceptions of relationships. Authority, for example, may under ideal conditions of two-way communication cease to serve as a sufficient protection for inadequacy. The dictum that a well-informed citizenry is democracy's protection against autocracy may also be applicable to the well-informed staff or the well-informed employee. And though "democracy" may connote things desirable in government, its connotations for industrial organizations in our society are far from clear.

Communication about Novel and
Routine Problems

Back in chapter 6, when our focus was on individual learning and problem solving, we pointed out that people *learn,* they use their memories of past problems to solve similar present ones.

Correspondingly, it is obviously true that if the problem in the experiment on two-way communication had been a familiar instead of a novel one, the results might have been quite different. A, for instance, could probably have communicated the English alphabet accurately and rapidly through one-way communication alone. In fact, it has been shown that if we use two-way communication on these rectangle problems again and again with the same group, *communication soon becomes one-way* anyhow. People stop asking questions. They don't have to. They have learned the code; so A and B understand one another.

From the point of view of speed and accuracy, then, one could make this tentative generalization. Two-way communication improves the accurate communication of previously uncoded or insufficiently coded ideas. But two-way communication contributes considerably less to accuracy *after* the code has been clarified—after new problems have been programed and routinized. Coupling this generalization with the notion that new problems occur more frequently in upper organizational echelons, we can also tentatively conclude that two-way communication is more useful within the management group than further down the line.

But let's not ignore two major constraints. First, one-way communication affects morale as well as speed and accuracy and *may* therefore be worth discarding for that reason alone. And, second, to what extent is it true in a particular plant to say that managers face more new problems per week than salesmen? Or employment interviewers? Or lathe operators in a job shop?

What Gets Communicated?

One aspect of the content problem deserves mention here, although it will be dealt with more fully later. The problem is that people usually communicate more than information to the target; they communicate feelings as well as facts. Suppose the artillery spotter, instead of simply announcing where the last shell had landed, decided to add a few typically human comments of his own. Suppose the spotter said to the gunner: "Look, you stupid s.o.b., your last shot was three hundred yards over. Where the hell did you learn to shoot?" That kind of communication of unsolicited information will complicate the psychological picture, just as will the communication of inaccurate information, sometimes causing the now frustrated gunner to change his target from the farmhouse to the spotter.

These problems of the content of communication are the subject matter of the next few chapters of this book—the chapters on (communication as a tool for) influencing people's behavior.

In Summary

Communication is a primary tool for effecting behavior change. We can isolate at least four independent dimensions of the communication process: content, noise, network characteristics, and direction.

One-way communication has some advantages in speed over two-way. It also has the advantage of protecting the sender from having to recognize his own faults. Two-way communication has the advantages of greater accuracy and greater feelings of certainty for the receiver. But two-way communication involves some psychological risks to the defenses of the sender.

Chapter 10

INFLUENCING BEHAVIOR

SOME DIMENSIONS OF THE PROBLEM

The purpose of this chapter is to scan panoramically some things that happen when one person, A, sets out to communicate with another person, B, for the specific purpose of changing B's behavior.

The problems under consideration here are largely tactical ones, like these: A sets out to get B to quit smoking; or A sets out to "discipline" B, who has again shown up late for work; or A sets out to stimulate his passive staff into more energetic activity; or A sets out to get B to like him better or to respect him more. When we watch A's undertaking such tasks, several common aspects become noticeable; some seem to center in A, others in B, and still others in the interactions between the two. Let's begin with a clear code. A is the chang*er*. B is the chang*ee*.

The Changer's Motivation

One oddity about people who seek to change others is their readiness to undertake the job without thinking much about their own objectives or their own motives. A friend of mine told me a story recently about his extended efforts to get his daughter to stop sucking her thumb. He had been worried about it for a long time and had seen the family doctor about it. The doctor had examined the child, found no physical damage, and advised the father to forget about the problem.

But when the child got to be about three years old, Papa began to worry about it again. He was worried, he said, about what thumb sucking would do to her teeth and jaws. This time he took her to a psychiatrist who talked to the child at some length and came up with the same advice the family physician had given: forget about it; it would take care of itself.

Six months later Papa decided on his own to try some of the popular methods for stopping thumb sucking. He put some nasty-tasting stuff on the thumb; he spanked her; and he made her wear mittens. But these methods didn't work either. Now he had come to me.

His objective *seemed* clear enough; it was to stop the child from sucking her thumb. But when pressed, he agreed that there were some secondary objectives that were perhaps not so secondary when he thought about them. He wanted the child to stop sucking her thumb, but he was not willing to pay any price to accomplish it. He was not willing, for instance, to exchange thumb sucking for stuttering or even for nose picking. Moreover, when we talked more generally about what he was trying to accomplish, he finally admitted that what he really wanted was to start making an adult out of his daughter, to start socializing her. He was disturbed because this three-and-a-half-year-old extension of himself was behaving in a way that he considered childish and shameful. He thought that other people disapproved of little girls who sucked their thumbs and that their disapproval *reflected on his capacity as a parent*. He finally decided, after thinking a good deal about himself, simply to stop the whole attempt.

Such confusion of motives is not at all unusual, even in business. A supervisor, under pressure from his own superiors, starts pushing discipline without thinking much about its effect on production. If an observer raises these issues, the foreman will argue that his goal is to get more work, purely and simply. But his behavior may suggest that some of the needs involved are personal and emotional, e.g., to get the approval of his boss.

A personnel manager tries to get his staff working hard on a suggestion system. His objective is to build a system that will help the company. But under a microscope one can see other objectives that the personnel manager may not admit very readily. He received a copy of *Business Week* from the president the other day with a note about an article on suggestion systems: "Joe, please let me know what we are doing about programs like this one."

Perhaps the most common form of unclarity about motives for changing others stems from conflicts between immediate and long-term needs. In most industrial situations, no matter how simple and specific the case, a secondary, long-term factor is likely to be lurking in the background. It is the factor of the continuing relationship. Any time a supervisor performs some specific act to get more or better work on a specific job at a specific time, he is acting like the big brother of chapter 2. He is influencing his long-term relationship with his employees. Unlike the big brother's, the supervisor's acts almost always have a large audience. And every specific incident in a supervisor's handling of his people can be thought of as one frame in the long movie which determines his people's general willingness (or unwillingness) to work, their optimism or pessimism, their approval or resentment. The difficulty is that work-a-day pressures tend to push executives, like parents, toward the short-term problems and toward the satisfaction of short-term personal and egoistic needs, at the expense of long-term objectives.

It isn't always easy to take the long view in the face of short-term pressures. Since every superior in an organization is usually a subordinate to someone else, each is likely to be intensely concerned with the short-term problem of doing what his superiors want him to do. And if the foreman feels squeezed by his superiors, he cannot simply ignore his own tensions in order to work for the long-term good. But, perhaps, if he can recognize for himself the several motives that may be relevant to an effort to change someone else's behavior, he can select a course of action that can better accomplish all the ends he wants to accomplish.

So if any generalized rule of thumb exists for the prospective behavior changer, it might be this one: Let him examine *his own reasons* for wanting to effect a particular change before plunging into the effort. Let him examine his own motives. If he does, he may be more likely to effect change successfully because he will be more clearheaded about what he wants to do; or he may alter or give up his efforts altogether if such an examination brings the realization that changing other people would not satisfy the needs he most wants to satisfy.

The Changee Is in the Saddle

No matter how much power a changer may possess, no matter how "superior" he may be, it is the changee who controls the final change decision. It is the employee, even the lowest paid one, who ultimately decides whether to show up for work or not. It is the child who ultimately decides whether to obey or not. It is the changee who changes. A can exert *more* or *less* influence on the situation. A can cut capers before B; he can cajole, threaten, or punish; but B (and he may be an irrational and unreasonable B) makes the ultimate decision about whether or not he will change. Moreover, it is A who feels the tension, whose needs are unsatisfied. So it is A who is dependent on B.

B, after all, is a whole person; and A's activities in trying to get B to change constitute just one set of forces in the multitude of forces that affect B's behavior. B, in effect, sits behind the solid fortifications of his own history and his own personality, integrating A's activities into all the other forces that act upon him and coming up with a new behavioral pattern that may or may not constitute what A wants.

Greater power in A's hands, greater control over B's vital needs does not necessarily give A greater control over B. B is never completely dependent. So the industrial worker finds numberless ingenious techniques for evading, avoiding, or retaliating against changes imposed by his superior.

Change Is Uncomfortable

Still another thing that commonly happens during the process of behavior change is that changees get disturbed. B, during the course of a significant change in his own behavior (whether the change results from A's actions or not), gets upset and anxious. A, the changer, may mistakenly interpret such action by B as a sign that his change efforts are a failure, that he has gone too far.

In fact, however, some disturbance seems to be a necessary accompaniment of change. The absence of signs of disturbance may, therefore, be a more negative warning than their presence.

Signs of upset in the process of change are visible in many situations. The child is likely to get upset when switching from diapers to the toilet. The bachelor suffers from sleeplessness and loss of appetite as he wrestles with the idea of marriage. The executive somehow feels anxious and upset, as well as happy, when he learns of his promotion to greater responsibilities.

Moreover, these upsets are likely to lead the changee into aggressive and hostile activity or into moodiness and withdrawal. A is often the logical target for tensions created by such disturbances; so B is likely to become aggressive and hostile toward A.

The explanation of these upsets takes us back to chapters 4 and 5. We have introduced frustration and conflict into the situation. People change when their present behavior begins to appear inadequate, either because they have been frustrated—something in the world has thrown a block across a previously open path—or because some new path has become visible and looks as if it *might* (conflict) be a better one. In either case a kind of behavior that had in the past been adequate has now become less adequate. If the present path is now inadequate, but no alternatives are immediately available, we have a classic frustration situation—and hence manifestations of aggression are to be expected. If one's present tack does not look as good as it did because another has begun to look better, we have conflict between the safety and security of the old path and the risk of an uncertain new one. Once again we should expect some emotional disturbance, the particular nature of which should be grossly predictable from our knowledge of the individual.

What Does A Need To Know about B?

Different changers in different change situations have different ideas about the importance of "diagnosis," of gathering information about B.

A's who use force as a prime device to effect change usually do not worry much about diagnosis. The effects of a whip, after all, are fairly predictable even if one doesn't know much about the psyche of the particular person being whipped. But at the other extreme one can find A's (and many psychiatrists are among them) devoting a large portion of their effort to finding out a great deal about the changee—about his background, his childhood, and his personality down to the finest detail.

In industry the whole range of changers are represented, with most exponents of "modern management" favoring the diagnostic side. One finds, for example, the common supervisory dictum "Get the facts before you act." That seems to mean that diagnosis is a useful predecessor to change.

A great deal can be said here, as elsewhere, in favor of gathering information about a problem before trying to solve it. But three easily overlooked points are worth considering. First, who most needs the information thus gathered, A or B? Second, what kind of information does A (or B) need? Third, how much information is worth chasing after, especially if the chasing process costs time and effort?

Behavior-change problems may be somewhat different from some other problems in this regard. Often it is more important for B to understand the problem than for A to understand it. If the ultimate control for change lies with B, and if it is for B to fit A's efforts into the larger framework of B's own perceptions, then B can best make a reasonable change decision when *he*, not A, understands what is going on. A may understand B inside out, but he may not be able to communicate that understanding to B or even to plot a very effective course of action. Somewhere along the line B has to line up the facts in a form *he* can understand and utilize. This is the problem with giving advice. A looks over B's situation, thinks (often correctly) that he sees it more clearly than B, and says: "What you ought to do is. . . ." B thereupon feels that his defenses have been violated or that A's advice represents poor understanding; or he takes the advice literally and utilizes it poorly and finally rejects both advice and adviser. Perhaps if A spent less time diagnosing B and more *helping B to diagnose himself,* the likelihood of successful change would be enhanced.

The second problem involves two kinds of information that are available to both A and B—information about facts and feelings. Facts in the usual sense of observable phenomena are likely to be much less important than feelings in change situations. Fears, doubts, feelings of confidence, inadequacy, ambition—these are much more likely to be significant information for behavior changers than the cold facts of duties or salary bracket. Moreover, these feelings may be hard for A to get at, even if he needs them. This is so partly because our language and our culture make verbal communication of feelings so difficult and partly because feelings often touch on people's psychological defenses.

An A who wants to know how B feels needs to have a sharp third ear. He has to be able to pick up information from such cues as the tone of B's voice, or the raising and lowering of B's eyebrows, or the secondary emotional connotations of B's words. Any A who sets out to find out why a B is doing what he is doing had best think of the job as something considerably more than a simple fact-finding expedition. He had better recognize that he will have to listen for some subtle cues and that, because they are likely to be subtle and indirect, they may be easily misinterpreted. Market-research people are struggling with just this problem as they worry through the concept of "motivational research" into consumer attitudes.

One of the best of many good things to be said for a serious effort by A to understand B's feelings is that those A's who undertake such diagnosis often end up changing their own objectives. An A who takes time to find out about an employee before disciplining him may end up changing his attitude toward the employee and hence changing his own behavior instead of B's. The guy isn't a lazy bum after all; he had reasons.

The "how much" question is an important one, too. In chapter 6 we pointed out that if we demand perfect information for a decision, we may never get to the decision. In the kind of human decision making we are talking about here, the same statement holds. To what extent must the manager be the psychiatrist of everyone in his department? To what extent need he know their sex lives to improve their working efficiency? Most managers implicitly recognize the diminishing-returns aspect of this problem. "Counseling," listening to people's personal problems, is tricky, for one thing—it has a way of changing the focus of a relationship from its value for business problem solving to its value in its own psychological right. More than that, after a while it costs a good deal more than it brings in in improved performance. If A needs to know about B, he needs to know the factors immediately relevant to the problem at hand. More might help, it is true, but it might cost far more than it is worth in the total business picture.

The Location of Responsibility in
Change Situations

In watching A's trying to change B's one may also notice that the responsibility for effecting the change seems to settle in different locations on different occasions. Sometimes A takes all the responsibility, and B none of it. Both A and B tend to see A as the person in charge and B only as an actor. On a road gang, for example, each laborer often seems to be saying to himself: "It is not my responsibility to work, it is the boss's responsibility to make me work. Therefore it is perfectly proper for me to do as little as possible, to do only what the boss can directly manipulate me into doing."

The location of responsibility in A is not limited to labor gangs, and it does not always occur against A's wishes. If anything, many A's accept the idea that it is their responsibility to change B and to see that he stays changed. Sales managers sometimes take this view in an extreme form. They properly consider it their job to stimulate salesmen but mistakenly assume that what is their job cannot also be the salesman's job. Since the effects of such stimulation seem to wear off, they feel it must be periodically reinforced. Hence one finds a great deal of emphasis by many sales managers on incentive gimmicks, on "inspirational" sales meetings, and so on. Very often even managers who talk a lot about "delegation" take such a view and succeed too well. Their salesmen end up taking the same view, i.e., that it is not their job to sell so much as it is the manager's job to use magic and gadgetry to get them to sell.

Clearly, the responsibility for change does not have to lie solely with the changer. It can be shared by changer and changee or even be taken over altogether by the person being changed. From the changee's viewpoint change is equivalent to learning, and learning, we agreed in chapter 6, is an *active* process. If teachers want to motivate their students to learn, one thing they can do is to try to get the student to take the responsibility for his own education, to come to want to learn on his own rather than to sit passively while the teacher pumps learning into his head. Many psychiatrists and counselors will even argue that there is no real hope for effecting much "deep" change in clients unless the clients take such responsibility. But in industry, organizational pressures and ideas about authority tend to make A's feel that the responsibility is theirs. They thereby encourage B's to take the easy, non-responsible course of action.

The advantages of shared responsibility are great for both A and B. For one thing, a B who feels that he wants to change is more likely to change effectively and lastingly than a B who feels no such internal tension. Moreover, no A is likely really to understand the subtleties of B's position better than B himself. No matter how successful A's communication with B, there are probably significant things left uncommunicated. So that if A takes sole responsibility, he may find himself trying to solve a problem working with less information about the problem than is available to B. If, on the other hand, B takes some of the responsibility for changing, he can take some of his own peculiarities into account, and perhaps A and B can find a new behavior that fills the needs of both.

In Summary

In this chapter the spotlight has been on a few common aspects of many behavior-change situations.

The changer, A, has the serious problem of knowing what

he is doing. Often A's literally do not know what they are doing or why they are doing it. Their motives may be partially unconscious and unperceived and their objectives equally so. Advance thinking through of one's purposes may lead to a reorientation of objectives or even to the abandonment of a change project.

Changees ultimately control the decision to change or not to change. A can influence that decision but he cannot make it. For the decision that B makes represents the integration of the forces imposed upon him by A along with a whole multitude of forces over which A has no control.

Some A's try hard to understand B's reasons for his present behavior before attempting to change that behavior. Others make no such effort but depend instead on observed similarities in all people. There are advantages to some degree of diagnosis of B. But if B ultimately controls the decision to change, then perhaps it is more important that B make the diagnosis of himself than that A make it of him. Moreover, the diagnostic process can be conceived of as a fact-finding or as a feeling-finding process. The position is taken here that feelings are as important, if not more important, than facts in behavior-change problems.

Final responsibility for changing can rest with A or B, or it can be shared. Behavior changers, especially when they occupy superior positions, are wont to feel that the responsibility for change must lie exclusively with them. But if B can be made to accept some of the responsibility for changing himself, the resulting change may be more lasting and more generalized.

Chapter 11

AUTHORITY

ONE TOOL FOR INFLUENCING BEHAVIOR

From the last chapter's discussion of some dimensions of influence, we turn now to a consideration of *means*. What are the tools of influence? How can they be used? What are their implications? This chapter focuses on just one tool, authority. Authority is worth a whole chapter because so many people in industry feel it is the *only* useful tool for modifying the behavior of other people.

Industrial organizational structures seem even to be designed with authority in mind. We build organizations in the shape of pyramids because that shape makes the exercise of authority easier. Pyramids create differences in rank and status, and the people in higher ranks can use their authority to influence lower ranks. Superiors in industrial organizations almost naturally turn to authority whenever a change problem arises with subordinates. The very idea of *delegating* authority rests on the assumption that authority can help people who have more of it to change the behavior of those who have less of it. In fact, we usually even define the "superior" in a relationship as the person with more authority.

Like other tools, authority can be used expertly or blunderingly. And like other tools, it must be used by men. Top managers have long since unhappily recognized that the delegation of large quantities of authority to middle and lower echelons is no guaranty of effective supervision. If anything, some executives seem to supervise better with less authority than with more. And, contrarily, some supervisors function better with more of it than less. The issue is not only how much authority but how it is used and by whom.

The Several Meanings of Authority

Let's start with some definitions, not to be academic but to try to clarify an important but fuzzy concept. Sometimes when we talk of authority, we are thinking about something formal, like *rank*. Authority can be defined by one's military rank, for example. The captain may not know exactly how much authority he has or even what it is, but he knows he has more than the lieutenant and less than the major.

Authority also has something to do with power, sometimes formal power, again like military rank: power that can be formally changed or delegated. "They," the "top brass," somebody up above, can change one's rank and thereby one's authority and thereby one's power.

Sometimes, however, we relate the words *authority* and *power* differently. We talk about someone with an "authoritative" (synonymous with "powerful") personality. Here we mean something like "influential" or "respect-evoking," but we do *not* mean formally delegable. We mean something the person carries around *inside* himself, not something he wears on his shoulders.

Besides this mix-up between formal and personal authority, another confusion results from the word. Sometimes we talk about authority from the perspective of the manager who uses it, sometimes from the perspective of the managed on whom it is used. When we identify with the user, authority looks like a mechanism for co-ordination and control. When we take the perspective of the subordinate, authority looks more psychological; it is a mechanism by which we are rewarded and/or punished for our behavior.

Once we have clarified and related these different meanings, we can go on to consider the uses of authority and the advantages and disadvantages attached to them. First, however, more clarification is in order.

Formal Aspects of Authority

Suppose we start defining authority by calling it one kind of power. There may be other kinds. We can narrow it further by defining it as formal, delegable, worn-on-the-shoulders power. By thus restricting it, our picture takes on this form:

Authority is power that enters the two-party relationship through the organization. It is an institutional mechanism that aims to define which of two members of a relationship, A or B, will be the superior. Authority is potential *extra* power, given by a third party (the organization) to some of its members in order to guarantee an *un*equal distribution of power; in order, in other words, to make sure that some people are chiefs and others Indians.

Sometimes the power thus delegated has nothing to do with relationships. For example, the organization may assign to A the power to spend some of its money for supplies. But very often authority does include power over other people, power to restrict or punish and/or power to reward. Thus the president announces to the superintendent, in the presence of the foremen: "You are permitted to decide to fire foremen or keep them; you are permitted to decide to raise foremen's pay to this limit or not to raise it." Now the superintendent has some authority—some additional, formal, potential power over and above any other power he may have carried into his relationship with foremen.

A difficulty arises at this point. An organization (or a powerful person) cannot delegate all the power it possesses, even if it wants to. A president can delegate only certain kinds of power by calling it authority. The forms of power over the satisfaction or frustration of another person's needs are legion. In industry power may take the form of control over income—a form delegable as authority. Or it may take the form of control over the terms of the relationship. That, too, is delegable as authority. It may be power to provide status or prestige. That, too, may be partly delegable.

But other sources of power are not so readily transferred; for example, the power deriving from an individual's competence and skill or from a member's sensitivity to the needs of another. Sensitivity cannot be delegated. One's name, or one's social standing in a community, or one's whole personality may constitute significant forms of power in a relationship, and they too are non-transferable. In fact, only a fraction of the ways in which one person can control another's needs are readily delegable as authority. The delegable forms include mostly external, non-personal kinds of power.

This analysis suggests that a superior who turns immediately and exclusively to his authority is either ignoring many other kinds of power he may possess or else he derives all his power from his authority. In either case his effective range of control over other people will be narrow.

Authority As Seen by Those Who Hold It

If we ask a manager if authority is useful to him, he will have some ready and reasonable answers, among them these: Authority is indeed useful because authority is a mechanism for co-ordination and control in organizations. People *have to* be gotten to work on time. They *have to* spend some of their time working, rather than telling stories or visiting the men's room. They *have to* carry out policy and make appropriate decisions. They have to do all these things if the organization is to move toward its goals in some kind of co-ordinated fashion.

Certainly if authority is used as a tool for influencing behavior, it is not for influence's sake but for the sake of the organization. Moreover, if it is used most often to restrict and limit individual behavior—and thereby it blocks or frustrates people—that is because organizations are what they are. Industrial organizations are places where people *cannot* do what they please, where people are required to submit to certain restrictive rules and standards. If people came to work when they felt like it or said what they felt like saying, no industrial organization could survive.

Given this view—and it is an extremely reasonable one—authority is a tool to restrict behavior (even if restriction frustrates), to create necessary homogeneity by leveling out individual variations. It is an important and efficient tool because it has the advantages of the shotgun over the rifle. We can broadcast restrictions, rules, and limits, and then use our authority to back up the rules when someone steps out of bounds. The mere presence of authority (precisely because it can be used to frustrate nonconformists) will keep most people within the rules most of the time.

The legal structure seems a fair analogy. Laws, in a sense,

constitute a threat of frustration for anyone in the population who steps outside the bounds. We need laws even though most people obey without threat. However, to carry the legal analogy a little further, even the threat of frustration can become insufficient when a specific law is seen by too many people to be too restrictive. The issue here is much like the issue of frustration versus deprivation (chapter 4). Restriction that only deprives is tolerable, especially if it has accompanying rewards; restriction that frustrates can backfire.

Authority As Seen from the Underside

We cannot observe authority in action just by observing the boss. Whether A has or has not blocked or frustrated B is determined almost entirely by B's interpretation of A's actions. The perceived world, we said in chapter 3, is the world that determines behavior. Thus the mere presence of the company president in a department may constitute a block for some people in that department. Or an extremely insecure employee, with a distrustful set of attitudes toward superiors, may interpret *any* act by a superior as a threat of frustration, even if the superior is busy patting him on the head. In fact, a superior almost always has to work harder than an equal or a subordinate in order to be seen as a rewarding, non-restrictive force. The reason again is the dependency of the subordinate on the superior. No matter how nice Papa may be, he is still Papa, and the belt of authority around his middle *could* be used as a whip.

Even though the boss's position carries continual implications of potential frustration, the intensity of such implications depends on the boss's own behavior. Certainly many organizational superiors use their authority in ways that obtain a great deal of confidence from their subordinates. Limited and consistent restriction can be seen by most of us as "reasonable," if the atmosphere of a department is generally satisfying of our social and egoistic needs.

Basically, then, most subordinates probably see authority in the same way superiors do, as a tool for restricting and controlling their activities. But though they may see the same thing, they attach different meanings to it. While the boss interprets restriction in organizational terms as control and co-ordination, the subordinates' interpretation may be far more personal. Authority is a mechanism for satisfying or frustrating their personal needs in a dependent relationship.

Some Pros and Cons of the Use of Authority

From the manager's viewpoint the advantages of authority, especially restrictively used authority, are huge. We have already cited one of them, the control and co-ordination advantage. There are many others, too.

For one thing, one doesn't have to know much about any particular Joe Doaks to be fairly certain that firing him or cutting his pay or demoting him will strike at some important needs and thereby keep him in line. But one might have to know a good deal about the same employee to find out how to make work more fun for him.

A corollary advantage, then, is simplicity. Authority as a restrictive tool does not require much subtlety or much understanding of people's motives. How simple it is to spank a child when he misbehaves, and how difficult and complicated to distract him or to provide substitute satisfactions or to "explain" the situation. Given a hundred children, how much easier it is to keep them in line by punishing a few recalcitrants than to teach them all to feel "responsible."

No matter how "improper," we cannot ignore the fact that exerting authority is often personally gratifying to superiors, and therefore attractive. The exercise of discipline can be reassuring to those who need reassurance about themselves. Moreover, authority fits neatly with a superior's needs, if he has any, to blow off aggression deriving from his own frustration. When the father spanks the child, not only does he change the child's behavior, he also provides himself with an outlet for tensions built up in him by his own boss, or by his wife, or by the irritating, troublesome child.

Similarly, authority is sometimes seen, perhaps properly, as a way for a superior to guarantee his superiority. If his subordinates know that a superior can and will punish readily, they are likely to behave respectfully and submissively, at least in his presence. The reassurance derived from these demonstrations of respect may constitute a great distortion in feedback channels, but it can be helpful to the superior's own uncertain psyche. The superior who takes an essentially supportive approach has no such reassurance. Like the good big brother of chapter 2, he may be complained to and complained against. He may get true feedback, even if it is unpleasant. He may have to tolerate emotionally upset people telling him stupid, even insulting things.

Restrictive authority has another kind of advantage: speed. A do-it-or-else order eliminates the time consuming dillydallying of feedback. But speed, as chapter 9 pointed out, may cost accuracy or morale. Where those issues are not critical, speed may be worth its costs.

Restrictive authority, we have said, also has the advantage of imposing orderliness and conformity upon an organization. By a threat to reduce some opportunities for need satisfaction, large numbers of people can be made to conform to fundamental regulations. A manager must make *sure* that his people stay through the required eight hours of the day. Even though the great majority may conform without external threat, the superior has to guarantee minimum conformity by all employees. The job of obtaining willing or self-imposed conformity without threat just looks too big to handle.

Moreover, this restrictive authority is efficient because it can be used on large numbers of people at the same time, even when one doesn't know much about the people.

If those are the pros, here are some cons worth thinking about. First, restriction may have some by-products. When A's activity interferes with B's efforts to satisfy important needs, B may not sit still very long. A often finds he has caught crabs instead of lobsters. He has changed behavior he had not intended to change as well as (or instead of) behavior he did intend to change. The child who is spanked every time he puts his hand into the cookie jar may learn to keep his hand out of the cookie jar, or he may learn to go to the jar only when Mama isn't looking. He may also learn (irrationally) that his parents are out to keep him from getting what he wants. Employees who expect to be censured whenever they are caught loafing may learn to *act* busy (and *when* to act busy) and also that the boss is an enemy. They are thereby provided with a challenging game to play against the boss: who can think up the best ways of loafing without getting caught; a game in which they can feel that justice is on their side and a game they can usually win.

Restrictions, then, can be effective in changing specific *actions* in the direction A wants (B will *act* busy), but often only to the minimum that B can get away with. It is less likely to change B's attitudes, and when it does it may change them in the wrong direction, in the general direction of distrust and hostility.

Moreover, the circular element described in chapter 2 often enters the scene when restrictive authority is called upon. Restriction includes the possibility of a downward spiraling relationship. A begins by trying to change B through threatening frustration. B changes to the extent that he feels he must, but because he has been frustrated he will feel aggressive and in one way or another he may try to retaliate. A uses more restriction, this time to control the retaliation. Again B is frustrated, and wants even more to retaliate. And so it goes.

It might seem that a serious downward spiral can occur only in relationships between equals. If B is extremely subordinate, he should not have enough power to retaliate effectively. But subordinates do have power in relationships, even though the power may be considerably less than the superior's. As long as B has any power, and as long as the relationship exists, he can retaliate. Sometimes he does it by joining together with other B's, perhaps to form a union. Sometimes he does it by cutting down or distorting the flow of feedback on which the superior depends so heavily. Often several B's work together informally. I know, for instance, of a group of middle-management people who succeeded very well in defeating a superior they had come to dislike. Their method was passive resistance. They simply did everything the superior asked them to do—*and no more.* For every problem that arose, each of the three went to him for a decision. They took no initiatives, solved no problems by themselves. The superior was soon forced into the impossible position of trying to do every job in the department by himself.

The tenuousness and the self-defeating weakness of reliance on restrictive authority becomes apparent right here. When his authority has been "undermined" by the "sabotage" of subordinates, the superior who has depended on authority is likely immediately to assume that what he needs is *more authority,* because authority is the only tool he knows how to use. But can the president, in fact, delegate any authority by which the superior can coerce his subordinates into doing more than they are told? More likely the president simply begins to view the *superior* as the person on whom it is now appropriate to exert his (the president's) restrictive authority.

Such cases are many, and they are understandable. It is a serious error to assume that the *greater* power in a relationship equals the *only* power. As parents we may start out feeling that power lies exclusively in our hands, only to change our minds radically when one of the children runs away from home or gets hurt. It is also a serious error to think that delegable power—authority—is a useful weapon in *all* conflicts.

Still another difficulty with restrictive authority is its relative irreversibility. It is just not so easy to pat a subordinate's head after spanking him as it is to spank him after patting. For human beings have memories, and since restriction tends to reduce feedback loops rather than to build them, a series of restrictive experiences for B may destroy the possibility of further communication between A and B. Once A has lost communication contact, *no* tools of influence are useful.

In fact, the irreversibility of restrictive methods sometimes creates difficulties even for those who preach a supportive, "human relations" approach to these problems. A restrictive industrial manager, exposed to human-relations propaganda, will sometimes suddenly see the light and change his methods completely. The scowl turns to a smile; the office door is thrown open; a ration of grog is distributed to all hands. Then comes the rude awakening. Subordinates don't behave right. They don't dance in the aisles. They get drunk on the grog. They "take advantage" of their new freedom. A then decides he was taken in by the longhairs. He reverts to the "right" way, the way he had been using to begin with.

Obviously this kind of sudden reversal from frustration to satisfaction is silly, just as it is silly to leave a candy-starved child alone with five pounds of chocolates. The child is likely to stuff himself. His behavior is then taken as proof that letting children have their own way does not work.

Added together, the pros and cons of restrictive authority lead toward these conclusions: In general, restrictive methods may be effective in situations that meet some or all of these conditions: (1) the change that A is trying to bring about is a change in specific overt action, rather than in generalized action or attitude. (2) The restrictions are seen by B as depriving rather than frustrating. (3) The balance of power is such that B's power is minimal and A's maximal. One might add a fourth condition, too: Restriction can be effective when speed and/or uniformity are critical.

In a way industry has already learned some of these lessons, mostly the hard way. Authority as a direct and open restrictive weapon is, in fact, used more consciously at lower levels than at higher ones. Lower levels are (or once were) the levels at which B's actions, more than his attitudes, are the targets. They are also the levels at which employees have generally already retaliated against frustration by organizing, so that restrictions, openly imposed, are *now* depriving more than frustrating. And lower levels were also the levels at which the power difference between A and B used to be greatest, though those conditions, too, obtain less clearly today than they used to.

At higher levels we have tended to be more interested in changing attitudes than actions, and we have perceived that B's have power, too. So, *broadly speaking*, we lean less heavily on restrictive authority as we move up the pyramid. A vice-president who shows up a half-hour late is not likely to be "disciplined."

In Summary

Formal authority is a delegable kind of power. Power to influence behavior may also derive from other sources, largely from the skills, personality, and possessions of the changer.

Restrictive authority is seen by managers as a tool for coordination and control. It has advantages in simplicity and speed and in personal gratification to powerful changers who feel unsure of themselves. It also helps to establish a minimum level of conformity by all subordinates to the superior's standards.

A major difficulty inherent in restrictive authority is the probability of secondary changes in attitude along with desired changes in act-behavior. Restriction may constitute frustration and may consequently be followed by aggression toward the changer. Restriction may then incur only a minimal amount of the desired behavior change while also incurring significant increases in hostility and decreases in feedback. Restriction may thereby destroy relationships.

Authority, as a restrictive mechanism, seems to be most useful in short-term, specific situations, where B's retaliatory power is minimal, where the change sought is change in specific overt action, and where the restrictions are perceived as depriving rather than frustrating.

Chapter 12

INFLUENCE WITHOUT AUTHORITY
CHANGING PEERS AND SUPERIORS

If authority is such a lethal tool, what are the alternatives? And what are the alternatives for those who have no authority? How does one influence those with equal authority? How does one influence the boss?

Some readers may already have discerned, and perhaps been disappointed by, the absence of rules of thumb in this section. The absence will continue, not wilfully, but because the nature of the influence process obviates magical little rules. The process of influencing behavior does not reside in one person. It resides in the *relationship*. If B's stood still, A's could indeed devise rules for influencing B's. But B's move, respond, retaliate, change. So if we are to come up with any rules at all, they must be rules governing the behavior of the A-B relationship, not just the behavior of one of the elements.

It is true that we could play probabilities. We could say to our salesmen: "This is your spiel. Run it off like a phonograph record. Seventy-five per cent of your clients will throw you out. Twenty-five per cent might be influenced."

But if a manager takes that view about influencing his sub-ordinates, or his peers, or his superiors, he is in for trouble.

Without expecting rules for answers, then, we can ask: What are the alternatives to the use of authority? How can some people influence others who have equal or greater authority?

The AA Model

Consider Alcoholics Anonymous. That organization effects deep and difficult influence with considerable success. Their objective is to cause drinkers to stop drinking. What are the methods by which such a goal can be achieved?

Many people have tried many methods on alcoholics. Wives have threatened to leave their drinking husbands. Churches have warned drinkers of everlasting punishment for their sins. "Conditioned reflexers" (I put the phrase in quotes because such views of conditioning do not do justice to conditioning concepts) have added cathartics to the alcoholic's drink so that he gets nauseous and sick.

All these are essentially restrictive methods, using power other than authority to restrict. They are concerned with symptoms rather than causes. They aim at changing overt behavior rather than the more fundamental need or attitude.

AA approaches the problem quite differently. Essentially, their procedure is the following:

They make the availability of their services known to the alcoholic (and he may choose not to avail himself of them).

If he chooses to attend a meeting, he listens to testimonials from ex-alcoholics (and he may be impressed by none of them—in which case he is again free to leave).

If he decides they know what they are talking about, he asks for help (but he doesn't have to).

He is given one or more "buddies"—ex-alcoholics like himself. The buddies make themselves available (if he chooses to call on them) to talk over his problem or just to hold his hand.

If he decides to try to quit drinking, it is not easy. So he calls on his faith in God, if he has any, and on his buddies. They provide help with support, with hand holding, with a supply of knowledge of the future—i.e., "Sure it's tough, but if you hold on awhile longer, you begin to feel different, and then it gets easier, *and we know.*" They also provide the knowledge that real change requires a really new way of looking at the world.

When AA is successful, the alcoholic stops drinking. Often he then helps others to stop drinking as one way of handling the new void in himself.

One finds no threat, no command, no authority in this process. The alcoholic stops drinking; he is not stopped. He is helped to change himself. He is helped by being shown alternative means, substitute behaviors, new sources of faith —by anything that will fit his needs. This is a predominantly augmentative, supportive process in which responsibility never leaves the changee.

Is Management Different from AA?

The businessman will point out several differences between the problems faced by Alcoholics Anonymous and the ones he faces. First, AA can afford to wait for people to recognize their own problems and to seek help. The businessman often cannot. He must bring about change even when people don't come to him seeking to be changed. Second, AA can let each man solve his own problem in his own way at his own pace. The business organization requires conformity to certain standard behaviors and to the pressures of time. Finally, the businessman will complain of the risk in this method, the lack of control over the changee. In AA's approach any alcoholic can just walk out the door any time he feels like it without changing at all. In business we have to be sure that people will do what needs doing; we cannot allow them to decide whether they would like to or not.

The alert reader will add still another objection: Where is the diagnosis, the understanding of causes so heavily emphasized in the preceding chapters of this book? In this AA situation effective behavior change seems to occur without any attempt to look into the source of alcoholism, into the frustrations and the conflicts that probably led to it.

These are partially valid objections, both to AA's method and to the whole-hog applications of the AA model to business problems. But before considering the modifications that need to be made to fit business requirements, it might be useful to consider the similarities between the AA method and those used by some other behavior changers.

Similarities between AA and Other
Approaches

The AA pattern, in its *broadest* outline, is a pattern that has independently taken hold—for good or evil—in a great many segments of modern American life. It showed up in chapter 6, with the emphasis on learning as an active, responsible process in the learner. It shows up in educational thinking, in the position that a student's education is an active function of the student as well as of the teacher. The teacher's role is to provide help and knowledge as the student requires it and as he can integrate it. The teacher's job is not to make the student a passive sponge to soak in a pool of pedagogical wisdom, but to help him to help himself.

Child-rearing practices have gone the same way. Today's pediatricians talk to mothers about "demand" schedules, easy toilet training, affection and support. Rigid discipline, even great emphasis on personal cleanliness, have gone by the boards.

Counseling and psychiatry have moved rapidly in the same direction, with "non-directive" therapy and most present-day psychotherapy. Similarly, penology and criminology, with their emphasis on rehabilitation through new skills and new adjustments, have moved in the same permissive, supportive direction.

Some may argue that these methods are precisely what is wrong with present-day America. They make us weak and soft and heaven knows what else. Perhaps they do. But if any businessman feels that these methods will be our ruination, he had better look over his shoulder at his own plant. The same ideas have probably crept in disguise into his own operations. His first-line supervisors are probably practicing "human-relations" techniques all over the place—especially on him. His market-research people are going motivational. They are using non-directive depth interviews and projective tests in dealing with consumers. Ditto his employment interviewers. His industrial-relations people are probably trying to apply essentially the same ideas to their relationship with the union. And his advertising people certainly are not using whips on the consumer. Even the businessman himself is probably saying things like: "To learn to swim, jump into the water," or, "Experience is the best teacher," or, "You can lead a horse, etc." All these are just other ways of saying that men must at least help to change themselves; others cannot do it all for them.

Applicability of the AA Model to Management

We said earlier that three major obstacles block the use of the AA approach in industrial problems. Let's examine these difficulties one at a time to see whether or not they really are difficulties and, if they are, to see what modifications are needed.

Here is a simple, but perhaps typical, industrial behavior-change problem:

> A new manager of a staff department grows increasingly concerned about the "weakness" of many people in his group. They seem stolid and unchanging, unimaginative and uncreative. They go on doing things as they have always been done, though it is obvious to the manager that many methods and procedures could be simplified, many new services could be rendered to line people. How can he make them less resistant to new ideas? How can he get them to take a new outlook toward their jobs? How can he get the lead out of their pants?

Getting People To See a Problem

Alcoholics Anonymous, for the most part, simply waits for the alcoholic to become unhappy with his alcoholism. Only then do they undertake to change him. Similarly, psychiatrists wait behind their office doors for the patient to feel bad enough to visit a doctor. But the social inefficiencies of such a process are obvious. Many people may be psychologically sick for a long time before the sickness becomes painful or crippling enough to make them look for help.

And it doesn't make much sense in education for a teacher just to wait for children to want to learn arithmetic or in business for an executive just to wait for his secretary to want to be more careful of her spelling.

And yet, although the manager cannot wait for people to see a problem, theoretically his people will not change very significantly unless they do see a problem, until they feel the tensions of relevant, unsatisfied needs. So the manager's first problem becomes: How do I make these people feel dissatisfied with their present behavior?

A variety of methods exists. Just waiting is one, and we should not discount it too quickly. Certainly many a young man in industry will notice by himself that a new superior is different from an old one and, apparently out of the clear blue sky, will come voluntarily in search of help, say, in learning how to write better reports. He may already have felt uncomfortably inadequate as he compared other people's writings to his own. Now he has his first opportunity to try to do something about it. The manager who had been wondering how to get this subordinate to improve his reports is now in a superb influence position. So, just waiting for B to encounter problems, to recognize his inadequacies, and to screw up enough courage to ask for help should not be thrown out altogether. Moreover, the very act of *not* acting, of waiting, especially by a new superior, may be seen by subordinates as a sign of tolerance and hence of accessibility.

But there are other possibilities besides waiting. One is to throw the subordinate into situations which will make some inadequacy obvious to him. The superior takes an active part here, but an impersonal part. The subordinate begins to see a problem because of the trouble he gets into with other people; the superior has simply caused these en-counters to occur. Thus, a manager may cause one of his people to recognize problems by *increasing* his responsibil-ity, by sending him out on difficult assignments, by expos-ing him to meetings with people who make no bones about their attitudes toward his staff. Such behavior by managers is unusual, for managers are wont to reduce the responsi-bilities of "ineffective" people much more frequently than they are to increase them, thereby reducing risk but also reducing the opportunity for learning.

Again, a superior can get a subordinate to recognize a problem simply through his assertion that a problem exists. Thus, a staff group which has been perfectly happy about the way things are going can be made to recognize a prob-lem if the manager simply announces that the group's work is unsatisfactory. The teacher can do the same for a student by giving him a low grade on an exam. The difficulty here is obvious. Although the manager will probably succeed in getting the group to recognize a problem, he will also suc-ceed (though he may not have attempted it) in having the group blame him for it. The group may decide that its work doesn't need to be changed but that the boss does. And sometimes they can do it. To get people to see a problem by threatening, directly or by innuendo, that if they don't change they will endanger their bread and butter is, of course, straight restriction and carries with it all the dan-gers inherent in reactions to frustration. The danger is espe-cially great when the source of the threat is the same indi-vidual who later wants to "improve" B's behavior.

This is the point at which a third party becomes useful. Parents are often abashed at how easily a new teacher can accomplish what they themselves have been unable to accomplish. Some of the credit given the teacher, or the family doctor, or Uncle Joe, does not belong to them as individuals so much as it does to their roles in the relationship. Anomalous as it may seem, a position of lesser power may often be a better position from which to effect a behavior change than a position of greater power. Our manager may try to start a change with a threat, but then he may have to turn over the rest of the job to the personnel department. The third party can often do much more to effect change from there on out than the manager himself can do. In a sense the manager's action has made personnel's job easy. For now personnel, like AA, receives a knock on the door from a B who has already decided he needs help.

There is something paradoxical in this line of reasoning. This chapter is about methods for effecting change without authority. And yet it seems that one cannot effect change unless some restriction has been going on, so that B feels unsatisfied.

But that is only half the picture. It is true that people are likely to start wanting help after they find out that their present behavior isn't as good as they think it is. But there is a second possibility, too. People can want to change because they learn to want more or better or higher goals. We may start looking for a new car when the old one stops performing. We may also start looking because Detroit has put out some shiny new ones. The manager can add new information to his staff's picture of the world. He can open new promotional avenues, new opportunities for learning, for socializing, for satisfying all sorts of needs that can often stir even the most stolid of old-timers into activity.

This is the problem of raising levels of aspiration. It is a difficult problem. It requires the changer always to keep such opportunities for growth and development open—always new ones, always better ones. For as long as B can foresee new, better, and *achievable* means to the satisfaction of his needs, he will be ready to change his behavior in the direction of those better means.

All this is to say that people don't change unless they get uncomfortable. One may use AA's method of standing by until the world makes them uncomfortable; or one may do it by trying to raise levels of aspiration so that B himself finds his present behavior inadequate and awkward; or one may get a third party to use his power to make B uncomfortable. Some one of these methods or a combination of them is a theoretical requirement for getting B to think seriously about changing his behavior.

Diagnosis: Why Is B Doing What He Is Doing?

The second objection raised to the Alcoholics Anonymous method is that AA seems to ignore the causes of B's alcoholism. A good deal of emphasis earlier in this book was placed on the importance of understanding the reasons for B's present behavior, either the factual or the emotional reasons. Now a model shows up in which relatively little emphasis is given to such diagnosis.

The problem really is this one: Who must make the diagnosis? In many cases, it is more important for B to understand the causes of his own behavior than for A to understand those causes. In the AA model the buddy provides the alcoholic with an opportunity to communicate any facts or feelings that may be relevant. If they are communicated aloud, it is true that the buddy may come to understand them, but, much more important, the alcoholic may also come to understand them. And if one already has a man who wants to change, then it is far more important that *he* understand what he is gaining or losing from his present behavior than that someone else understand it.

This is not to say that A needs no understanding. It is only to say that A's understanding of B's problem is often not nearly so important as B's own understanding of it.

Let us return here to the problem of the new manager of an ineffective department. His job is to revivify the depart-ment—without changing personnel. How much does he have to know about why his people are unimaginative, un-enthusiastic, unproductive?

He has to know more about *how* they feel than *why* they feel that way. He does not need a case history on every man so much as he needs enough understanding of feelings to estimate the meanings his actions will evoke. He has to know whether his people have just been waiting for a break and are all ready to grab it or whether they have settled firmly into a path of safe stolidity. He has to know some-thing about their dominant needs and dominant fears. He has to know these things primarily in order to know how to communicate his conception of their inadequacies to them. For to suggest great new responsibilities to people who are fearful even of their small old ones may not get them to rec-ognize a need for change but only to deny it more com-pletely. *What's behind these feelings is usually better left as B's own business.* The present feelings, more than their causes and origins, are the most important working materi-als of the industrial behavior changer.

Who Controls the Change Situation?

The third objection to the AA method is that AA seems to have so little control over the alcoholics' behavior. At any step along the way B is free to reject the whole process and to leave the situation without changing. In industrial situations, allowing B such opportunities would seem an extremely risky process. But those risks are worth thinking about.

Consider again the new department staff manager. First, as manager, he can always veto what his people decide to do. He can give his subordinates opportunities to change themselves, and, finding that they fail to change in accordance with his wishes, he can then still resort to his authority. So the only risk added by giving B more leeway is the possible loss of time if the method fails.

On the other hand, if the kinds of behavior changes sought were only changes in overt behavior, then there might be a good case for tight control. If all the manager wanted was his people's putting their shovels into the ground and lifting them up full of dirt at specified intervals, and if the manager could afford to stand over them to make sure they carried out the ritual, then obviously he could actually exercise pretty close control. But in practice the kinds of changes the manager usually seeks are changes in brain as well as muscle behavior. He wants his people *to make decisions differently* than they did before, and he knows perfectly well that many of the decisions will have to be made in the manager's absence. Though he can watch to see that a man uses his shovel right, he often cannot watch to see whether he is using his brain right. Since that is the case, is it actually riskier to let subordinates decide they want to change and then to make decisions that fit their changed perceptions of the world? Or is it riskier to force them to change, so that when they face a new decision they face it with a mixed feeling of wanting to do it and of resentment against having to do it?

The answer seems clear. The manager's control, in the sense of his ability to foresee his subordinates' behavior, is far greater if he has given them an opportunity to accept or reject change (and knows where they stand) than if he has required change without obtaining "honest" feedback.

Even Self-Imposed Change Is Uncomfortable

AA does not have an easy time changing people. And people do not even have an easy time changing themselves. Since any behavior change usually represents giving up some previously adequate behavior in favor of some new and untested behavior, any behavior change will be accompanied by some degree of tension and anxiety. So it is with the switch from one job to another—butterflies in the stomach on the day or two preceding the first day on the new job.

Although he uses a permissive, augmentative approach in trying to effect a change in his subordinates, our manager must still expect B to show this kind of tension and anxiety. The changer probably cannot prevent anxiety in B, but he can help to alleviate it by encouraging and supporting B's efforts to change.

A Generalized Pattern

So the AA method has some limitations and some difficulties for industrial use. But perhaps by making some modifications we can set up a general set of conditions for effecting behavior change in continuing relationships:

1. *B perceives a problem.* AA waits for people to perceive a problem. In industry one must often take action to get them to recognize that a problem exists and that conse-

quently a change is necessary. We suggested several possibilities, all the way from simply telling B that his present behavior is inadequate to manipulating the world so that he runs into inadequacies in his own behavior. But the changer must always beware lest the problem B perceives is the changer himself.

2. *B takes responsibility for considering alternative ways of behaving (and if possible seeks A's help in discovering additional alternatives).* When B has decided he has a problem calling for change, it is for him to consider the possibilities for change and for A to provide help.

3. *A and B mutually communicate the implications for both A and B of one new method of behavior versus others.* Since A is the person who is seeking the change, and since the change that B selects is important to A, A must have an opportunity to feed back to B the implications of one alternative or another. Thus possibly B may decide to change, but to a behavior that is *still* unacceptable to A. This unacceptability is one real factor in B's deciding whether or not the alternative is feasible.

4. *B selects an alternative which A can accept.* The responsibility for deciding what B shall do and how he shall do it still remains with B. Especially if A is a superior, B's selection will have to be acceptable to A, although *acceptable* may not be the same as *ideal.* This is a little like collective bargaining but even more like a discussion between husband and wife about where they shall take their vacation. If a location can be found that is entirely acceptable to both, all to the good. If the location is only a satisfactory compromise to each, that is still pretty good. If no compromise is possible, then A, if he is in a position of authority, can always revert to the simple use of the veto.

5. *B tries to change. A supports.* It is at this point that A's role shifts from that of provider of information to helper and supporter and reassurer. For it is here that tension and anxiety may show up in B. After taking a few baby steps in the new method, he may decide that this new behavior is hopeless or ridiculous. A can help by providing knowledge of the future, reassuring, making B feel that he is progressing (if he is actually progressing). It is here, too, that A can expect to come under overt or covert attack. It is A after all who has "forced" B to try this new, awkward, and inefficient way of behaving. The great mistake that A can make is to insist he is not to blame and to argue the facts of the case. What B needs is help, not argument.

6. *B finds the new method successful and integrates it as part of his behavior; or he finds the new method unsuccessful and abandons it.* After being nursed along in his attempt to behave differently, B's skill may increase and he himself may find the new method serving his purposes better than the old. B can then be said to have changed. But if B finds that the new is not so good as the old, he may revert to the earlier method, if that is still possible, or he may move to a third method. If the latter is his choice then the whole process begins again.

These six steps constitute a crude and incomplete set of conditions for behavior change in continuing relationships. It is a difficult set of conditions to bring about. But the important question is whether it is more difficult and more time consuming than the beguilingly simple use of authority. If the time and energy that must be devoted to the unforeseen by-products of authoritarian methods is added to the total, the restrictive process may be even more difficult than the supportive one. Moreover, one of the most important advantages of supportive methods is that they tend to become easier with time. For B's who have "been changed" by this method are likely to develop feelings of confidence in A that make future changes in the relationship easier. Such feelings of confidence may even allow A to use authoritarian methods effectively because they are no longer seen as frustrating.

In Summary

Alcoholics Anonymous seems to do a good job of changing people without much call upon authority. Their method appears to be uncontrolled and uncertain, but with modifications it may be much more applicable to industrial problems than one might guess.

The basic assumption underlying the AA approach is that people must take most of the responsibility for changing themselves and changers therefore must be helpers rather than manipulators. A superior's authority thus becomes a supply of means by which to help subordinates satisfy their needs through work rather than a supply of ammunition with which to threaten them.

Chapter 13

MONEY INCENTIVES
ONE EFFORT TO INFLUENCE

Managers, acutely conscious of the paycheck, have tried to turn their control over it into a mechanism of influence. They have devised all sorts of rules for trading money for work, incentive systems among them.

In fact, of all the ways of setting up a work situation that encourages hard work, the one that industry has formalized most is the money-incentive system. Money incentives have come to occupy a central place because money is a common means for satisfying all sorts of diverse needs in our society and because money may be handled and measured. Money is "real"; it is communicable. Many other means to need satisfaction are abstract and ephemeral. Moreover, money incentives fit with our culture's conception of what work means, with the definition of work as non-satisfying and restrictive activity given by people in exchange for means like money. The means thus earned allow the earner to satisfy his idiosyncratic needs off the job.

In this chapter we shall look at two kinds of money incentive plans—individual and multiple incentives—to see how they fit with the preceding chapters and to see how and when they ought to be useful tools for influence. The first step in such an analysis is a consideration of money as a motive.

The Place of Money in the Hierarchy of Motives

Most readers are probably familiar with some of the many surveys designed to find out what workers want from their jobs. Social scientists and personnel people have been quick to point up the results of such surveys—results showing that workers rank money only fourth or fifth among the variety of possible rewards obtainable from their jobs. Workers, including supervisory and research personnel, are likely, in these surveys, to place things like "fair treatment" or "good working conditions" well above money.

It seems to the writer that these are misleading findings. Where management once may have overrated the significance of money (sometimes feeling that this was the *only* reward due a man for his labors), these rank-ordering surveys directly suggest that money is somehow *less* important than some other things. The difficulties with this reasoning are two: the presumption that man's motives can be broken down into a static order representing his permanent and unchanging attitudes and the fact that we live in a society which approves the expression of interest in working conditions and supervision and disapproves the expression of interest in money. No "good" supervisor in today's industry will easily admit that his primary motive is money even if it is.

People's wants are neither static nor clear-cut. Instead they are dynamic and conflicting, as Part I emphasized.

Money is important to most people only in relation to the current state of other needs that money cannot satisfy. Any manager would be foolish to accept a list of his employees' rank orderings of motives at face value and try to "do something about them." For wants are seldom permanently satisfiable, even if the ordered list correctly indicates people's current motives.

Money *is* an important potential motivating force in industry, but not because of its rank on the "most wanted" list. Money is important psychologically for the same reasons that it is important economically: because it is a symbolic substance, a common basis for the exchange of goods and services that are differentially required by different individuals. Its degree of importance relative to other motives is not within our present ken of meaningful measurement.

Individual Incentives As Tools for Influence

Let's start by granting that individual incentive systems have, in fact, frequently increased production in American companies. Let's also grant that they frequently lead to trouble. Our purpose here can be to consider why they sometimes work and why they sometimes cause more trouble than they are worth.

The two assumptions underlying individual incentive systems are these: (1) people want money, and (2) people will expend more effort to obtain more money.

There is nothing wrong with these two assumptions except that they are usually not enough. If a *directly perceivable*, positive, and causal relationship can be arranged between a man's productivity and money, the man's productivity will be greater than when no such relationship exists—other things being equal. The trouble, of course, is that other things are not always equal.

Perhaps by specifying these "other things," we may be able to make them equal. Experience with individual incentives suggests that the other things center on interdependency. We can, for discussion purposes, break the interdependency issue down into these three factors: (1) other people around B; (2) other needs within B; and (3) unrecognized needs within A. Let's look at them one at a time.

B plugging away at his machine is usually not alone. He is in a social environment. B's activity has some effects on other people around him. And he is, in a different way, as dependent on these other people as he is on the boss. He does not shed his group membership when he goes on incentive. So the direct incentive path to money, though desirable, may be partly blocked by the counterinfluence of other members—members who, out of "obstinacy" or "irrationality," do not trust or like the incentive rate. It is no easy task for any of us to put up with the label of "rate-buster" or in other ways to bear the sanctions of the group we need to live with.

But even if workers are working alone, when we tie money rewards directly to individual performance, the individuals involved frequently find themselves in conflict. They now have a new and simple path to more money (which they want); but the path takes them away from some other things they also want, like taking it easy, socializing with the boys, and so on. These other social and egoistic needs, unlike money, are not easy to see and measure, which is probably why early industrial engineers missed them.

The third "other" thing, management's own motives,

shows up very often too. It shows up best when an incentive system works too well. When the girls begin to produce at 300 per cent of the standard and their premiums make their take-home pay out of line with other departments, then managers are likely to recognize that they did not want just to influence every individual to do his best. They wanted individuals to do their best *within limits* and according to the total pattern of the company.

Let's take an example that is not unusual. Consider eight girls removing casings from skinless frankfurters. The frankfurters are molded in cellophane-like casings which must be peeled off after chilling. The girls stand alongside a conveyer, pick up the frankfurters, hook a fingernail under an edge of the casing and strip it off. This is the kind of straightforward, repetitive job that is almost ideally suited to an individual incentive rate. So the industrial engineers work out a standard, succeed in getting union and employee approval, and put an incentive rate into effect.

The rate works well for a while until one of the girls hits upon the idea of taping a small razor blade to her finger. The "other people" factor shows up at this point. This creative technological improvement is immediately adopted by all the other girls (who are not, for good reason, as "resistant to change" in this case as they are purported to be in many others), and productivity per girl increases several hundred per cent. Now the take-home pay of the girls is far out of line with the pay of other employees doing comparable or even more skilful tasks in other departments. Management's motives now need re-examination. If management changes the rate, the union will accuse it of reverting to rate-cutting practices and of reneging on its contract to pay for productivity. And so on.

The Logic and Illogic of Individual Incentives

Psychologically speaking, the example shows how the logic of individual incentive pay is wrong as well as right. It is right in the sense that it usually ties meaningful rewards to the kind of effort that the rewarder wants. It is wrong in what it omits: other people, other worker needs, and managerial needs. In its failure to take interdependence into account, the incentive system is not based on the assumption that the workers are independent individuals. The assumption is that the total job of a company can be broken down into individual subparts, each subpart just the right size for one individual in the organization. The work of the organization will be accomplished best (this argument runs) when each man does his job as effectively as he can.

Gestalt psychologists, especially, like gleefully to point out the fallacy in such reasoning. The whole is not the sum of its parts, they argue, but something much more, because the parts are interdependent. A tune is more than the notes that make it up; the bicycle remains a bicycle even after every one of its original pieces has been replaced. Contrarily, all the parts are not a bicycle, not until they are put together in one particular way. If every man looks at his own small task alone, ignoring its relationship to other tasks, the greatest total productivity will not be attained.

It is easy to show the same phenomenon in experimental situations, just as long as intercommunication and interaction are required. For example, suppose we give each of five men several pieces of a puzzle. No man has enough pieces to complete his own puzzle, but among the five there are enough pieces to complete five puzzles.

Suppose we set up an individual incentive system. We say to each man: "You will be paid in accordance with the speed with which you can put together your puzzle. The man who makes his puzzle first gets first prize, the man who makes his last gets the booby prize." Under these conditions, with each man concerned about his own immediate productivity but necessarily caught in the trap of having to give up some of his pieces in order to get others he needs, the total productivity of the group in X minutes is usually less than five completed puzzles.

Change the incentive system now so that each man is given an equal share of the prize money, the prize money being determined by the total number of puzzles they can complete in X minutes. Five completed puzzles are the likely result.

But it is only when there is such interdependency, such a need to trade off pieces with other people, that this disadvantage of the individual incentive system shows up so clearly. For if we give to each man all the pieces needed to compete his own puzzle, it may well be that he will complete it fastest under conditions of individual motivation. If management can indeed faultlessly divide and plan the parts of an operation so that each part is actually independent of any other part, then management can truthfully say, "All that we want this worker to do is to produce as many of these pieces as he can produce."

Such conditions are rare in the industrial world. We still find them occasionally in home work situations, and they are sometimes approximated at lower levels of industrial organizations. But only approximated, because most managements, when they reflect on it, want people to do more than their jobs. They do not really want the individual employee to go on blindly punching out blanks when his machine needs lubrication; they *do* want him to take a few seconds off to show the new employee at the next machine how to cut down his enormous scrappage; they *do* want him to report a fire when he sees one.

In the puzzle experiments just mentioned, an interesting thing may happen. Subjects often refuse to accept the individual incentive rules of the game. Many of them simply don't serve their own "best interest"; they insist on trading pieces they know will produce puzzles for two other people, even if they can't complete their own. Moreover, they begin to look sheepish and unhappy if they sit with a completed puzzle before them, being stared at balefully by the others they are blocking.

As one goes up the scale in an organization to higher levels of responsibility, these points become far more obvious. At higher levels we seldom say, "Do this—and don't do anything else." For at higher and more technical levels more and more decision making must be left to the individual. He must define for himself more of what a good day's work is.

Although we cannot very well rank people's wants, we can be fairly safe in assuming that money is not all they want all the time. Even as early as 1927 the Western Electric researches were pointing out that the introduction of individual money incentives could create psychological conflicts by forcing people to choose between money and the important social standards of their own group: between cooperation and competition; or between the need for approval of one's group at work and the approval of one's wife when she sees the pay check.

Like most conflicts, these too may be solved by unexpected means. One compromise for a person caught in such a conflict is to work out some way to beat the system and yet maintain or even improve his relationships with others. The development of a new jig hidden from management can satisfy both needs. Aggression is another way of working off the tension evoked by such conflicts. And who is the ideal target?

Moreover, the control of individual incentive rewards is perceived by employees to lie almost exclusively in the hands of an unpredictable and not always beloved managerial big brother. One should therefore expect to find ingenious and powerful forms of resistance. Incentive plans then may become pawns in games of strategy, with management seeking always to plug potential loopholes in the system while employees, in ways that can be unbelievably imaginative and creative, drill new holes in "impossible" places. As a consequence, I think, many industrial engineers find themselves caught up in a frustrating, never ending, and unpopular holding-action strategy. If the socially determined production ceiling has become a commonplace in plants with individual incentives, so has the unhappy, slightly embittered industrial engineer.

In two ways, then, the simple maxim "A good day's pay for a good day's work" becomes hard to implement. First, we have to specify, as managers, whether we want a good day's work from *every* man, or a good day's work from *all* the men. The two are not the same. Second, even if we want a good day's work from every man, money isn't always enough to get it, especially if the means we provide for getting money conflict with other available means to social and egoistic satisfactions.

If this picture of the individual incentive seems unattractive, the reader should keep the alternatives in mind. In many, many situations, when the alternative is a flat rate, the individual incentive can and does yield significant improvements, both in productivity and morale. When employee confidence in management's integrity is high and when the "atmosphere" of an organization is co-operative and friendly, the addition of an individual incentive may do much good and little harm.

Unit-wide Multiple Incentives

Consider the profit-sharing plan as an extreme contrast to bare individual incentives. Consider, for example, a small company of, say, three hundred employees which chooses, instead of individual incentives, one of the many varieties of such plans. Assume it chooses the Scanlon plan, which is itself an extreme within the profit-sharing group. In a sense such a plan does not properly belong in a chapter on money incentives, for though it begins with money incentives and though money incentives derive from it, it can be better thought of as a plan for the psychological reorganization of a company.

The elements of the plan are these: (1) A monthly bonus for *everyone* in the plant based on an index of the over-all productivity of the plant—an index that is a satisfactory measure of improvement in the organization's efficiency. (2) The introduction of production committees. If every man's take-home pay is tied not to his individual productivity but to the productive efficiency of the company as a whole, then the production committee becomes the mechanism for tying everyone's efforts to the goal of productivity.

Notice that this plan includes the same assumptions made

in individual plans. But profit-sharing plans also add two others: interdependency and social and egoistic needs.

These two additions are surprisingly important. The underlying proposition of individual incentives reads something like this: Individuals will work harder if they are individually rewarded with money for harder individual work. The profit-sharing modification is of this order: Organizations will work harder if they are organizationally rewarded for harder organizational work.

The two propositions do not even contradict one another. The second is an extension of the first. We do not have to prove one right and the other wrong; we have only to decide whether we are dealing with *independent* or *interdependent* individuals and with simply motivated or multiply motivated ones.

The second proposition assumes that individuals in industrial organizations are both socially and economically interdependent. It therefore defines an individual's job differently than the first. His job is no longer to punch his press as productively as possible; it is to punch his press in a social environment, to think about ways of improving the operation of his press and the company, to help whenever helping other people in the plant wil contribute to the over-all efficiency of the organization, and finally, when faced with unusual decisions, to try to make those decisions which will contribute to total efficiency.

One result of such a plan is an increase in feelings of responsibility for the total operation on the part of all members of the organization. For now it is harder to make management the scapegoat for all problems. If production, and therefore the bonus share, drops, there is no tight rate to blame it on. If some people work too slowly or stupidly, it costs everyone something. What should everyone, not just management, do about it?

This increase in employees' "ownership attitude," however, is not an unmixed blessing. Even though most managers insist they want their people to develop one, an ownership attitude in each employee means that each employee may take a serious interest in things management considers its private property. It may mean, for example, that the machine operator now expresses interest in the sales manager's decisions. He may question such decisions. He may want an accounting for the sales department's failure to bring in a large order. At this level secondary and tertiary changes in atmosphere and organizational structure are likely to occur. Notions about secrecy, about prerogatives of one group or another, are likely to be battered down.

If profit-sharing plans succeed in developing what they set out to develop, a strongly active desire on the part of everyone in the plant to improve the plant, what then? Where individual incentives so often sharpen the line between management and employees, these profit-sharing plans tend to obviate it. They tend to push the whole organization in the direction of oneness, in which everything is everybody's business. The new control problem may not be how to get people to work on time but how to keep them from henpecking management.

When a management is struggling for productivity, when employees appear obstinate, inconsiderate, and entirely insensitive to management's needs, the development of an ownership attitude in employees may seem wonderfully utopian. But the reality creates difficulties. The senior officers of more than one small company that has adopted such plans have spent some sleepless nights and gone on even blander diets precisely when they have achieved what they sought—a working force intensely and creatively motivated to help the organization to succeed. Management feels the pressure when it has to face up to the reality of long-sought honest feedback. They find that they are hearing not only the happy news of dollar savings but the unhappy public exposure of past managerial inadequacy. For as every phase of production is examined in the bright light of joint committees, almost any management team is bound to discover case after case in which its decisions were not quite so good as they had seemed to be. Yet the fact remains that the multiple incentive system has paid handsome dollar dividends to management and worker alike. Its cost is that management and everyone else must operate in a glass house.

The words "multiple incentives" were used advisedly in the subheading of this section. Although the money incentive is central to the development of such plans, they also encompass changes in the whole organizational structure. Incentives in the form of greater opportunities for independence and for greater participation in planning and decision making are other outgrowths of these group-wide systems. In these ways, they represent an almost total rebuilding of the relationships among members of an organization.

Several of these plans have by now been tested in many small companies, generally with good success. They have not been put through the harder test of a depressed economy, however, nor have they yet been applied to very large firms. Psychologically they make sense in that they open channels of communication and create a situation in which at least one goal, the goal of greater productive efficiency, is spread more widely through all levels of the organization.

They move people toward an ownership attitude by the simple expedient of providing a kind of ownership.

But they are no panacea. They create new, difficult psychological and organizational problems while solving others. They lead us into the pervasive problems of working groups. It is one thing to find a group of people with common goals. It is another to find them working together efficiently toward those goals.

Incentives and Methods of Influence

This chapter started out to relate money incentives to the ideas about influence and behavior change outlined earlier. What are the relationships? There are several.

Neither individual nor multiple incentives make direct use of restrictive authority. Both offer rewards for work rather than punishment for non-work. Both seek some impersonal, measurable, objective criteria on which to base rewards. Both give up, thereby, some of the control that management often says it wants.

But at that point the two plans part company. Earlier we agreed that *shared* responsibility between A and B encourages broader and deeper change in B than responsibility kept by A alone. Multiple incentives share responsibility. Individual incentives do not. They keep the responsibility for behavior change in the hands of the changer rather than the changee.

Second, individual incentive systems call first for A to take the responsibility and then paradoxically to *give up* some managerial authority by setting impersonal, open-for-inspection incentive rates. They, in effect, contradict the dictum that authority should equal responsibility. Even if that dictum is not too meaningful, the fact remains that management takes responsibility for the incentive and then lets go the reins of control, sometimes thereby getting unintended results. Multiple incentives, though also giving up control, are more flexible, allowing for change by encouraging feedback and by emphasizing the mutuality of influence. Moreover, multiple incentives implicitly accept the idea that the changee is in the saddle in that they say to B, in effect: "Here are the rewards of productivity, if you want them. Our job together is to find a mutually satisfactory way of getting them." Restrictive authority plays a minor role. Productivity is the focal point of the problem, not the conflict between manager and employee. They also, like AA, lay more emphasis on the whole man, taking his social and egoistic needs into account far more than individual incentives.

Finally, multiple incentives recognize the interdependency of members of modern businesses. They try to deal with, rather than deny, that interdependency. They encourage direct communication and co-operation. They try to set a common goal. And herein lies the hardest problem of all—the problem of trying to get all the members of an organization to operate like one good man.

In Summary

Money remains a significant but not exclusive incentive to work in our society.

Individual money incentive systems are most appropriate where workers can operate independently of one another and where their jobs can, in fact, be designed so as to permit independent operation. Difficulties begin to arise when individual incentives are applied to interdependent people on interdependent jobs. Then productive work by each person on his special job (even if it could be attained) may not add up to productive accomplishment for the whole organization. Company-wide multiple incentive plans are psychologically different from individual plans. Individual plans tend to isolate the individual and his work from the organization and its work. Company-wide plans tend to focus everyone on a common organizational goal rather than his own individual one. This common concern for the organizational goal makes for basic changes in worker-management relationships, for increases in the range of satisfactions available to people in an organization, and for new and difficult problems of interaction.

As influence mechanisms, individual incentives are more likely to effect overt actions than basic attitudes. Multiple incentives, closer to the AA model, may have deep and wide effects.

Part III

PEOPLE IN THREES TO TWENTIES
EFFICIENCY AND INFLUENCE IN GROUPS

In Part III we change our perspective in two ways. First we shift again in breadth, changing focus from the A-B relationship to the group—the A-B-C-D-E, etc.—relationship. And, second, we simultaneously shift our observation point outward, so that instead of observing B through A's eyes, we look at groups from the outside, trying to account for the things that happen in them.

In the last section we saw that influencing behavior is difficult enough when we are dealing with just one B. But it is clear, too, that most organizations cannot deal with people one at a time. The essence of organization after all is people many at a time. This section is concerned with interdependent people, five, ten, or twenty at a time, trying to operate efficiently.

This intermediate range is worth a separate section for several reasons: First, the small group is an incomplete but simplified model of the large organization. Second, we have a good base of research on small groups to draw upon. Third, the small group, in its own right, is playing an increasingly important, but problematical, part in modern business.

Staff meetings, problem-solving committees, informal planning groups, work groups—all seem to have multiplied and gained importance in the last couple of decades, and for good reasons. Businesses have been growing in size, for one thing, many past the point at which one person can keep his finger on everything. They have been growing technologically, too, so that the specialist has come in to the picture. Where buying, manufacturing, merchandising, and selling were once all common-sense operations, often all performed by one person, they have now become technical specialties each requiring specialists and subspecialists.

Size and specialization have forced the individual manager to give part way to the group, to recognize his dependence on his subordinates. One head is no longer big enough to get all the facts, to analyze them, to decide, and to act. Hence the information-gathering staff group and the problem-solving planning group and all the others—each made up of many brains trying to act like one superbrain.

It therefore seems fair to say that "problem-solving groups" are a new managerial tool. True, business has used committees and other small groups for a long time, but it is only recently that the small group has been consciously singled out as a major problem-solving tool. One more comment is in order, this time about the place of small groups in industry.

People in business often express intense feeling about committees and group meetings. The majority seems to be on the antigroup side, the same majority that grudgingly accepts the necessity for some kind of committee meetings but holds out as long as possible against them. But they are counterbalanced by a growing vanguard of "group-thinkers," people with an almost mystical faith in the potency of committees. Committees, for them, can do anything better than anybody.

But size and technology dictate the use of the group, whether we like it or not. So the problem is a "how" not a "whether or not" problem. The "how" issue can be divided into two subproblems. The first is how to make groups work. The second is how to fit them into the hierarchical design of most organizations. The first subproblem, how to make them work, is considered in this part. The problem of how they fit is best left for Part IV, on large organizations.

This section accepts groups as facts of industrial life. It considers first some alternative structural designs that affect the efficiency of small groups (chap. 14); then some operating problems that arise in trying to lead and participate in them (chaps. 15–16); finally we take one applied managerial problem, management development, and look at it from the perspective of the small-group psychologist (chap. 17).

One general purpose in this section is to throw some light on conditions that affect the problem-solving efficiency of groups. In so doing we will come up against some buzz phrases that are being tossed around in industry these days, like "conference leadership" and "groups dynamics." Those phrases are useful, but they are often served up as bare-boned rules of thumb guaranteed to make any group do anything, anytime.

Once again, as the reader will see, the problem is more complex than that. Although we can understand a good deal about groups, no neat formulas work very well for controlling or influencing them. But some mapping out of the processes that go on in groups may be helpful to people who spend many of their working hours trying, in groups, to solve problems.

Chapter 14

COMMUNICATION NETS IN GROUPS

DESIGNS FOR GETTING THE WORD AROUND

Like the relationship between two people, the relationships among members of a group are limited by the kinds of communication that occur. In the chapter on two-person communication in Part II, we pointed out that communication has several dimensions, only one of which is the content of what is said.

The same holds for groups. Group members can talk about all sorts of ideas, but they can also use one-way or two-way communication no matter what they talk about. They can, moreover, carry on more or less noisy and redundant conversations. And, the reader will recall, group members can communicate over different *networks*.

These networks, it turns out, do indeed affect the ways groups solve problems. By experimenting with networks, we can tell a good deal about the efficiency with which a group will operate on a problem and a good deal about how individual group members will feel. So an analysis of communication nets can serve as a good bridge between problems of individual behavior and problems of organizational behavior.

Experimental research in the field has only a short history. Many of the findings are highly tentative and not subject to ready generalization. But students of industrial organization should be aware of the history, despite these inadequacies, because it points to the accessibility of organizations as subjects for quantitative experimental research. In fact, studies of group communication networks are just one phase in a body of research, as yet unintegrated, concerned with organization for decision making and action. The scope of these larger researches goes beyond industrial organization into the nature of "systems" in general, whether the system be the single cell, the single person, the machine, or the organized human group. It promises, in this writer's opinion, to produce some extremely useful results.

What We Mean by Communication Nets

Communication nets are a *structural* aspect of a group. They tell us how the group is hung together. Consider, for instance, the difference between a boss who sets himself up with his staff like this:

and one who prefers to divide his four staff people into two seniors and two juniors:

The lines here represent lines of communication. These diagrams are structural. They tell us nothing about the people involved—just something about the "system." What differences might such different setups make in the boss's flow of information? In his flexibility? In the originality of the ideas he gets?

Consider also the effects on subordinates of being in one communicational position or another—like B in the two charts. In one case he can talk to his superior directly, in the other he must go through channels.

The issue here is not whether the several channels in these group networks are one-way or two-way channels but whether the problem of existing channels affects the performance of the group. For example, suppose that for a group of five men all channels are two-way channels. Then this question still remains: What system of channels will be the most effective system for these five men? Will such a group solve problems best when everyone has an open two-way channel to everyone else? Like this:

Or is *this* system better?

Or this one?

Even though each of these networks provides enough communication channels to permit intercommunication, the arrangements and numbers of channels differ, and so, therefore, may the effectiveness of the group as a problem-solving body. Moreover, some of these networks fit better with the usual company organization chart than others; some would look very strange indeed on an organization chart.

In practical terms the question now is this one: How does the communication network affect the efficiency of a group's performance?

Testing Communication Networks

The best way to answer such questions may be temporarily to strip away the complications found in real life. Then one can set up small experimental committees and put them to work in one or another of these different networks. By providing each experimental group with some standard problems to solve and then measuring performance, one can get some ideas about the relative efficiency of one of these networks versus another. In the past five or six years such experimental work has been carried on, and the results have been both consistent and interesting.

The reader might like to try to decide for himself, on a common-sense basis, just what results one should get with one of these networks or another. So, for illustrative purposes, consider these two networks of five people each:

Such groups might be analogous to groups of field staff people, each located in a different branch or district but all reporting eventually to the same boss at headquarters. Let's say communication is by telephone. In both networks, A, E, B, and D are district people, and C is someone back at the central office.

In an experimental setup, one can give each group the same problem, a problem which requires some information from each man before it can be solved. Usually it is some sort of puzzle, in many ways analogous to a pricing problem in a rapidly changing supply and demand situation.

Which of these two groups will solve this kind of problem faster? Which group will have the higher morale? Will there be a leader in No 1? In No. 2? Which particular positions in group No. 1 or No. 2 will be high morale positions? Which will be low morale positions?

Here are the answers that have come out of experiments like these:

Network No. 1 will be the faster of the two.

On the whole, the morale of group No. 2 will be higher than that of group No. 1. People will be more enthusiastic in group No. 2.

Only one person in group No. 1 is likely to get a big bang out of the job, and that man is C. The others, A, B, D, and E, will probably feel bored and left out of the center of things.

Man C in No. 1 will probably be the leader of that group. Everyone in the group will be likely to turn to him. In No. 2 the leader (the one who gets the answer first and sends it out to the others) can be almost anybody. In fact, there may be a different leader each time the group runs through a problem, or else no identifiable leader at all.

Another finding in these researches is most intriguing in

its implications for industry. Two groups are put to work in the circle (No. 2) and star (No. 1) patterns. Their task is as follows: Each man is given five solid colored marbles of which one color is common to all men in the group. The group must find the one color that all 5 members have in common. They then write notes to one another over the available channels, saying things like this: "I have red, green, yellow, blue, and brown." Eventually they discover that all have red marbles. After playing this game several times, the groups in both networks become proficient and fast. At this point, the marbles are changed. Instead of simple solid colors, they are given mottled marbles, of odd shades, difficult to describe. Now two men looking at identical marbles may describe them quite differently. One may use the term "greenish-yellow," the other may call it "aqua." "Noise," in other words, has entered the system in the form of a semantic problem.

The interesting finding is the difference between these two networks in their ability to adapt to and meet this change. The circle handles it nicely, so that after ten runs or so it is back to high efficiency. The star can't seem to cope with it, still making a large number of errors after many trials. This result certainly suggests that the structure of an organization influences its adaptability as well as its other forms of efficiency.

Communication structure, then, does affect a group's efficiency, at least in this kind of situation. But much depends on the definition one gives to the word "efficiency." Some communication networks allow for *faster* operation than others, but the advantage of speed may be gained at the cost of accuracy and/or morale. People are *happier* in some networks than they are in others, and some networks therefore are more likely to keep going longer without blowing up, but these networks may be slower or less accurate than some others. This conflict between "morale" and "efficiency" may indeed turn out to be a generalized conflict in industrial organizations. Some networks have fewer *errors* than others. Some are more *flexible* than others. All these words may have something to do with what we mean by "efficiency."

Why Different Networks Cause People
To Behave Differently

If we look at these results in the light of Parts I and II, they are not hard to understand. Why is network No. 1 faster than network No. 2? For one thing No. 1 is like a one-way communication system. Although people can talk back individually to the central man, they cannot talk to one another. No. 1 imposes an orderliness on the group that wipes out extra messages. In No. 2 no such clear organization is imposed. People can send messages to two people; they can get around more and thereby spend more time.

But in sending more messages members of No. 2 also are taking advantage of more checkpoints of the kind provided by two-way communication. Thus, they can locate and correct more of their errors.

They also have in No. 2 more chance to participate and take responsibility. They are less dependent on one person since they can check with one *other* person. So they are more satisfied and happy, just as people were in the two-way communication example in chapter 9.

On the other hand, the central man in network No. 1 is quite happy—and for the same reasons. He has responsibility, he has several sources of information and several checkpoints. He is independent and powerful.

In these ways, then, the mere mechanical fact of *structure* can act upon individuals by making them more or less dependent, more or less certain of where they stand, and more or less responsible. The same fact of structure can also act upon the total operational efficiency of the group, causing it to work faster or slower, more or less accurately, and more or less adaptably.

Once again, though, it is worth pointing out, as we did in chapter 9, that structure seems to affect people's feelings in one direction and their speed and accuracy in the other. No one has yet found a structure that maximizes speed and accuracy and, at the same time, morale and flexibility.

Networks in Industrial Groups

One may argue that these laboratory findings, though interesting, are not particularly relevant to the problems actually encountered in industry. In most face-to-face industrial groups only one communication network seems possible, and that is a fully connected network like the one on p. 194, in which everyone can communicate directly with everyone else.

But the argument that this is the only actual network, even in committees, does not hold water. A clear, albeit informal, notion about who can talk to whom exists in most groups. In fact, in face-to-face meetings, although the *official* network is a fully connected one, the *actual* network may be some other one altogether. Communication networks are much like organization charts: there is likely to be a formal, officially charted organization, and there is likely also to be an informal, uncharted organization that nevertheless plays a significant role in the functioning of the company.

In a committee meeting, for example, a chairman can usually manipulate the communication setup so that in practice each person talks only to him and not directly to other people. And even if the chairman tries to be "democratic," the same result may occur unintentionally because of differences in rank or power among members of the committee. Privates don't interrupt generals whenever they feel like it, no matter what the official communication network.

In continuing work groups, the possibilities for changing communication nets are better than in meetings. Almost any network is possible if the group in question is the continuing membership of a particular department.

However, the members of a great many industrial groups seldom meet face to face. Where there is physical separation, one would expect the structure of the communication net to have far more direct effects.

"Good" and "Bad" Networks

What, then, are the characteristics of the "best" communication networks? That question demands another: Best for what? If the question is what is "best" for small meetings and conferences, where everyone's ideas are worth something and where the same people will probably get together again next week, then the answer seems clear. The best networks are likely to be the ones with at least these two related characteristics:

First, equalitarian networks are probably preferable to hierarchical networks. That is, networks like the circle, where everyone has access to about the same number of channels, are preferable to networks like the star, where one person has many neighbors and the rest none.

Second, those networks that provide everyone with at

least two direct communication channels are probably better than those that give some people only one channel to the rest of the group.

Several different networks meet these criteria. And there are real differences even among these. But as a group, networks that meet these standards seem—in experimental situations—to yield higher morale, greater willingness to work, and a series of other advantages over networks that do not meet them.

But if by "efficient" we mean fast in getting started and fast in its operations, our conclusions about the best network must be quite different. Then differentiated, non-equalitarian networks like the star look better. For they impose a clear-cut organization on the group, defining each person's job and leaving little leeway for wandering away from that job. As a consequence, those groups get started faster and work faster once they have started.

Similarly, the experimental findings would lead to other predictions. For instance, consider a superior, A, who puts himself in the position shown here:

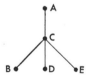

Any superior who does this may be leaving himself in serious danger. And his assistant, C, may find himself in a very powerful spot. For the assistant has more and faster access to internal organizational information than his boss or anyone else, and by being a little selective in what he transmits (purposely or by oversight), he can end up controlling the organization. Sometimes one sees this situation with the president's private secretary. By being in a position to screen all incoming and many outgoing messages, she can be a formidable personage.

Preferential access to information, after all, is a major source of power in any organization. In experiments in the star network, any man in the central position, C, is likely to become the functioning boss. His personal characteristics do not matter much. He learns more, faster, than anyone else. In real life, his communicational power may be balanced by someone else's authoritative power. Curiously, one will often find groups so organized that the position of greater authority is *not* the key comunicational position, even where power maximization in the hands of authority is the objective sought.

These ideas are related to some ideas about feedback talked about in chapter 9. Information is transmitted more broadly and apparently more accurately, and people are happier about sending and receiving it, when the people involved have some degree of control over what is happening; that is, when they have some feedback, or when they have checkpoints to help them increase their certainty about what they are getting, or when they have opportunities to contribute to what is going on. Free feedback clearly helps in this direction, and now one can add that "equalitarian," "multichannel" communication networks seem also to help toward the same end.

A word of warning may be appropriate here. It may seem to follow from what has been said that the very *best* network is the fully communicating one, wherein everyone can talk directly with everyone else. Although this is *probably* true for certain types of problems in relatively small groups, it may not be true as groups grow larger. Purely practical considerations, like how much one person can send or receive at one time, might require limitations in the number of channels to be used in larger meetings, or even in small meetings for special kinds of problems.

Another warning: To date the research on communication has not dealt much with "real" situations. Problems of authority and responsibility that exist in industrial organizations clearly complicate real-life situations. So we must necessarily be cautious about jumping off into generalizations from such experimental research. Nevertheless, the very fact that some aspects of organization can be dealt with quantitatively in the laboratory seems a promising advance in a field so recently limited to experiential, "clinical" examination.

Unfortunately we do not know much about the networks that will or will not work for large organizations. Some of our little ones "look" centralized, some decentralized. But we can't put a thousand people in a laboratory, or at least we haven't yet.

Although it is probably true that many of the results would hold up if we could test them on large groups, many of them would not. We would run into the problem of *oversupply* of information if we expanded the star network to even twenty-five people with only one central man in position C. We would probably need some intermediate people to absorb irrelevant information and organize the remainder for C. Similarly, if we had a hundred men in a fully connected network, we would probably get chaotic results, at least until a good many channels had been voluntarily closed off. And we cannot even draw some networks for larger groups. Some, like this one, are unique to

a particular number of people. How does one draw that same net for ten people?

Self-Defense and the Design of Networks

If these notions hold, one may ask why work groups are not more often of equalitarian, multichannel design in industrial organizations. One good reason is that these designs conflict, as do many aspects of small-group operation, with the pyramidal, highly individualized structure of most industrial organizations. Another good reason is that speed and control are often more critical than morale or even creativity.

There is also a not-so-good reason that may be worth special mention. Two-way comunication in equalitarian networks is often dangerous and threatening to some people in the group. For instance, people in higher positions in an organization may prefer hierarchical communication networks like the star pattern because it helps to maximize their power in the group (assuming that a superior will put himself in a position like C's). Patterns like this one serve the same purpose as one-way communication. They keep a boss off the psychological hook. His weaknesses are hidden better in a position like C's in the center of the star than in any position in the circle. He can screen information from others. He can blame errors on others, and maybe he can get away with it. The other people in such a group may have no way of checking on the real source of either an error or a bright idea. Often people argue for the star pattern over the circle on grounds of speed or business-like efficiency when an underlying reason for the preference is the protection of someone's self-esteem. The same reasoning may hold for subordinates. It is easier for them, too, to hide in a hierarchical network.

In Summary

The simple structure of the communication network in a group, independent of the persons in the group, seems to set limits on the group's performance.

Groups whose problems require the collation of information from all members work faster when one position is highly centralized and the others relatively peripheral. But the morale, the self-correctiveness, and perhaps the creativity of such groups may be better when the communication network is more equalitarian and when each member has more than one source of information.

Highly centralized groups may often be used for their consistency with general organizational designs, their speed, and their controllability; but they are also used as psychological defense devices to protect superiors' "weaknesses" from being exposed to subordinates, and vice versa.

Chapter 15

THE CONTENT OF COMMUNICATION IN GROUPS
WHAT WORDS GET AROUND

The *structure* of communication in a group is one thing, the *content* another. In this chapter, content is the issue to be treated. What information ought to be transmitted over any particular network? What information is or is not relevant to the solution of a problem? When a group sets out to solve a problem, after all feedback and network questions have been resolved, it still must decide what should be sent through the network.

This may seem a simple problem. Yet anyone who has ever been on a committee must have noted how discussion can bog down into argument, name calling, and story telling; how some points are stated and restated and others never get heard. Are arguments, name calling, funny stories, and redundancy relevant or irrelevant to the solution of a problem that people have come together to solve? If they are not relevant, how can they be kept out? What is relevant? And how can what is relevant be kept in?

Noise and Redundancy

Information theorists, we said in chapter 9, use the term "noise" when talking about things like the static one may find on a telephone connection. Some things that get communicated in group meetings are much like telephone or radio static—the wind, the argument, the *noise* that gets stirred up and interferes with communication of "really relevant" information.

Besides being noisy, the content of group communication tends to be redundant. The same information is communicated again and again. In meetings, the same point may be made half a dozen times in half a dozen ways in the course of a single discussion.

Noise and redundancy look like signs of inefficiency in the communication process. Ideally, we would like to see groups solve problems like intelligent individuals. They should do the things described in the chapter on problem solving in Part I. They should search, systematically, for alternatives, using an appropriate set of categories; then they should follow a set of reasonable decision rules for dealing with the alternatives. They should use their memories. And they should *learn*, so that they can deal with new problems better than they did with old ones.

Those things do not always happen. Or at least so much committee activity seems devoted to noise and redundancy that those orderly problem-solving processes are obscure and even secondary. It is understandable, therefore, that most business people would like to see noise and redundancy cut to a minimum as quickly as possible, so people can get on with solving the problem at hand. The difficulty is procedural. How does one minimize the sound and fury of day-to-day life in an industrial organization: the boasting, the credit seeking, the boot licking, the kowtowing, the blustering?

Minimizing Noise in a Group

Two general approaches have been used to minimize noise, and the two are at almost opposite extremes. The most obvious and most common procedure is simply to set up rules disallowing most noise. The rules may be formal parliamentary ones or informal ones. The chairman says, "We will stick to the facts in this meeting. We will keep personalities out of this. We will cut off people who talk too long or too much." His purpose is to eliminate noise, and his weapon is his authority to enforce organizational rules. This seems a sensible, business-like approach to the problem, but it needs more consideration.

Another, not so business-like, method for handling noise is to take the position that noise should not be kept out of meetings but let in and identified. Here the chairman says, "If you want to blow off, blow off. If you want to boast, boast. If you want to deal in personalities, deal in personalities. But when anyone does any of these things, let him or anyone else point it out so that everyone will know what he's doing." This second method also deserves serious consideration.

Noise-making behavior by people in groups, like all other behavior, is goal directed. People boast because they feel that boasting will get them something they want—recognition, or power, or status. People lick boots for reasons, too; perhaps they think boot licking will make someone they need like them a little better. When several people join to try to solve a problem through committee action, there may be one central problem that is common to everyone on the committee, but there are also individually perceived problems that each member brings in with him. People, we said in Part I, perceive the world in relation to their operant needs. If other members of a group are in a position to help or hurt a particular member, that member is likely to be alert to their power. The noise in a group may therefore be made up, to a large extent, of efforts of individuals to satisfy their personal needs in the presence of the group. Thus, this kind of noisiness can only be considered wasteful or irrelevant when the group problem is defined as the only real problem. Such a definition is simply unrealistic. This second level of individual problems exists, and attempts to solve them—although irrelevant to the group's problem—constitute, so far as individual members are concerned, a perfectly relevant use of the communication system.

We may object to persons using a group for their own ends, or we may object to the methods that some individuals use to solve their personal problems—methods like name calling or yessing. We may also feel that the methods people sometimes use are not effective methods even for accomplishing what those individuals want to accomplish. Nevertheless, those methods are attempts by individuals to solve problems, and to rule them out by authority may be to rule out the individuals as well as the noise. For if these "irrelevant" needs are so important to a person that he tries to use the group as a sounding board for them, then to deny him that opportunity can only do one of two things: it can make him lose interest in the group and the group's problem, or it can make him disguise his communications so that they *sound* relevant to the common problem.

Authority or parliamentary procedure or social pressures

may drive individual motives underground, but such methods do not necessarily eliminate them. Instead of open argument and open emotion, one now gets calm, seemingly rational discussions, but discussions which somehow manage indirectly to discredit opponents or to defend positions beyond any point of reasonable utility.

Everyone who has served on a committee has seen this kind of velvet-glove activity many times. Sometimes it takes the "it's an excellent idea but . . ." form, or, "Well, of course we *could* go about it your way but. . . ." Such tacks are much harder to handle, much less likely to contribute to honest unanimity (or honest disagreement), than an open haggle.

It is quite impossible to exclude individual noise from group discussion by force or by parliamentary procedure. If these devices eliminate noise, they eliminate it as ear plugs do—at the cost of much relevant information. Problems may appear to be solved in such restrictive situations when the "solution" is actually a hodgepodge of compromise and half-truth. As in the feedback example in chapter 9, if we want the information, we may have to bear the emotion.

Hence, the other choice: let the communication channels carry whatever people want to communicate. Let everything in, but tag the different classes of information, so that everyone knows what's what. Seek out the causes of noise and get rid of the causes. When people don't need to make noise, they will stop and get down to the problem at hand.

Such a policy need not be as chaotic as it sounds. Perhaps it is more orderly to convert chaos to system than to cover it with system. The question is not anarchy versus order so much as the orderly handling of anarchistic factors in a group. Getting groups to say what they feel is not easy, however, especially if time is limited. But patience and some respect for people's ultimate willingness to accept responsibility can help a good deal. Post-mortems and bull sessions devoted to what was right or wrong about the last meeting are useful techniques for this purpose if the group meets periodically.

I remember one group of six men working on a research project full time. The project called for the six to break up into pairs and travel to some field locations for a few days. The group spent hours trying to decide who would go where with whom. Afterward, in a bull-session review of the day's progress, someone pointed out that it was silly to have thrashed around so long over this trivial point. This stimulus finally brought a previously hidden issue out in the open. Everyone liked Joe, and everyone wanted to be the one to travel with Joe. But nobody would admit it; so they had used all sorts of "rational" arguments all day about why one pairing arrangement or another wouldn't work. Of course this recognition came several hours too late, but it helped to prevent occurrence of similar stalemates later. Post-mortems like this become easier with time. In fact they can often be worked in as part of the meeting itself, so that people are always watching for and pointing up underlying feelings contemporaneously with their discussions of content problems.

Groups that operate with fairly free expression and recognition of feelings follow a somewhat different pattern from more carefully controlled groups. They start slowly, characteristically with considerable hodgepodge and disturbance and little measurable progress. But they can accelerate fast once the air is cleared. Controlled groups, on the other hand, show steadier, step-by-step progress that seems more orderly from the outside.

Barriers to Communication in Groups

It may be profitable to examine the same problem from the other side. Instead of asking, What causes irrelevant noise? one can ask, What blocks the communication of relevant information? This is the same question we asked in chapter 9: What blocks feedback?

Looking at the problem from this perspective can be useful; for, while it is true that too much is often said in groups, too much may also be left unsaid. The subordinate says, "Yes, I understand your instructions," but later it turns out that he did not understand. The salesman does not think it important to tell the sales manager about the change in the customer's attitude. The production worker does not report that his machine is acting oddly because he forgot to lubricate it. The patient says, "You're the doctor; you tell *me* where it hurts." These kinds of relevant information left uncommunicated are the opposite of noise. The atmosphere of a group may be too quiet—too quiet in the sense that problems do not get all available information brought to bear upon them.

Sometimes the barriers that limit communication are simple mechanical ones. Thus, when the communication system is a one-way loudspeaker, the simple absence of channels in one direction makes it mechanically impossible for the receiver to send relevant information back to the sender. Letter writing is another process that includes at least a partial mechanical barrier. People can write letters in two directions, but the process necessarily involves a time lag that constitutes a partial barrier to the communication of information that may be useful only if it arrives quickly.

Such mechanical barriers, however, are probably the least important barriers to communication in human groups. The most significant barriers are the more ephemeral psychological ones like these examples:

First, there is a *status barrier* between superior and subordinate that limits communication in either direction because of fear of disapproval, on the one hand, or loss of prestige, on the other:

"If I ask that question these people will think I don't know enough to be boss, so I'll act like I know the answer already."

"If I admit this to the boss, he'll be wild. He'll think I've lost my touch."

Then there is the *interpersonal hostility barrier*. This is the one that goes:

"I won't give that guy the satisfaction of admitting he's got a good idea. And I certainly won't let him in on my idea."

And there is the *parliamentary methods barrier*. It sometimes takes this form:

"I can't speak until I'm recognized by the chair; and if the chair never recognizes me, my information will never come out. If the chair does recognize me later, I'll still say what should be said now—even if it's irrelevant later."

We need not elaborate on the way parliamentary procedures, which were intended to promote and simplify communication, have been used in social and political affairs selectively to prevent and complicate communication.

These kinds of barriers are trouble makers in human groups. They cannot be dammed up or set aside at will. They do not even have the saving grace of remaining stable and fixed. Instead they move and change with moods and feelings of group members, so that now one set is in operation and now another.

The answers to such barriers may be the same as the answer to too much noise. They could be circumvented if they themselves were communicated. If two people, for example, can reach the point where they can tell one another what they think of one another, they may be able to work out an understanding that will allow them to communicate successfully. But ordinarily they do not communicate these feelings—they do not especially in the industrial culture. Instead, they say, "Stick to the facts! Don't get emotional! Let's be business-like!" This cultural attitude is probably the biggest communication barrier of all because it prevents the communication of interpersonal feelings, and uncommunicated interpersonal feelings, in turn, complicate and sometimes prevent the communication of facts.

The Short and the Long

Sometimes when we think of a committee we are thinking of a group that meets three or four times and is then finished. For these committees we can ignore much of what has been said here. There probably is not time for people to work off feelings, anyway. But if the committee is a continuing one, these issues become important. Then some time spent lubricating and adjusting the mechanism may be well worthwhile, and so too may be the usable storage of results.

So we need perhaps to separate these two kinds of groups in the way we separated one-shot from continuing relationships in the chapter on influence. In a one-shot situation A need not look far beyond his nose; his job is to make the sale. In a one-shot committee, members need not look far ahead either. They can concentrate on the solution of the problem at hand and put on the perceptual blinders of parliamentary rules to block off the irritating intrusion of human emotions. They don't even have to remember *how* they solved the problem.

But if they are going to work together for a while, they need to take a wider perspective. They need to develop a general program for solving many problems. So they need, like individuals, to pay attention to their own processes; they need to search out and learn *ways* of solving classes of problems even more than they need a quick and good solution to the particular problem right now at hand.

In Summary

It may be a mistake to equate orderliness with efficiency in group processes.

The "irrelevant" noise made by people in groups may represent attempts by members to satisfy personal needs. If that noise is forbidden expression, it may go underground but continue to distort the group's operation.

Conversely, there may be too little noise in a group; i.e., available relevant information may not be forthcoming because of barriers in the communication system. Some of these barriers may be mechanical, but many of them are psychological, like barriers created by status differences or interpersonal jealousies.

In either case, too much noise or too little, the preferred course would seem to be to promote rather than limit communication, i.e., to accept and deal with information about personal feelings and personal needs as well as information about pertinent facts.

For short-lived groups, the solution to the problem may take top priority. For longer-lived ones, programs and processes for solving classes of problems deserve precedence.

Chapter 16

OPERATING PROBLEMS OF GROUPS

GETTING WORDS AROUND EFFICIENTLY

When an executive must chair or participate in a committee, he is usually up against an influence problem calling for careful strategy and tactics. He comes into the meeting with some objectives he would like to achieve, either personally or as a representative of some faction. If he is a salesman he would like the interests of salesmen to prevail over the interests of production people. If he represents industrial engineering it is that group's purposes he is serving.

Under such circumstances an executive may sometimes conclude that his ends will best be gained by sabotaging the committee on which he is participating. Sometimes an analysis of the situation will lead him to compromise some of his objectives, and sometimes full co-operation with the committee may seem the most promising course. No matter what his objective, and none can universally be labeled more right or wrong than any other, he can probably plan and execute his strategy best if he knows his own strengths and weaknesses and the strengths and weaknesses of committees.

This chapter attempts to outline, for the use of the committee participant, some characteristic operating problems of committees (and other small groups). These problems, insofar as they are problems of influence, have much in common with those considered in Part II. They raise questions about the strategic use of authority, about the mutuality of responsibility, and about AA types of influence.

Although committees may differ radically in size, purpose, design, membership, and procedure, they have some problems in common. The similarities are divided here into four categories: problems of objective; personnel problems; problems of navigation; and problems of decision making.

Problems of Objective

If a committee of executives starts out to decide whether or not to institute selection tests, their objective seems, at first, perfectly unambiguous. Then someone discovers that one member has quite a different conception of selection tests from other members of the group. Ten minutes later someone raises these questions: "Is our objective to decide on selection tests only? Or are we really here to revise all our selection procedures? Are interviews and application blanks tests, or are they outside our scope?"

Ten minutes later still, someone wants to know: "What does the boss really have in mind when he asks us to look into this? How much money is he willing to spend? Is he willing for us to do a major research job? Or does he want us to buy a packaged product even though it may not be very good?"

And still later someone with an irate note in his voice asks: "What are we trying to decide anyhow? Is it whether or not tests are a good idea? Or is it what tests to buy?"

And so on at intervals throughout the meeting. What seemed precise and unambiguous turns out to be diffuse and shadowy.

Defining objectives becomes more or less difficult with the nature of the problem the group faces. But almost every time we find a decision-making committee in action, we also find periodic difficulties with the definition of objectives.

Moreover, we find another sort of difficulty involving objectives. Besides these overt questions, a series of covert problems is often present. A major one is the problem of subgroup objectives versus group objectives. Thus, in collective bargaining everyone may overtly agree that the objective is to work out a best solution to common problems. But everyone also knows that other major objectives are in operation and that they are in conflict. The union wants to get the best deal it can get, even at the expense of management. And management wants the best deal it can get, even at the expense of the union.

Similarly, in a meeting in which several departments are represented, we often find unverbalized objectives lying just below the surface. The sales department wants to make sure that it doesn't lose any of its control over pricing. The production people do not want the salesmen to be in a better position to dictate production schedules after the meeting than they were before. And so on.

A third level of problems also exists. This is the level of the individual operating as an individual. "How does the boss really feel about this issue? What decisions will please him most? Is my objective really to take the direction that I think is best, or the direction that will most please the boss?" Or, similarly, "Where does this particular proposal fit into the larger political picture? Who will get hurt if we take one direction or another? Who will be helped?"

Clearly the "right" way to cope with these problems will vary with the motives of the coper. Sometimes an individual or subgroup can profit most by blocking the definition of objectives. One can hardly find a better way to keep a meeting from going anywhere than to raise a new specific issue every time the committee gets close to clarifying its purposes. On the other hand, one can equally well befuddle a meeting by overemphasizing objectives—especially if a member chooses so to broaden and complicate them as to take the meeting altogether out of the range of possible accomplishment. The problem is that objectives create difficulties for groups so long as they are differently understood by different people in the group and so long as some of them are not out on the table. Once everyone in the group has a reasonably good feel for the limits of the problem and for the variety of objectives present, something can usually be done about them.

Helping to clarify objectives, perhaps by restating someone else's statement, can help a group to get started and can also put the restater, the clarifier, in a position of strength in the group. Similarly, conscious efforts to talk about covert objectives (as we pointed out in the last chapter), if one suspects their presence, can help a committee to function more efficiently; although the person who does this job takes more risks with covert than with overt issues. If one member suggests, for example, that someone else's personal needs are predominating, guards will be quickly thrown up, and the discussion may thereby be led into fruitless defensive argument. So a group member or chairman who feels that someone in the meeting has ulterior motives had better word and time his suggestion carefully. If he himself is the person with ulterior motives, he may do himself and his cause some good by expressing them—if his cause will be helped by an efficient meeting.

The point is that groups are not likely to go anywhere unless they know where they are going. Even a single human being may have trouble defining his own objectives, and the problem gets much more complicated in a group. Whether it is advantageous for a group member to clarify objectives in the group or to confuse them, to express his own personal objectives or to hide them, these are questions each member of a group must weigh for himself.

From the perspective of the whole group instead of any individual member, the problems to be solved are these: (1) to have every man in the group know where the group is going; (2) to have every man in the group either want to go where the group is going or say where he wants to get off; (3) if there are people who want to get off early, either to change objectives so these people can go along or to let them off and start over; and (4) to take another look every once in a while to see whether objectives need to be changed or modified.

Several actions can help a group in these directions. If people try to communicate about objectives, both personal and official, then at least the problem is out on the table where it can be seen and dealt with. Objectives are likely to be communicated readily if they are not jammed down people's throats by chairmen, if they are treated as a normal part of the agenda, and if the general atmosphere of the meeting encourages this kind of feedback. If, in other words, they operate more like Alcoholics Anonymous and less like the old-time, iron-pants boss.

A census of ideas about the group's objectives taken early in a meeting can also help get these issues out on the table quickly. Often, in meetings, the first idea raised becomes the take-off point for discussion, thereby eliminating expression of some other possibilities. Since the first highway may not be the best one, it can be useful to map out several alternatives before starting the trip.

Problems of Personnel

Another class of obstacles that seems to block small-group operation centers in the personalities of the participants. Such personnel problems include factors carried into the group by the members, like the leader's personality, his dominance or submissiveness, the intensity of his desire to be liked, and so on. They also include problems of individual members' talkativeness, shyness, argumentativeness, and defensiveness.

There are problems of communication, too, stemming from differences in rank, age, expertness, and prestige in the company. And certain problems may arise *within* the group —somebody's idea is ignored, somebody else's is laughed at, somebody else says absolutely nothing and just smiles, thereby frightening some of his colleagues and encouraging others. Finally, this general personnel category includes problems of group mood: elation, depression, and regression into dirty stories or golf or anything except the subject at hand.

No way of avoiding such problems has yet been found, but there are ways of minimizing them. From the group point of view, they are problems only if relevant ideas and information are omitted or distorted as a consequence of them. Often, of course, such problems do affect both the kind and degree of communication. The quiet man who sits and smokes his pipe may seriously affect the rate and even the nature of the ideas that are contributed. For out of the corner of his eye each member may be watching him for some sign of approval or disapproval. Depending primarily on any member's own feelings of security or insecurity, this point or that may be modified, withheld, or overemphasized because of the quiet man.

Or shy man A offers a suggestion which is ignored. He offers it again and it is again ignored. Like the adolescent in the chapter on frustration, one can see A gradually withdraw, thereafter to come out of his shell only infrequently and only in order to jab at someone else's ideas.

What, then, can be done, not so much to prevent such problems as to deal with them? Again the answer seems to lie in the communication process. For if a group can communicate about its personnel problems, the problems may be resolved. But they cannot be resolved so long as they remain hidden and uncommunicated. This again is the problem of dealing with noise. These issues can be opened for group discussion, or they can be denied entry. If a group chooses to deny them, if it chooses to cut off argument, to require that emotionalism be kept out of the meeting and that dirty stories be excluded, then the group is ignoring data relevant to its own operation. And data about itself are as important to the solution of a group's problem as they are to the solution of any individual's problem.

Discussion of such personnel issues need not mean that the group has to examine the remote causes of people's feelings. As in the case of A trying to influence B, the original *causes* of B's feelings are often irrelevant, but the feelings themselves need to get aired. Thus, when some members of a group leave the field by going off into jokes or gossip or pipe dreams, it is not absolutely necessary to find out why they are doing it. It may be necessary, however, to recognize that such digressions are not accidental. They represent attempts to satisfy needs, to get rid of tension. It may therefore be wise to permit time to be "wasted" in the release of such tensions, instead of forcing the needs to find outlet through the medium of "rational" discussion. Recognition and acceptance of people's feelings and encouragement of an atmosphere of permissiveness seem to be sensible directions for a probelm-solving group to take.

A group that operates this way may seem strange sometimes. It does not progress steadily, but in bursts, with periods of highly concentrated work interspersed with periods of digression or argument or laughter. If a superior should happen to walk in on such a group meeting, the chances are about even that he would be impressed or disturbed by what he found.

As it is for problems of objective, the census is a handy device for getting personnel problems out on the table. It is useful for a group to stop once in a while just so that people can say how they feel—how they feel about the group's progress, how they feel about the methods the group is using, how they feel in general. Periodic stops to examine feelings need not be formally instituted; in fact, they occur quite naturally if we let them.

A third method for coping with personnel problems is, surprisingly, to *de-emphasize* pre-meeting preparation. It seems, at first, to make sense to urge group members to think about the committee agenda in advance and to come "prepared." But preplanning can also be a source of serious personnel difficulties. For "preparation" may mean that each man works out his individual position before the meeting and then comes into the group to try to sell his position to the rest. If that is what preparation means, every member of the group now has a position to defend. If his position is rejected he may feel he has suffered a personal, egoistic defeat.

Group leaders especially are given to overpreparation. They often feel that the responsibility for success rests solely with them. Consequently, a new chairman is likely to go home and think out alternative answers to the problem before the meeting and to select the answer that seems best to him. He then comes into the meeting with the wrong expectations about the right answers. Whereupon a whole host of reactive personnel problems arises.

"Preparation" can have other more useful meanings, too. A leader can plan a group meeting without creating much difficulty for himself or his group. It is one thing, for example, to come armed with all the information one can muster to feed into the hopper and quite another to come armed with conclusions. Moreover, to be prepared with a general *procedural* plan for conducting a meeting is different from coming with a specific step-by-step outline. Group members are likely to accept information or a general plan but to resist the imposition of conclusions or tight, inflexible procedures. Moreover, if a problem is big enough to call for a meeting, a chairman who has the answer in advance is often incorrectly prejudging the complexity of the issue.

This whole personnel question involves one of the issues talked about in the section on influence—the location of responsibility. Groups are likely to function with a minimum of personnel difficulty when the responsibility for action and procedure lies with all the members rather than with any particular individual. The responsibility then remaining for the chairman or the leader is to help provide and police a communication system that will evoke all the information the group needs to make its decisions.

Problems of Navigation

Groups get lost in the problems they try to solve. Often they have difficulty locating their position after they have decided where they want to go and have started out to get there. The problems here include timing, meeting deadlines, laying out sequences. They are programing problems. They can be called problems for two reasons: First, they represent sources of inefficiency in a group. Once a group has decided on a destination, it can get itself so involved in going there that it gets lost. It doesn't notice the wrong turn or the circularity of its movements. Second, navigation is a problem because of the relationship between people's self-orientation and people's feelings. Group members feel uncertain and anxious if they don't know where they are. They may feel they are making no progress when in fact they are. Or they may feel that they are drifting purposelessly. These feelings are often direct consequences of poor navigation.

Skilful navigation is something of an art. A chairman (or any member of a group) who begins to feel that his group is getting lost has several ways of trying to do something about it. He can just wait and hope the group will find itself. He can ask the members to stop and go somewhere else. Or he can ask them to stop and try to find out where they are going. If they then decide they like where they are going, they can pick up where they left off; if they don't like it, they can change.

This third alternative is a sensible one for several reasons.

Failure to do anything includes the possibility that people who begin to feel lost may also begin to withdraw from the scene. Simply vetoing the present course is bound to create some kind of debilitating emotional reaction, either further withdrawal or aggression. But just asking for a pause to reconsider is likely to yield few side effects and may actually enhance the group's progress.

Any navigational act, however, especially if it comes from a leader, involves some risks for the actor. For navigational interruptions constitute restrictions on the group, and restrictions may make the restricter unpopular. But periods of unpopularity, after all, are the fate of a group leader. He must choose between the long-term gain that will come from over-all efficiency and the short-term popularity he can invite by abdicating his leadership and ignoring uncomfortable problems like deadlines.

What this navigational problem amounts to, then, is that somebody—the leader or anyone else—has to keep his eye on the group as well as on the problems the group is trying to solve and has to report back what he finds.

Decision-making Problems

Another source of difficulty in groups arises at those points at which a decision seems appropriate. Discussion of a point has been more or less completed, and the time to come to some conclusion has arrived. Sometimes groups block impossibly at these points. They seem unable to recognize them or unable to make any decisions if they do recognize them. And sometimes the decisions that do get made do not seem to be meaningful. People don't pay much attention to them, or they don't act upon them once they leave the meeting.

The problem is to get decisions made when they are ready to be made and to get them made in a way that will lead to follow-up action by the people in the group after they leave the group.

Group leaders may approach this problem in one of two extreme ways. Sometimes a chairman will push hard for decisions, allowing a specified period for discussion and then asking immediately for a vote. At the other end of the scale is the leader who never gets to decision-making points, either because he doesn't recognize those points or because the discussion of an issue just never seems to be fully completed. Like the individual problem solvers in chapter 6, in other words, groups may fail to search for alternatives long enough or may demand an optimum solution well beyond their realistic level of achievement.

Most businessmen favor the limited discussion and vote method of the parliamentary variety. They recognize that the best is too hard to get; so they are satisfied with a brief search. The primary weakness of that method is that, although the decision finally reached may be a satisfactory solution to the problem, it may be a decision in appearance more than reality. When a decision is forced quickly and when the method of deciding is by vote, what is left for the minority except psychologically to reject the decision? If they were "rational" human beings, of course, they would accept the majority wish and carry out their part in it. But most of us, even though we may try consciously to accept a decision with which we disagree, have trouble getting very enthusiastic about it. In a sense the minority is challenged to prove that the majority decision is wrong. Such a challenge is easy to meet when the time comes for individual action, simply by acting in ways that "prove" the decision cannot be made to work.

Moreover, if decisions come too early, before people feel that they have contributed what they have to contribute, before they have organized and clarified the issues for themselves, then the decisions reached may indeed be superficial and unsatisfactory. They are therefore likely to be forgotten quickly or passed over lightly once the meeting is over. Vague feelings of hostility and resistance may also follow, feelings that may lead consciously or unconsciously to sabotage or denial of the decision.

A good deal of research evidence shows that decisions are carried into action most effectively when they are group-consensus decisions, when all members of a group can somehow settle by their own efforts on a choice with which they all agree. On the other hand, decisions imposed from the outside or decisions imposed on a minority by a majority or decisions imposed by the leader are not likely to be lasting or effective, for the same reasons that restrictive authority is a poor tool for effecting important changes in attitude.

Consensus decisions are not easy to achieve. People in groups have an unhappy tendency to disagree with one another, either overtly or covertly. And yet, if the group's problems require that every member carry out of the group a desire to act positively on the group's decision, then it is imperative that everyone accept, both consciously and unconsciously, the decisions reached in the group.

Often, it is true, we must fall short of ideal decision-making procedures. Deadlines and other immediate pressures force us to make majority or individual-leader decisions. But this will occur less often when we have built an atmosphere that makes consensus easier. Open two-way communication, clarification of people's feelings, freedom to object—these contribute to the ease with which consensus can be approached. Sometimes even the most efficient group will run into a decision for which consensus seems impossible to achieve. Someone just cannot or will not agree with the position being taken. Here again, however, even if total agreement cannot be reached on the problem, agreement can often be reached about the need for some kind of decision. Then, at least, the minority has expressed its position, has announced that it is not ready to change that position, has had a chance to express its own feelings about its position, and has agreed that some decision short of unanimity is necessary.

Leadership and Individuality in Groups

Usually someone writing about groups devotes much of his attention directly to two issues we have circumvented here: first, the issue of group leadership and, second, the issue of maintaining individuality in a group setting. In a way we have already talked indirectly about each of them, but a final word is appropriate here.

What is leadership, anyway? Is it some characteristic of a person, like decisiveness or assertiveness? The answer we have given here is negative. When we talk about leadership, as when we talk about communication, we are not talking about an individual but about a relationship between individuals. So leadership becomes a job, a function, not a set of characteristics. Sometimes, as in the network experiments, leadership is just a function of position in the network. When positions are equal, group leaders are people who do certain jobs in a system of related jobs, principally the job of building and policing an information-processing system that solves problems. If there are any general characteristics of "good" group leaders, they are sensitivity, personal security, and intelligence. For those characteristics probably do help people to build and police functional communication systems.

Authority does not make men leaders. Skill in *using* authority or personal attributes to build a problem-solving organization probably does help to make men leaders.

We should remember, too, that the leadership job is only one job in a group. In fact, if the leader thinks he has to do everything, he probably won't do his job very effectively. We don't have to watch groups much to realize that some people are idea men, others are navigators, still others bring wild ideas down to reality, and so on.

If all these other jobs are part of the leader's job, then we can appropriately think of leadership as everybody's job. If it is the leader's job to encourage other people to assume these specialized roles, then leadership is the encouragement of the development and the carrying-out of such roles and *not* the doing of all of them.

Some writers on groups argue that leadership in a group is in fact everybody's job and that the "good" and "democratic" leader soon has no job. Our argument here is a little different. The group leader has a job to do that is different from other jobs in the group. He should recognize it as a distinct job and do it.

The individuality issue is a tougher one. Many people, observing the tendency of Americans to do more and more in groups, worry about the restrictive social pressures groups may impose on the expression of individuality. Groups can force conformity by punishing anyone who steps out of line.

Yet we need people who step out of line, who think for themselves, who are daring enough to have unpopular ideas.

Certainly groups do exert pressures to conform. And certainly most of us think twice before we risk our membership by breaking the rules of groups we value. Perhaps, however, it is possible for groups to value individuality, too. That they often do not may speak loudly for their emphasis on conformity for its own sake rather than for their emphasis on the solution of problems.

What we must watch out for is the notion that groups have to be always happy to be productive. If happiness becomes an end in itself, then conformity is likely to follow; for conformity means in part that no one can do things to make others unhappy. It is not a happy state that groups need, but a capacity to blow off frustrations so that they can maintain valid communication and thereby adapt to change.

In fact, the thesis of this chapter, in essence, is that groups solve problems best when members feel free to communicate what they think within very wide, not narrow, bounds. Of course, it will also help if the members are people who can and do think. If they are people frightened of authority and frightened of accepting responsibility, they will probably substitute conformity for thinking anyway.

In Summary

No matter what a group member's purposes may be, familiarity with the operating characteristics of groups can be useful.

Problems involving objectives are one major category. Objectives often seem clearer than they are. These problems can be dealt with by building discussion of objectives into the agenda, by taking an early census of members' conceptions of the questions to be worked out, and by periodically re-examining objectives.

Personnel problems are a second major category. These include problems of personalities, mood, individual needs, and the like. Again, open, permissive communication seems indicated to encourage consideration of these secondary but relevant questions.

Navigational problems also plague groups. Groups can get so involved in content matters that they may lose direction. Periodic stops, to shift from content to process, can alleviate these difficulties.

Decision making raises additional problems in groups. Unanimous consensus is an ideal goal if action and initiative outside the group is sought.

Group leadership is seen here as a specialized job in a group, not as a set of personal attributes. Conformity is seen as one result of the emphasis on group happiness and morale as ends in themselves. If problem solving is the end, leadership becomes functional, not personal, and conformity gives way to a search for ideas, unusual or not.

Chapter 17

A problem for the reader:

> You are the training director of a large multiproduct company. You are a lucky training director, because top management is intensely aware of the need for training at all levels. Top management also thinks well of you.
>
> You are called to a meeting in the president's office one day, where you find the president, the personnel vice-president, and some of the senior line officers of the company.
>
> The president says: "Joe, we've decided to go all out on intensive management development. We've spotted a dozen younger men around the company, every one of whom looks like at least vice-presidential timber. Right now they're in third- or fourth-level jobs, as assistant department heads or department heads in some of the smaller de-

partments. They're lightweights now, and we want to make heavies out of them. And we have to speed up the process. We're going to need several top-level people in a year or two. We're willing to stand the salaries of these men up to six months, even if they don't do any productive work. You can have them. Do anything you have to do to make top-flight managers out of them. You can keep them here or take them out into the country somewhere. You can hire consultants and experts; you can send them off to a university if you think that's best. Just turn them into men who can take over in our top spots."

This is the assignment—a carte blanche. Now what would you do?

A problem like this can be broken down into three or four major subquestions. These seem to be the questions a training director would, sooner or later, have to answer:

1. What is a top-flight manager?
2. Under what conditions can people learn to be more like top-flight managers?
3. What are the most useful methods for influencing people to think and act like top-flight managers?

The Top-Flight Manager and the Present Generation of Managers

The first question is probably the hardest one. What is a top-flight manager anyway? If the training director can answer that one, he can set the goals of his training program. But how does one find an answer to such a question?

Some people thought one answer lay in finding the common personality characteristics of successful business leaders. But as the conception of leadership became more sophisticated, most people abandoned that idea, having found as many different personal characteristics as they did leaders.

More recently, instead of working on specific traits or characteristics, researchers have devoted much effort to describing the social background and over-all personalities of successful and unsuccessful executives. If clear-cut results emerged, a trainer might then try to use them as a model toward which to train his people. But the results have not been clear, nor would they be very useful for this purpose anyhow. Models of the personalities that can do a job are not, after all, models of a job. Besides, our engineering methods for achieving those models are pretty poor; so even if we could feel satisfied with building people who are like successful managers, we couldn't do it anyway.

Another direction in the search for answers is analysis of managerial *jobs* rather than of managers themselves. Once we have located and defined the significant aspects of managers' jobs, we can go on to imbue our acolytes with the knowledge and skills that are appropriate.

This search for adequate job descriptions has taken two major forms: job descriptions based on what present managers actually do and descriptions based on analysis of what they *ought* to do. The first has the advantage of practical empiricism. We can *see* what successful managers do. It has the disadvantage of limiting the goal of management development to the present limits of present management. We know the world is changing; we know that even the best-managed company will be faced with all sorts of new problems in the years to come. So why limit our goals to producing new managers who, ten years hence, will be able to do only what present managers do already?

The second alternative, to draw up an idealized version of what the good manager should be able to do in the world of 197?, is no mean task. It has no neat empirical basis. Different people project the future of our economy in different ways. It is somewhat, but not entirely, a shot in the dark.

It is not surprising that many present managers prefer the first choice while many educators prefer the second. For the present manager, what is a better standard for managerial behavior than his own behavior? For the academician, what is more appropriate than analysis and prediction?

The author of this book is an academician. So here is an attempt at a generalized but incomplete characterization of the manager's job in the present and near future. It is not entirely made up out of my own head; neither is it solidly based on experimentation. But my guess is that it will jibe fairly closely with the views of many present-day managers and many other academicians.

A Characterization of the Manager's Job

We can partially differentiate managerial from other jobs by emphasizing the *change* quality of managerial problems as against the relatively static quality of tasks at lower levels. The manager deals largely with unknowns instead of knowns. He is a solver of *unprogramed* problems.

We can also differentiate the manager's job from the executive's job. For the word "executive" implies that the executing function is primary. The managerial job should be *more than an executive one*. It should also include information-gathering and problem-defining functions. Once programs have been worked out, the manager is likely either to "execute" them himself or to pass them on to other "executives."

The manager ought to do more than search for problems and alternative solutions to them. He must translate his understanding into *decisions for action* and thence into *action* itself. This part of the description is the Hollywood version of the manager—not an untrue version, but an incomplete one: the man of decision choosing instantly from among frying-pan and fire alternatives; the man of action implementing his choices in a continuous series of crises; never even given the scientist's freedom to experiment in a no-chips-down laboratory situation.

But the phases of problem and information seeking, searching for alternatives, decision making, and action do not sufficiently differentiate the manager from the rest of us. According to chapter 6, all men seeking to satisfy their needs operate on more or less the same problem-solving basis, though perhaps less dramatically and often less skilfully than managers. They gather information about a situation, search for satisfactory alternatives, act, and then, on the basis of information fed back to them about the effects of their acts, remodify their subsequent acts. "Success" for any man varies with his skill in developing broad and valid sources of information, with his skill in developing and choosing among alternatives, and with his skill in taking action in the chosen alternative.

The factor which differentiates the manager from the rest of us is the *organizational setting* in which he works. Unlike most men (including scientists), the manager operates from a *power position* within a pyramidal structure. He is blessed (or perhaps cursed) with the authority we discussed in chapter 11. Those below him in the pyramid usually see themselves as being more dependent on him than he is on them. And whether he likes the power position or not, he is in it, and many forces in his environment operate to keep him in it. But though he appears to have great and independent power, the actual balance of power in the industrial world seems to have shifted rapidly downward, making the manager's position somewhat awkward. The paralyzed brother has recovered the use of some of his muscles. Where once he knew every operation in his business better than anyone else, the manager cannot now come close to such sagacity. Where he once may have needed help only in the information-gathering and executing phases of his operation, he now often needs it even in the analytical phases. He operates, as we pointed out in chapter 8, in a position that is peculiarly dependent while *seeming* to be independent.

From that position he must somehow perform his functions through his influence on other people. For his task is not a one-shot task but must be performed in a way that will permit him always to return for more. Nor is the typical manager the top manager; he is dependent not only on subordinates but also on his peers and superiors. He expects, and is expected, to act as an extension of his superior's ego. He is expected to think creatively and originally but also to act as his boss would act in a similar situation. The young manager is perhaps even more an apprentice than apprentices at lower levels in the hierarchy. He learns from older managers in a close, personalized relationship. All these psychological factors complicate the problem-solving activities of the manager by requiring him always to deal with difficulties coming from his flanks as well as from the front.

Although the manager's personal ambitions are part of the man rather than the job, they cannot be ignored. For in the hierarchical setting, it does not always follow that the best problem solver (that is, the best solver of industrial and business problems) becomes most successful most rapidly. Most industrial organizations have not been able to escape a kind of double standard for success. While good work does not go unnoticed, good work is not the only thing to be noticed. Executives are judged for their business performance but also for their methods and manners. And even managements that try hard not to judge on such bases seem unable to escape their subordinates' beliefs that such things count heavily. Young managers, anxious to move ahead, believe that the boss prefers certain styles of behavior to others, even if he does not.

This gross characterization of the manager's job suggests that a management-development program ought to be devoted to helping people learn to solve "typical" managerial problems in a "typical" managerial setting; to helping them develop skills in gathering information about diverse areas, skills in analyzing the information they gather, in searching for alternatives, in acting upon their choices. Further, since in large, technologically complicated organizations these skills most often involve many other people, the whole developmental process needs to be accompanied by training in getting the willing help of other people—if "getting willing help" is something learnable. Finally, since the manager's position is such an odd one, of both power and weakness, of independence and dependence, programs for the development of managers should include work in "how to maintain equilibrium and objectivity in the presence of temporal and psychological pressures."

How Do People Learn?

Our second question was, How do people learn to be top-flight managers? Chapter 6 was devoted to the learning process. In that chapter we tried to answer the question,

"What are the minimum necessary conditions for 'higher' learning?" We said that a "learning machine" would probably need a memory mechanism—some device by which it could retain some traces of the information previously brought to it through its sense organs—and an output mechanism to allow it to act upon the world. It would probably have to be stingy, to try to reduce effort. It would need a choice mechanism and some decision rules. And, finally, it would need something like motivation—it would need some goals, some preferences (though they may be built in by the engineer) for certain things over others. In the absence of any one of these characteristics, the capacity to learn, the capacity to modify behavior "sensibly" after experience, apparently could not exist.

When we put these ideas together, we have a partial answer to the question, How do people learn? We can think of learning as a "reorganization" of perceptions. *When new or old things in the perceived world are related to one another in new ways, the person has learned.* When the aspiring manager stops seeing problems through a clerk's eyes and starts seeing them through a department head's eyes, then he has learned something about being a manager. For one difference between a developed manager and an underdeveloped one, we argued earlier, is that managers must tolerate and deal with *unprogramed* frontier problems. The change from lightweight to heavyweight in industry is largely a change in perceptual organization—in the angles and distances from which business problems are seen and in the definitions of problems.

This conception of how people learn has some useful implications for training people for the "ideal" manager's job. First, it emphasizes the relations of parts rather than the content. It says in effect that people can learn something new even when there is nothing new to be learned by putting old things together in new ways. The child learns something new when, without adding to his vocabulary, he patterns his words to form sentences.

In fact, skill in handling patterns of things helps people to solve new kinds of problems. When children understand the relationship between the height of a rectangle and its base, they can find the areas of many kinds of four-sided figures. When they have simply memorized a formula, their ability to generalize is more limited. The conception of learning as "perceptual reorganization," then, also implies that a trainer should emphasize *understanding* as distinct from *knowledge* in the learning process. It leads to an emphasis on simultaneous concern with all aspects of a problem rather than the building-up of individual elements; and by so doing it values mistakes, for mistakes provide insight into relationships.

Our question about how people learn is not yet fully answered. The factor of *motivation* needs to be brought in. Aimless wandering by the trainee, with no destination in mind, is not likely to yield (from the trainer's point of view) very useful managerial learning. People seem to reorganize their perceptions best against the skeleton of a goal or objective. The mere fact of experience, without relevance to needs and motives, does *not* seem to yield much learning.

What we are saying now is something most of us implicitly believe anyway. *People learn when they have a problem to solve.* Knowledge and skill can be packed usefully into the human organism when some goals provide a sensible system for organizing them. In the absence of such goals, the human filing system has a hard time deciding where to categorize its experiences. Management training might therefore begin with practice on managerial problems.

Influencing People To Think and Act Like Managers

Learning to think like a manager, we just said, can probably be helped if people have unprogramed, managerial problems to solve. If our hypothetical training director accepts that idea, he has at least one anchor point from which to start developing a training program.

But granted that people learn by doing, seeing the effects, reorganizing, and doing again, how does a trainer influence them so that they will do, then observe and remember the effects, reorganize, and try again?

Our answer to that question should stem from Part II on influence, especially from our consideration of the AA model. In that section we pointed out that changes in attitude seem to be brought about most readily in an atmosphere in which B sees a problem and takes much of the responsibility and A supports with knowledge and approval. Since what we want to do with fledgling managers is to make them see and work at problems from a new managerial viewpoint, the AA model should be applicable to our training director's problem.

If he uses the AA idea as well as the related learning-is-reorganization idea, he can begin to lay out the framework of a general training plan. First, his training program will focus on managerial problems. Second, the trainer's role will be much like that of the AA buddy's—not the boss's, but the coach's.

Where Do Groups Come In?

These two ideas—the focus on unprogramed problems-to-be-solved and the trainer in an AA type of role—have of themselves little to do with groups. Yet this chapter appears in a section on group behavior.

Groups do come into the picture in trying to answer the very first question posed at the beginning of this chapter: What does a top-flight manager have to do? Part of our answer was that he has to solve managerial problems through groups. Size, technology, and lots of other factors have combined to make the manager more dependent on other people. He needs their help in defining problems, searching for alternatives, and acting out decisions. This is not to make the manager just a "co-ordinator" who needs only to "get along" with people. He has to be a thinker, too, but in an especially—whether he likes it or not—"groupy" environment.

So now we can add to the framework for the training director's program. First, he focuses on *managerial problems;* second, he *shares responsibility,* à la AA; third, he sets up a program that requires trainees to work largely *with and through groups* to solve problems adequately.

One more point is worth making here. Working with groups means influencing and being influenced by other people. In turn, we have already argued that "successful" influencers need to be aware of themselves, of their own motives, their own fears. So the training director might want to go back still another step in his program. He might want to include *opportunities for people to re-examine themselves* as individual human beings.

Alternative Training Techniques

With this sort of framework in mind, the trainer can begin to select some combination of methods and techniques to use as his training tools. Most training directors would doubtless, at this point, begin to reconsider the available alternatives currently in use in industry. They include job-rotation plans, classroom-education plans, apprenticeship plans, multiple and group plans, and problem-solving plans. They can be found in varying degrees and combinations because they are not entirely independent of one another. Some are techniques that can be used within others; some are primarily administrative devices that leave training itself largely to other people. Consequently, it is not proper to try to label any of these mechanisms as better or worse than any others. Any of them can be carried through naïvely and poorly, or well and with wisdom.

Probably the most widespread formal method of management development, even today, is *job rotation*. An executive-in-training is systematically or unsystematically rotated through many jobs at many levels of the organization. In some plans he simply observes the jobs; in others he may work actively in them for a period of several months or a year.

Underlying these plans is the belief that a variety of job experiences provides the trainee with an opportunity to learn "all about the business" and is therefore good preparation for managership. The advantage to a manager of knowing his own business is obvious. It is questionable, however, whether knowledge of the internal workings of his own organization is *all* he needs to know. It is even questionable whether independent experience in each of several jobs provides a man with knowledge of the relationships among the jobs, a kind of knowledge probably more useful to a manager than knowledge of any specific operation. Moreover, rotation plans may—although they do not necessarily—suffer from a kind of passivity and aimlessness resulting from the absence of a clear-cut central goal. Thus, for example, when a man works in a department for three months as part of a rotation scheme, he may learn quite different things from what he would learn either as a regular employee or as a manager who had to look into the department to solve some specific managerial problem. The rotated trainee is in danger of learning superficially, like a tourist in a foreign land. Organizations that use rotation systems often become aware of this difficulty. If they are wise they either lengthen the rotation schedule or set up special assignments which require trainees in rotation to be more concerned with the managerial aspects of the job than with its operational aspects.

It is sometimes claimed that a simple rotation plan is a good way of separating the men from the boys. Those trainees who are poor tourists, who learn only the minimum, can be differentiated readily from those who take initiative and find things to learn, even if those things have not been defined for them. It may well be true that a rotation plan is a useful selection method. The people who take initiatives, who think up problems on their own, may stand out quickly. But that is selection, not training.

Classroom training, including lectures and discussions, is, like rotation, both useful and incomplete. As the rotation system emphasizes experience, most classroom training emphasizes the provision of knowledge. Both knowledge and experience are relevant to the development of management. Both add to the trainee's breadth of perception of the world. But like rotation, classroom courses are likely to be psychologically sealed off from the solution of managerial problems. For in the classroom, learning is tied largely to the trainee's desire to be successful in the class. Only later, when he is faced with managerial problems in which class-room knowledge *would* have helped, is he likely to be fully aware of how many really useful things he could have learned if he had known then what he knows now. Three months of reading and lectures are likely to train inefficiently unless they *accompany* rather than *precede* the need tensions that come from having to solve a management problem. It is paradoxical that industry, which in the eyes of many educators presents an ideal training ground, should be turning to the classroom as an educational device while educators themselves are complaining that the classroom is an inadequate educational mechanism.

Again it is worth pointing out that the adequacy of the classroom must be judged not only against the content and method of classroom teaching but also against the motivation of the student. If a manager-in-training goes to a classroom in search of help with a problem he has already defined for himself, then the classroom, like the AA meeting, can be extremely helpful. But if the student is the passive party in the classroom relationship while the trainers try to pump him full of knowledge, it is likely to be an inefficient method. For learning cannot be exclusive of the needs of the learner. And what is learned best is what is relevant to the current needs of the learner, not what may be relevant to his future needs.

Apprenticeship systems, often combined with rotational systems, are another base for developing managers. Sometimes trainees are attached for extended periods to a particular executive, to serve as his assistant, to live in his office, and, insofar as possible, to do his work. Such systems may provide good opportunities for the trainee to practice working on managerial problems. They may also provide the motivation for acting like an executive. But the quality of the coaching is variable. Political and personality factors limit their usefulness, for the variety of executive problems the trainee is given is left largely up to the executive to whom he is attached. If the executive is either uninterested in the apprentice or feels threatened by him, that particular apprenticeship will provide few learning opportunities.

Still another effort to provide motivation and opportunities for practice in a group setting is the junior *management "board."* A group of lower-level people is elected or appointed to a kind of second board of directors which meets periodically to consider any business problems it chooses to consider, to gather information about those problems, to analyze them, to come to decisions, and to make recommendations to the senior board. While holding their lower-level jobs, young men thus get an opportunity both to tax their own brains on executive problems and to work at the peer level with a group of other "part-time" managers. This approach has the advantage of giving young men an opportunity to view the world as a manager, to be faced with and wade through problems of impending change, and to create changes of their own.

A Problem-Centered Group Training Program

Finally, and this is the model that best fits the requirements outlined earlier, a modification and expansion of the management-board method can be constructed by centering all training on unprogramed managerial problems, by requiring the trainee in a *real* situation to work back from a difficult problem to the kinds of skills and knowledge he needs to solve it. Thus, for example, our training director can ask the president to assign a group of trainees to work on precisely the kind of big and difficult problems that the officers themselves or consultants would ordinarily work on. The problem might be a re-evaluation of the company's personnel program or a re-examination of the sales operation.

If such a project is assigned a group of young men who have never before been faced with a task of its scope and complexity, and if the young men are provided with AA-type resources in the form of company officers and technicians to whom they can go for help, then they will be faced with an almost ideal motivational situation for learning. For if the problem is broad enough, it will require of the trainees knowledge of the business, knowledge of the outside world, knowledge of the sources of information that are available within the company and without it, practice in gathering information from people in the company and perhaps from customers and competitors, practice in analyzing and organizing this information and in selecting among alternative choices, practice in communicating the information accumulated, practice in implementing their recommendations (if they can influence top management to accept them), and finally practice in organizing an unorganized group of young men in accordance with the interests and capacities of the men themselves.

With help, the presence of a large and difficult task and the requirement that these young men jointly carry it out can increase motivation to learn all these things. In fact, it is quite an easy step to work back to another level, to the level of the individual personality. Areas of weakness in individual trainees show up in such a program; so the individual trainee can see them. And if the training staff is wise and helpful, it can utilize this opportunity to encourage each man to re-examine himself and his relationships not only with peers but with superiors and subordinates. It can provide counseling and test data, if people want them. Certainly a large part of skill in working through others lies not only in the individual's understanding of himself but in his understanding of other people's perception of his behavior.

Notice, too, that this model is hard to administer. It works backward. Time schedules cannot be pre-planned down to the hour. It is a plan-as-you-go operation. Time is devoted to areas of skill or knowledge when and to the degree that they become relevant to solving the problem. They cannot all be predetermined. So the trainer has to be on his toes to provide resources, like books and experts, as they become needed, and they are needed whenever the trainees hit a snag in trying to solve their problem.

In Summary

Anyone concerned with developing managers must deal with three key questions: How do people learn? How can a trainer train? And what is a manager?

Learning is defined here as a process of reorganizing perceptions so that new problems of relationship are formed. Training, therefore, necessitates providing trainees with problems that require perceptual reorganization for their solutions and providing these problems in a situation in which relevant knowledge and experience are also available —including knowledge and experience about groups.

The "ideal" manager can be defined in many ways. The emphasis here has been on those phases of the manager's job involving the gathering and analyzing of information, decision making, and action, with a recognition of the unprogramed nature of his problems, his continuous dependence on other people, and the pressures imposed upon him by his position in a hierarchy.

Part IV

PEOPLE IN HUNDREDS AND THOUSANDS
PROBLEMS OF ORGANIZATIONAL STRUCTURE

This final section deals with some questions of organizational theory and some human problems that industrial organizations manufacture along with their other products. Of course, all the problems we have already talked about—problems of individuals, of relationships, and of small groups—also occur within large organizations. But the large organization superimposes some special difficulties on these others, difficulties that seem to be the product of the large industrial organization itself.

Only a few of the problems created by the organizational milieu are discussed here. And even these are only touched upon lightly. For they are massive problems about which far too little useful knowledge has been accumulated.

The perspective of this section is a little different from that of its predecessors. This time we take several structural characteristics of industrial organizations and try to see how they affect people and vice versa. We shall deal with authority, responsibility, the hierarchical nature of industrial organizations, their size, and so on. Then we shall go on to consider how structure and people might be modified and how some new concepts might be useful.

The characteristics we shall discuss are common to most industrial organizations, and, although some of them are equally characteristic of other groups, together they seem to differentiate industrial from other organizational structures. Moreover, they are characteristics that necessarily affect the people who compose the organizations. Size, for example, in its own right, creates communication problems different in kind as well as in degree from the communication problems found in very small groups. The pyramidal shape of industrial organizations similarly creates some distinctive human problems.

The first of the three chapters in this section, then, aims at isolating some special psychological problems that emerge in large organizations; the second considers some alternative ways of coping with those problems; and the third raises questions of organizational theory per se. What's wrong with present theory? What better alternatives are there? The third chapter is speculative but perhaps very important. For the way we think about organizations is changing rapidly. These changes promise to make even recent ideas, like decentralization, obsolete.

Chapter 18

ORGANIZATIONS AND INDIVIDUALS
HOUSES THAT DO NOT ALWAYS FIT
THEIR OCCUPANTS

Many Americans spend about half their waking lives at work—in factories, offices, or stores. This chapter deals with some of the special problems people meet trying to satisfy their needs in these organizational settings.

Much of life in organizations is not very different from life on the outside. Getting along with one's self and with other people is no more or less of a problem within organizations than without. But the organizational environment exerts some pressures of its own, over and above these others. Organizations are a source of stimulation in their own right. Their effects are less easily discernible, perhaps, than the effects of particular people or particular things. Organizations are more like neighborhoods than specific neighbors. But like neighborhoods, they can significantly influence behavior.

Unlike the neighborhood, however, the industrial organization is a place to work, not a place to live. Many people in industry therefore claim that the effect of organizations on people's comfort is unimportant unless comfort is related to productivity. Often, for example, industrial managers hold that the eight hours a day people spend in business organizations are not hours designed for need satisfaction to begin with. They are *working* hours. Americans distinguish work from play precisely because work is not intended to provide contemporaneous need satisfaction. When a man goes to work he should therefore feel that he is sacrificing his eight working hours in order to earn the wherewithal to obtain satisfactions *off* the job.

This clean-cut separation of work from play encounters two difficulties. First, it carries with it the unrealistic assumption, talked about in Part II, that people can actually make such a separation on some neat, rational basis. People cannot shed their personalities at eight o'clock or their personal, non-organizational goals and interests. Even if they sign a frustration-in-exchange-for-pay contract, they are not likely to be able to fulfil their commitment. "Illogically" (but with the *internal* logic described in Part I) they go on using up organizational time trying to avoid personal frustration and to find positive satisfactions on the job.

Second, even if a manager could get his people to accept their jobs as necessary periods of frustration, he probably could not, if chapter 4 is right, get them to stop responding to frustration with aggression. Feelings of aggression are also outside the scope of the contract.

The questions raised in this chapter, therefore, remain appropriate: How is the organizational neighborhood likely to affect the residents' opportunities for need satisfaction? And is it likely to affect behavior? We already said, in talking about communication nets, that the answer to the second question is "yes" for small groups. But what about large ones?

To try to answer these two questions this chapter looks at several common organizational characteristics that exert direct pressure on people's behavior: First, the hierarchical, pyramidal shape of industrial organizations; second, the ideas of individual authority and responsibility that are an integral part of most industrial organizations; and, third, the sheer size of many modern American business enterprises, both in population and physical extent.

Pyramids and People

All American industrial organizations are shaped like pyramids. They become narrow at higher levels. Coupled, intentionally, with this narrowing design is a more or less conscious effort by people at higher levels to encourage people at lower levels to climb. This effort need not be great to be successful because early training and education have already encouraged climbing behavior. Industrial organizations simply continue the process by offering greater rewards at higher levels, rewards that are perceptually real for most of us. They also help the process along by selectively screening out those with less intensive climbing desires.

These two factors, narrowing toward the top and desire to reach the top, combine to create *competition* for advancement. Such competition is likely to be less intense when the whole pyramid is rapidly growing and more intense as the growth rate decelerates. For when the whole pie is getting bigger, everyone can move with it. When the pie's growth ceases, but the diners' appetites do not, competition for a piece of it is likely to be more intense. Fortunately, however, the world is bigger than the company; so even when an organization has stopped growing, its members may continue to climb by leaving the organization—a characteristic and accepted phenomenon in some industries (merchandising is probably the outstanding example) but one fought by management in others.

Still another escape, in static or slow-growth periods, can be found through personnel selection. It is possible to find competent people who do not like to climb or whose levels of aspiration will tolerate a more moderate rate of climb. Some American unions have found a need to remake or replace some of their people at the point at which the battle to organize gave way to the problem of consolidating the union and establishing more "gentlemanly" relations with managements. The old-time battler, useful and effective in winning the war for organization, became a difficult problem when war gave way to diplomacy.

It should not be necessary to add, after the section on influence, that "remaking" people is not always a hopeless process. Experienced industrial counselors will probably agree that helping people to lower their levels of aspiration is one of their most common tasks. Counselors must deal with the young man who did not become superintendent after one year and the older man who did not become president—but whose best friend did. People can, in a great many instances, successfully learn to accept something short of supremacy.

If individual competition results from the combination of the pyramid and egoistic climbing needs, how does such competition affect the productivity of the whole organization? It does not seem safe simply to generalize the advantages of inter*organizational* competition and apply them to inter*personal* competition. A football team may compete successfully with other teams, but it does not follow that it will compete best if its members are in competition with one another.

Interpersonal competition also hits another complication that interorganizational competition manages to avoid; the problem of personal conflict between egoistic and social needs discussed in chapter 5. While parents and education have encouraged us to compete, our dependency has also encouraged our social needs. Climbing at the expense of others is un-Christian and un-sportsmanlike. So required interpersonal competition may disturb people and evoke feelings of guilt, feelings that are not usually present in competition between firms or other large organizations. Again, though, if the criterion is the total productivity of the organization, internal conflicts are relevant only if they hurt productivity.

Still another complication deriving from interpersonal competition is that people at higher levels in companies are the umpires and judges. In competition between organizations no such complication exists. The impersonal "market" is the judge of success. But within organizations the climbing game is played differently. The climber is largely dependent on the personal evaluation made of him by people at higher levels.

This personal element in the climbing process is much like what dependent children encounter. How "good" the job of mowing the lawn is depends largely on parents' reactions. It is a good job if they say so and a bad one if they say so. The youngster may learn that "good" depends as much on parental moods or on his ability to ingratiate as it does on the neatness of the lawn.

Considering all these complications, under what general

conditions can increasing interpersonal competition be expected to increase organizational productivity? At least three conditions come to mind: If the jobs of the competitors are *independent,* not interdependent; if *objective,* not subjective, *standards* for advancement can be established; and if *success* for one *can be separated from failure* for others; then interpersonal competition should result in a net increase in productivity.

Suppose, for example, that a sales manager decides to select an assistant from among ten salesmen. The salesmen know that one of them will get the job, but they do not know which one. Competition for the assistant's job would probably increase total productivity if:

1. The salesmen operated in independent, non-overlapping territories.

2. The manager could devise and communicate an objective standard for selection. For example, he might select the man with the greatest sales increase in the next six months over his past three-year sales average. An objective standard is not easy to achieve. It requires a method for equating territories; it must avoid the pitfall of encouraging salesmen to overload some customers and ignore others for the short-term prize, and so on. And it must mean what it says: the subjective judgment of the manager must not count.

3. The salesmen see the objective standards as reasonable and fair; the salesmen prefer the assistant's job to the satisfactions derived from being out in the territory; and the salesmen do *not* feel that they are hurting one another in the process of striving for the promotion.

Such conditions are difficult to meet, and to the extent that they are not met, the productive advantages of interpersonal competition would be decreased.

In general, these conditions are probably easier to approximate at lower than at higher levels. Jobs are often more independent of one another at lower levels; measures of performance are easier, too. But even at those levels, questions of job separation and individual incentives create difficult, perhaps impossible, problems. At higher levels, where interdependent decision making plays a larger role, a design for ideal competitive conditions is even less likely to be successful.

For at higher levels, jobs are unique rather than standardized. They change, too; new problems show up. The right decisions, even after they have been made, are often hard to judge objectively. And probabilities play a larger part, so that a series of successful decisions, or of unsuccessful ones, *may* occur by chance. All these things force managers to evaluate high-level subordinates more personally, more subjectively.

Further, the same characteristics of pyramids and people create difficulties for superiors as well as for subordinates. One of the rewards for the superior's own successful climb is the right to rule the roost, the right to the attention and respect of subordinates. That reward must be partly given up when the manager is asked to set up impersonal, objective standards for his subordinates.

Managerial resistance to setting up objective standards, even where they are possible, is understandable. The best man objectively may not be the best team member (for we want co-operation, too) or the easiest to work with. A successful pattern of people in a group, even if each is not perfect, may be more productive than a group of "perfect" but poorly related individuals.

Even where competition is an effective stimulus, the reward of promotion up the administrative ladder may not be a reward for some useful people. Research people and other

professionals often fall into this group. The goals of many
of them lie in their professions, not in the administrative
hierarchy. But the organizational pyramid builds in the assumption that higher levels in the organization are more important levels, more deserving of higher income and higher
status. It becomes awkward for the pyramidal organization,
therefore, to have a man at a lower level regularly contributing more than men several levels above him in the structure.

This picture of the costs of interpersonal competition can
be easily overdrawn if one does not take into account the
many other purposes the pyramid serves. It is a shape that
simplifies many problems of communication and control. It
is, on the face of it, a logical structure for handling the
many levels of decision making that must go on in an organization. So, despite all the difficulties that are consequent to
the competition created by the pyramid, there is not sufficient reason for abandoning it, especially since no good substitute is available. Nevertheless, some actions can be taken
to minimize competitive difficulties. These will be discussed
in the next chapter.

But if the emphasis on competition often causes trouble,
the simultaneous emphasis on co-operation causes more. For
like inconsistent parents, managers talk out of both sides of
their mouths. While they want "aggressive," "competitive"
young men, they also want people who "get along," who can
"play on the team." The worst part of these clichés is the
conflict they produce for the young man who wants to get
ahead. Shall he be competitive or co-operative? Does the
manager himself know what he wants, or ought he to spend
some time, like our good influencer, re-examining his own
motives and objectives?

Authority and Dependency

A second characteristic of industrial organizations is the hierarchical, unequal distribution of power among the members. Roughly, power follows the pyramid: higher levels have more of it; lower levels, less. Chapter 11 pointed out that this distribution is brought about primarily through the delegation of authority. Through authority, in addition to personal power, given people at higher levels, power is generally distributed through the organization so that more stays at the top than sifts to the bottom.

The other side of this coin is the psychological one. This distribution of power through authority means that people lower in the organization probably feel more dependent on higher levels than the other way around. So the hierarchical system of authority, in serving other organizational purposes, also causes feelings of dependency.

One important outgrowth of dependency, we have said, is ambivalence: the tendency simultaneously to like and dislike being dependent. That most of us like dependency is apparent when we lose it—when the lonely, independent assignment (like the presidency of the company) ultimately comes our way. That most of us also dislike dependency is shown by our efforts to attain the presidency.

Dependency, by splitting people down the middle, can affect organizational behavior in important ways. It can cause tensions in relationships between subordinate and superior, limiting freedom to communicate and increasing concern about the meanings of the superior's behavior. The signs of these difficulties show up everywhere in industry. At the office party the boss drops in and the atmosphere changes; some people drift away; others talk a little louder or a little faster. Idiosyncracies in the behavior of peers are passed over quickly, but the boss's oddities become legendary; his moods become prime subjects for gossip; his occasional off-hand comments are scrutinized microscopically for their hidden but significant implications.

These behaviors are clues to the subordinate's perspective on the same problem higher management usually defines in terms of merit rating or personnel evaluation. Both perspectives recognize the extent to which life in an industrial organization is life in a medium of dependency, of continuous evaluation—a partial replication of childhood when every act was judged to be good or bad by adults. Such a medium necessarily must draw some of the subordinate's attention away from job functions so that he can focus it on methods of improving his position with superiors. To a greater or lesser degree, any assigned job becomes, in this medium, two jobs: One job is to carry out the assignment, to get the job done; the other (but not always secondary) job is to please the superior. Maybe the two tasks can be melded into one, or maybe the second one can be minimized (some alternatives are considered in the next chapter), but basically dependency causes concern over being judged in any task undertaken within the industrial setting.

Dependency on other people for the satisfaction of one's needs is not unique to industry. It is characteristic of many other phases of American life. Nor is it a new phenomenon. Nevertheless, this problem may be more important today than it was a few generations ago. The veteran businessman's claim that today's young people are too "security conscious" may be valid. Certainly some sociologists agree that Americans today are more "other-directed"—more concerned with other people's judgments and with meeting other people's standards—than they used to be. This concern about approval, about security, about conforming to the "right" kind of behavior intensifies dependency. While such attitudes may simplify the superior's task of controlling behavior, they may complicate the task of bringing about creative, independent behavior.

Another factor bears on this question. Partly to protect their relationships with their own superiors and partly on rational grounds, superiors tend to demand that subordinates objectively *justify* their actions, often in advance of the actions themselves. The superior expects his subordinates to be "business-like" in their *methods* as well as their results. This requirement may force people's dependency underground; so they act more and more independently, though they really would like a shoulder to weep on. The results of chronically unexpressible feelings of dependency can be serious, sometimes physically harmful, for the individual.

The same conditions can be organizationally harmful, too. Most executives are probably familiar with the problem of reporting back to top management some unhappy discovery about the adverse effects of one of top management's pet ideas. Often it is personally dangerous to communicate such information, despite behests by superiors to report the facts "objectively." Even the good subordinate may end up with a watered down, selective report of what he observed, though he cloaks it in the paraphernalia of facts and figures. And if the findings reflect on the subordinate himself, rather than the superior, objectivity becomes even more unlikely.

One result of this "evaluation fear" may be the loss of a most useful organizational tool—the sensitive, intuitive judgment of experienced people. Pressure on the superior to evaluate and on the subordinate to get a positive evaluation can team up to destroy unverbalizable judgment in favor of rational, objective justification.

For instance, the fact seems to be that we do not know very much about how advertising works. But to be business-like, advertising people often have to act as if they do. There would be nothing inherently dangerous in such play-acting if the actors knew they were acting and if they knew they were really using their uncommunicable knowledge and experience. Instead, they often behave as though they could write down and communicate all the relevant facts. The result, for the present, is that many business decisions have more the appearance of rationality than the actuality.

The Jigsaw Puzzle of Responsibility

A third related characteristic of industrial organizations is that they live by the principle of individual responsibility. This is the belief that a task can be subdivided into person-sized pieces, each piece independent of every other and each piece just the right size for an individual. Some doubt exists about whether such an atomistic breakdown is possible in complex modern organizations, and some doubt also exists about whether organizational charts which purport to demonstrate such a breakdown are reality or mirage.

The idea of individual responsibility probably grows out of the fact that industrial organizations are built from the top down, with a continuing need for control from the top. But as the size and complexity of organizations grow, control from the top becomes more difficult—at least the complete, unequivocal control that includes exclusive ownership of all significant decision-making rights.

With growth, management must ask: Now that we are so

big that we must allow lower levels to make some decisions, how can we do so without giving up our independent sovereignty? The idea of responsibility to correspond with authority seems to be the best answer that has been found. Top levels give subordinates some of their decision-making prerogatives, but they hold on to control over the relationship itself. Delegation of authority and responsibility are not irrevocable. They do not include a tenure clause. Thus, the dependency of the subordinate on the superior can remain almost intact. Moreover, by delegating specific, carefully defined areas of responsibility to individuals in individual-sized pieces, control from the top can be maximized. With one individual responsible for each separable phase of activity, difficulties can be spotted quickly and correctives can be applied to a manageable unit—an individual.

This is practical reasoning. In a structure controlled from the top, it makes sense to subdivide the total job into parts, to hold one individual responsible for each part, and at the same time to maintain control over means to the individual's key need satisfactions.

But these same ideas have some secondary effects. The principle of individual responsibility assumes that all decisions can be made by individuals. It assumes also that the whole of an enterprise equals the sum of its separable areas of individual responsibility. These two assumptions lead the traditional concept of responsibility into difficulty in modern big business.

One difficulty arises when the assumption that the whole equals the sum of its individual-sized parts meets the factor of technical specialization. At that point the individual-sized parts stop being entirely independent of one another and become interdependent. The subparts and the sub-subparts begin inextricably to intertwine, and so, too, do individual areas of responsibility.

Consider, for example, an organization that is subdivided primarily along functional lines. It is made up of three major functions: procurement, manufacturing, and selling. Vice-presidents are in charge of these functions. Over time the company's products begin to grow in numbers, so additional people are assigned responsibility for supervising particular classes of products—"product supervisors." Still all products derive from the same raw materials; many are manufactured on the same production lines; and all are sold by the same sales force. Who is now responsible for the manufacture of product X—the manufacturing people or the product supervisors? Who is responsible for deciding how much raw material to procure for product X, especially if procurement of raw material for X automatically requires procurement of raw material for Y and Z? If the product supervisor is held responsible for the over-all success of his product, but not for procurement, isn't he in the position of having responsibility without equal authority? Moreover, if the manufacturing vice-president is responsible for manufacturing, then what is the product supervisor's relation to him?

Overlapping circles of responsibility seem to show up more and more as organizations increase in size and complexity. Individual jobs become more and more dependent on other, previously unrelated jobs. Staff and service activities come into being, and defining their authority and responsibility becomes a nightmare.

Within the general medium of continual personal evaluation, subordinates must come more and more to demand wider and wider realms of authority in order to fulfil their responsibility. Private little kingdoms thus begin to emerge.

Department heads get protective about their prerogatives and about other people moving in on their territory.

These complications are to be expected if a man knows he is being watched and judged continually and also knows that his job is defined in such a way that he cannot hope to do it adequately through his own efforts. He is dependent on his superiors for promotion and advancement and dependent on his peers for help in getting his job done; but he is evaluated by his superiors as though he were not dependent on either. So the plant superintendent is in continual conflict with the industrial-relations manager, because the superintendent's performance is partly dependent on his relations with his union. The industrial-relations manager, on the other hand, to do his job adequately, cannot permit plant-to-plant variations in labor contracts, even though a particular plant could profit from a special contract. The product manager is in continual conflict with the general sales manager because his products are not getting the sales attention he thinks they deserve. But the sales manager feels that he cannot do an adequate job unless he controls the way his salesmen subdivide their time and effort among products.

Size

Still another set of human problems derives from the large numbers of people whose activities must be co-ordinated in modern industrial organizations. Large groups are harder to systematize and control than small groups. Large groups can, in fact, be different in kind as well as degree from small ones. We pointed out earlier that some communication nets, for example, are unique to small groups. They are not applicable to a ten-man group, let alone to a hundred men.

For a group of five people, ten channels of communication are possible; but when the number of people increases to ten, forty-five channels open up, and when the number is one hundred, four hundred and ninety-five communication channels are possible.

The point is that big groups are different from small ones. As organizations grow, some of the principles by which they are organized no longer apply. One writer has drawn some analogies from biology. He points out that Jack the Giant Killer's giant is sixty feet tall and well proportioned. He is ten times as tall as Jack, ten times as broad, ten times as thick through. His volume and mass are a thousand times those of Jack. But being built like Jack, his leg bones are probably ten times as wide and ten times as thick, or a hundred times as big as Jack's in cross-section. So now the giant has to carry a thousand times Jack's weight on supports only a hundred times as big. He probably cannot stand up. Simple proportionate increases in the size of each point do not necessarily make the system grow successfully. The same writer goes on to suggest that as industrial organizations grow, ideas such as span of control, the suggestion box, etc., which may have been useful at one point in an organization's size, lose their usefulness and require complete redesign.

Size, then, goes on to generate many varieties of individual human problems. Increased size increases every man's distance from people who influence his organizational fate. Although immediate superiors have a lot to do with determining where he goes, decisions beyond the immediate superior or even beyond the immediate superior's superior set limits on the speed and direction of his movements. Direct communication with those distant decision makers is almost impossible. The subordinate's anonymity increases, and so does his uncertainty about what will become of him. Each man knows that he is being evaluated and also that he can have little effect on the information his evaluators use or on their interpretation of that information. So size adds to the tensions already instigated by the atmosphere of evaluation.

Size also separates people at the same level from one another. Because free and open communication among all persons becomes more complicated with growth, any man at any level becomes more isolated from others involved in other activities at the same level. So people's opportunities for a "general" business education, for varieties of experience, are fewer. Opportunities for an overview of the whole operation become more difficult. A modern foreman, for example, can easily live his life in a present-day organization and never meet a man who sells the product he is manufacturing. When related people and their related activities are mutually unknown, their perceptions of one another may become dangerously distorted.

Size, by increasing the complexity of communication, increases the probability of *mis*information as well as the probability of decreased total information flow. As the number of people between a decision maker and his source of information increases, the probability of error and mistiming increases—a phenomenon that is most important because of its multiplying effects on attitudes as well as on the quality of business decisions. People, chapter 9 showed, get frustrated and angry at one another when they have difficulty in sending or receiving information. Field people come to feel that the home office is made up of dunderheads, and the home office reciprocates the feelings. Managers recognizing these difficulties may try to compensate by forcing more information through the channels. They may require more periodic reports, set up forms, and themselves make it a point to disperse more information to more people. But though this counteraction may alleviate the problem, it may create additional difficulties—an oversupply of material that the recipient finds difficult to evaluate or even to read. As long as the structure itself makes for long and difficult communication lines, changes in the structure itself would seem to be the only cure.

In Summary

Some characteristics of present-day industrial organizations necessarily affect people. Some of these effects are bad, either because they damage people or because they interfere with the problem-solving activities of organizations. Perhaps none of the bad effects is so bad that it outweighs the advantages of control and economic integration that the same characteristics also provide.

The characteristics discussed are the pyramidal shape of organizations, with its tendency to increase interpersonal competitiveness; the hierarchical distribution of authority, with its tendency to increase dependency and "evaluation fear"; the idea of individual responsibility, with its assumption that a large and complicated task can be cut down into non-overlapping, individual-sized pieces; and the sheer size of modern organizations, with consequent difficulties of communication.

In general, each of these characteristics carries a potential for intensifying conflict and frustration in individuals and for increasing psychological pressures on the manager.

Such psychological difficulties seem to be on the increase because size has increased, because the attitudes and expectations of the new generation of employees are different from those of the old, and because increasing technology requires more and more subdivision of functions into smaller and smaller parts.

Chapter 19

ADAPTING ORGANIZATIONS TO PEOPLE
EFFORTS TO REMODEL

Feelings of competition, of uncertainty, and of intense dependency are organizationally important because they directly affect the way organizations do their jobs. An assistant sales manager, for instance, doesn't bring the market-research people in on a problem they should be in on because he feels the market-research people are screwy longhairs to begin with and because he fears they will claim credit for the solution when the problem is eventually solved. So the assistant sales manager fails to get some relevant information he could have gotten, and his decision consequently suffers. Or a branch office waits six months for a piece of equipment it needs tomorrow because no one in the home office wants to take what they feel is the risk of okaying or denying it. Or the plant superintendent, concerned about his feelings of technical inadequacy, doesn't want the snooty young laboratory boys prowling around the plant upsetting his work force. Or a department manager, faced with a frying-pan–fire decision, calls a meeting of related departments so that the decision can be "shared," i.e., so that top management won't be able to find the right target for its wrath.

The reader can doubtless add indefinitely to this list of business activities that are directly and significantly influenced by the feelings of members of the organizations. These feelings in turn are partly by-products of large, hierarchical organizations acting upon the complicated personalities of men. They are among the reducible but not removable costs paid for the economic yield of such organizations.

The problem can be looked at this way: Organizational factors like authority and pyramidal shapes force management people toward personalistic, subjective, and more or less concrete, short-term, and often defensive behavior; but the changing business environment demands the opposite behavior. It demands that businessmen make multiple decisions and more objective, long-term, planful decisions. The problem is how to modify the organization so that it makes the second kind of behavior more likely.

The ways organizations push people toward individualized, subjective, and overly concrete thought and action have already been discussed, but whence the assertion that the external environment pushes in the opposite direction?

The reasons are many. The first is one we have already referred to, technology. Businesses are more technically complicated than they used to be, so individuals are specialists in smaller parts of the whole job than they used to be. Perhaps not very long ago a new product, for example, could have been launched by one smart operator doing all the jobs himself, but most products today require a variety of research technicians, development and pilot-plant engineers, market researchers, package designers, copywriters, transportation people, merchandisers, and lots more. So whether the people involved like it or not, technology is, at least temporarily, pushing them toward complicated interdependent action—toward the meeting, the committee, and the group. The word "temporarily" is used because there are signs that another technology, namely, information-processing technology, may ultimately *reduce* interdependency and complexity.

Something else that has been happening over the last two or three decades is a sort of "social leveling." Unionism, social legislation, public pressure toward "humanizing" industry, and full employment may be among the more important causes. They have leveled out the power differential between superiors and subordinates in industry. They have, in general, made superiors more dependent on subordinates, though perhaps in any individual case the subordinate has not noticed the change. This leveling of the power differentials has also pushed people toward more group action (collective bargaining, foremen's meetings, and company-wide incentives) and also toward less arbitrary, less personalized decision making.

If these environmental forces are real, we are left with a conflict. To do what "ought" to be done, individual managers within a company need to do more co-operating and less competing; they need to be more problem-centered and impersonal and less subjective and personal; they should think more abstractly and more distantly and less (or perhaps as well as) concretely and immediately. But if an individual manager wants to climb the organizational ladder, it is hard to prove that the opposite way—the competitive, personalized way—is not the best way.

Consciously or unconsciously, many organizations have tried to cope with these problems in many ways. They have tried to modify their structures, to tighten them up. One alternative that has been taken by some companies seems psychologically nonsensical. As their organizations have grown bigger and more complex, they have put *more restriction on individuals*. They have set up more elaborate systems for evaluating people (as distinct from functions); more detailing of individual responsibility and authority; more restrictions on the range of any individual's personal bailiwick; more limitations on communication through more emphasis on "proper channels"; and more demand for black and white rationale for the individual decision maker's decisions.

This re-emphasis of traditional organizational principles may be a trap, like the Chinese handcuffs—the harder one pulls the tighter they get. Do we really meet the problem of overlapping authority, for instance, by trying continuously to un-overlap it with increasingly lengthy and rigorous job descriptions?

What other alternatives are available? There would seem to be four general ones: First, we can change organizational structure so that it conflicts less with its human occupants. Second, we can change personnel and fill jobs with people who somehow are psychologically better able to deal with the conflicting forces that the organizational structure imposes. Third, we can change the "climate" of the organization so that organizational pressures are eased though the basic structure stays intact. Fourth, we can program previously unprogramed areas, thus simplifying the organization.

Structural Changes in Organizations

From a *psychological* viewpoint, perhaps the biggest organizational change that has shown up recently is the change toward *decentralization*. Decentralization is the downward transfer of decision points. What decisions and how far downward are variables. A "centralized" company is one in which many decisions, perhaps all or most unprogramed decisions, are made only at the highest points in the organizational pyramid. As more classes of decisions, especially unprogramed ones, are transferred downward, the organization is more decentralized.

In one sense, decentralization is an admission of organizational defeat. To decentralize is to acknowledge that we cannot handle large numbers of people well enough to win all the economic prizes that logic tells us are the rewards of size. By decentralizing we lose theoretical sources of efficiency—more fully centralized services, more complete information, more fully utilized facilities and equipment, and even better utilized human skills. Logically, at least, a highly organized and centralized organization would offer a multitude of such advantages. Equipment would not have to be fully replicated. "Expert" central services could be provided. Specialists handling the most minute of subspecialties would guarantee the most advanced information possible about problems, and so on. But many large companies are finding that these theoretical efficiencies cannot actually be achieved with our present degree of organizational know-how, so that, in practice, decentralization seems to yield a better net return than centralization. But the development of the problem-solving computer (chap. 6) and other programing techniques may radically dampen current enthusiasm for decentralization.

Decentralization of large organizations makes *psychological* sense because it shortens and simplifies human communication. It brings subordinates closer to the people who control their organizational fate. It lays greater emphasis on competition among groups and less on competition among individuals. It directly increases the independence and autonomy of at least one level of the managerial ladder and indirectly probably increases the independence and autonomy of many more. It puts more emphasis upon evaluating people by their results rather than by their work methods. Thereby decentralization clarifies, if it does not lessen, the dependency of the subordinate and allows him more control over the judgments being made of him.

Decentralization of middle management makes the large company resemble several smaller companies. The creation of small, autonomous decision-making units puts the heads of the units in a position close to that of the independent entrepreneur. If top management really accepts the decentralization principle, it will worry less about the methods used by the decentralized units and more about their results. And it leaves the lowest man in the organization closer to the top by the simple expedient of lowering the top.

Separation of staff from line personnel is another organization change (not a particularly new one) that can help to resolve some of the psychological problems that organizations create, though it sometimes complicates them. Definitions of "line" and "staff" are often vague, but staff people generally are those limited to "advisory" or "supportive" duties. They cannot give orders or make operating decisions as the line personnel can. But staff people do have jobs they are expected to get done. In effect, then, the staff is usually thought to be an exception to the organizational adage that authority must equal responsibility. Staff people *can* be given responsibility without commensurate authority. They are asked to go ahead with their jobs using whatever power tools other than authority they may be able to find. This position at least constitutes recognition, albeit only partial recognition, that authority cannot be perfectly subdivided into individual-sized portions.

Another effort toward resolving the conflict between organizational structure and the changing environment is the emergence of the *committee* as a recognized, built-in part of the organization. It may be troublesome and awkward, but the presence of committee boxes on organization charts indicates awareness that the total organizational job is not the summation of individual jobs. Built-in committees are a sign, too, of recognition that responsibilities must sometimes be shared, even if shared responsibility is hard to control. Committees began to appear first at the tops of organization charts—executive committees and the like. Perhaps one of the reasons is that top people feel *they* can behave responsibly in a dangerously free committee atmosphere, but they are not sure about people on lower levels. Another reason is probably the nature of top-level tasks. They are likely to be novel and unprogramed.

Even at lower levels the modified group decision has been growing in industrial organizations. Officially such decisions remain individual—the individual manager is still held responsible for them. But in practice many decisions made by individual middle managers are mediated, influenced, and pressured by subordinates. These are not group decisions in the extreme jury sense; but all that is left of the old entirely unilateral decision is the official skeleton of individual responsibility. The number and degree of such modified group decisions varies with the managers in question. But the tendency until recently has been for managers to give away to their subordinates (sometimes under duress) a considerable portion of the prerogatives they used to hold close to their vests.

One other kind of informal organizational change initiated at lower levels is helping to ease some of these psychological problems. Independent subordinates seem often simply to break organizational law by *opening up horizontal communication channels,* despite the organization chart. They need them to do their jobs. A district sales manager and a plant manager, for instance, who report through completely separate organizational lines may occasionally take the bull by the horns and decentralize themselves by dealing directly with one another, without going through channels. If they are lucky, i.e., if the move pays off, top management may never bother them. It is surprising how many organizational changes come about this way, despite the risks they entail.

One of the most important ways in which organizations can be modified, and a way not yet very widespread, is by the *addition of internal "sense organs"*—feedback devices (really two-way communication channels)—for detecting internal organizational conflicts almost as soon as they arise. Many of the problems discussed here probably cannot be eliminated altogether, but their intensity and frequency can be decreased if the organization has some ways of spotting its own internal pains. Perhaps it is more fruitful for an organization to locate and correct its difficulties than to try to avoid those difficulties altogether.

Organizations can build internal eyes-on-themselves (analogous to the kinesthetic and proprioceptive senses in people) in several ways. A "department of organization" (a relatively rare phenomenon today) can serve such a purpose. It can search continually for the problems the mother structure is creating—for gaps in authority or for overlapping authority. It can watch for red flags from departments that are getting excessively squeezed by the organizational structure. It can look for places where committees can operate better than individuals and for places where individuals can operate better than committees. It can feed back to the brains of the organization some information about the effects of the organization's own behavior. Unfortunately, many departments of organization don't do these jobs. They draw charts instead.

Personnel departments can sometimes perform the same or a similar function. They can (but again many do not) continuously serve as a feedback channel for psychological and human-relations problems resulting from organizational design, so that the design can be continuously modified to alleviate the pressures that create such problems. They can serve as a second and more direct channel for *everyone* in the organization.

Most organizations already have reasonably effective means for sensing changes in the outside world. And in small organizations the possibilities for face-to-face communication provide them automatically with this kind of sensitivity. But growth forces depersonalization and formalization of communication—so that only business "facts" are likely to get through.

Replacing Personnel

If the conflict between organizational pressures and human behavior is real, then there is another alternative for dealing with it. People differ from one another. So a second alternative is to change the people in the organization, replacing those whose work suffers from these conflicts with people who are not bothered so easily.

Psychological conflict, after all, is psychological, i.e., it is not "real." If two people encounter the same situation, one may feel the effects of internal conflict and may show the effects in his performance. The other may feel no such effect. Might we then find people who could do their jobs without falling into interpersonal competition, or into excessive concerns about their dependency, or into the fruitless search for more and more authority? Perhaps we can find *job-oriented* people whose motivations are primarily aimed at solving problems and only secondarily toward getting ahead or making an impression.

People who are vitally, "professionally" interested in problems-to-be-solved and not interested in authority or advancement or recognition are rare people to begin with; and they are not particularly the kind of people that most businessmen seem to want.

The stereotype of the scientific researcher fits this pattern. He is not likely to be as loyal to the organization as he is to his profession and to the problems he is trying to solve. He may not conform particularly well to organizational standards of manner or behavior but only to the standards he believes appropriate for solving the problems he wants to solve. If he feels that his superior constitutes an obstacle to the solution of a problem, he is more likely to attack the superior than to give up the problem. So he may not be popular with his superior. Moreover, in our American culture, the number of people who find their primary satisfaction in the job-well-done is probably smaller than the number whose satisfaction derives more from the recognition their jobs can bring them.

Managers can select people in at least one other, almost opposite way. They can select "authoritarian" people: people who have strong tendencies to conform to the organization's standards, who will be loyal to their superiors rather than to their work, who will do what is expected of them without much concern about whether what is expected looks reasonable or not, who live by rigid, somewhat uncritical rules. The "typical" office manager is our stereotype here. This is the "taut ship" tack in personnel selection. It is likely to yield results as good as the brains at the top of the organization or as bad.

Changing the Organizational Atmosphere

A third class of alternatives presents itself. One can change the climate within an organizational structure without significantly changing the structure. The structure can operate loosely or it can operate tightly. Rules and regulations can be numerous and detailed, or they can be few and general. Personal competition can be actively encouraged or it can be tolerated as an unpleasant by-product. Proper communication channels can be outlined in detail and enforced, or simply encouraged. Perhaps this is the area in which one great hope for resolving some of these problems really lies. If top management recognizes the need for large hierarchical structures, it may also recognize the difficulties that such structures impose on individuals. Then it can try to use the structure it has built in a way that will minimize personal distortion and maximize the focus on problem solving.

People in organizations will focus their efforts more on business problems if they feel more secure in their jobs and more independently in control of their own destinies. Parts I and II tried to show that the nature of our whole society, the nature of man, and the nature of industrial organizations all contrive to make people see work problems from two angles: first, they are work problems, but, second, they are psychological problems of so handling the work as to increase personal need satisfaction. The relative emphasis given the second problem seems to vary inversely, we said in Part I, with feelings of security and independence.

These secondary feelings push objective decisions toward subjectivity. They can be decreased to the extent that a decision maker feels secure about his position in the organization and feels that he can operate without worrying about evaluation by his superiors. The question then becomes: What are the atmospheric conditions that generally make people feel secure?

Several tentative answers to that question can be derived from the preceding sections of this book: One source of security and independence is *knowledge*. If we know more about what is going on, we have more alternative paths toward our goals, in case we should encounter an obstacle. Moreover, knowledge can be a source of security even if the knowledge itself is unpleasant. Managers, for example, must sometimes choose between announcing an impending layoff in advance or keeping quiet about it until the last minute. Usually the grapevine carries undependable and uncertain information even if management chooses to shut up about it. But certain knowledge (i.e., knowledge directly from management), even about something as threatening as a layoff, may yield greater feelings of security than uncertainty.

A chance to learn is a related source of security because again it is a source of control over one's fate. People who know more, who can do more things, are adding to their capacity to hedge against obstacles.

Participation in decision making is another source of security and independence. Participation is a source of control over the environment. It gives one a better picture of people on whom one is dependent—a better picture of what one is up against in trying to satisfy his needs.

But greater security derives from other sources too. It also results from increasing *confidence in one's superiors*. People can feel more secure when they know their leaders are competent. Demonstration of technical competence by superiors in organizations can in its own right allow subordinates to become more conscious of job problems. But even if I feel that my boss is competent, I may not feel particularly secure in my relationship with him, unless I also know that he likes me. So an atmosphere that is generally approving rather than disapproving becomes another condition of greater security. By this view, those people are more likely to work who do not feel that a call to the boss's office is a sign of impending trouble.

A related source of security is one we talked about in Part II—an atmosphere in which *expression of feelings* is encouraged and accepted instead of suppressed and denied. When one does begin to feel personally insecure, the problem can be dealt with more easily if such feelings can be expressed to peers, to superiors, or even to subordinates. But if worries need to be withheld from others in favor of an external façade of cool rationality, they are more likely to breed and multiply.

Still another major source of security is *proximity between behavior and the effects of behavior*. Knowledge of effects is important because it provides people with a mechanism of control that enables them to change behavior in accordance with the demands of the situation. In industry the effects of our behavior on other people are often invisible because of the barriers that block feedback. If feedback from people about people were a regular and accepted part of an organization's operation, the ultimate result might be a rise in the general level of security and independence. Similarly, an incentive plan is more likely to operate as intended if the subordinate can quickly and directly learn the effects of his work than if results show up indirectly and only after a long delay.

Another point is so obvious that it may not deserve mention. But one way of getting people to think about job problems instead of personal problems is by *evaluation of people's job behavior* rather than of their personal behavior. Perhaps the point is worth talking about because of the recent emphasis on the social and personal characteristics of executives. This emphasis on selecting "good" people (people who "get along") has led to confusion between personal qualities and behavioral effectiveness.

If this book has only furthered that confusion, it has done so inadvertently. For one of its purposes has been to show that there is no "good" personality or "bad" one. The issue is who can work best under what conditions, not who has the "qualities of leadership" or who wears the right tie. The department-store manager may make a mistake when he tries to hire "nice" girls to work in the bargain basement. He may be far better off with tough, crotchety, old characters who are not particularly nice to customers and who are impervious to the pressures they have to face. But personnel managers often feel that some kinds of people are basically good and some are bad, and then go on to select and evaluate on the basis of standards designed to separate the two classes. The same problem extends beyond over-all personnel policy. How many plants are there in which employees do *not* feel they have to look busy when the boss walks in?

How many junior executives do *not* feel that the shine on their shoes is decidedly relevant to their advancement? The author recently asked seventy-five middle executives this question: "On what bases do you really think you are most carefully judged by your superiors?" A very large number put conformity to the superior's personal standards at the top of the list. Effectiveness at a cocktail party can apparently still get confused with effectiveness as a purchasing agent.

These mechanisms aimed at creating an atmosphere of security and independence can be applied informally or through specific policies. Many of them depend mostly on the over-all attitudes of management. Occasionally, though, the whole nature of the subordinate-superior relationship is changed by a conscious major change in policy. The multiple-incentive plans talked about in chapter 13 are a case in point. These top-to-bottom incentive plans, with individual shares based on the total productivity of the whole organization, apparently go far beyond simple company-wide profit sharing. One result seems to be a much more intense focus by everyone in the organization on the job-to-be-done, with a consequent de-emphasis of interpersonal dependency on specific superiors.

The reader may have noticed a resemblance between the last few pages of this chapter and the first few pages of chapters 1 and 2. The resemblance is not coincidental. We're still drawing a dynamic picture of human behavior, although the context has changed from fatherhood to management. Most of us would like our children to be independent, creative, and co-operative without being particularly hostile, tense, or frightened. In the first section we took the view that such children can best be raised in an atmosphere of satisfaction rather than frustration, although some frustration is inescapable. In industry some frustration is inescapable, too, but management may be able to come closer to obtaining independent, creative, job-oriented effort by providing more opportunities for satisfaction—physical, social, and egoistic—than for frustration and deprivation.

"Good" organizations are not organizations that never have problems. There are no such organizations. But perhaps realistically "good" organizations are those that recognize their problems and own some mechanisms for locating and dealing with them. Like fathers, managers cannot hope to control all the experiences their people have in the work environment, let alone out of it, but they can design a structure and an atmosphere in which irrelevant problems can be dealt with and disposed of so that individuals feel free to work at their jobs.

Programing Middle Management

The fourth alternative is new, radical, and growing fast. The reader will note that these problems focus on the middle of the pyramid, the part that has grown most rapidly in recent years. A way to deal with those levels is to make them less important—in numbers and in decision-making responsibility; to take planning away from them; to *program* them. Then their personality problems will be irrelevant.

The evolving technologies of information processing (see the chapter that follows) should lead that way. Ten years hence, the man in the middle of the pyramid may be as routinized as the industrial engineer has made the hourly worker today.

In Summary

The psychological by-products of modern industrial organizations include interpersonal competition, feelings of dependency, and feelings of uncertainty. These feelings generally press toward personalized, subjective, and concrete decision making. The changing business environment, however, seems to call for more objective and more long-term decisions.

Changes in organizational structure can help to resolve this conflict. Decentralization, staff and line separation, more use of committees, and creation of "departments of organization" are changes in the direction of resolution.

Selection either of more stolidly problem-oriented people or more authoritarian people is another kind of effort in the same direction, though it is less practicable.

Changes can also be made in the organizational "atmosphere," changes designed to increase feelings of security and independence.

Finally, programing middle-management jobs may make the psychological problems of middle managers relatively unimportant to the organization.

Chapter 20

RECENT DEVELOPMENTS IN ORGANIZATION THEORY

CAN WE BUILD A BRAND NEW HOUSE?

In the last two chapters we considered the marriage of people to organizational structures. We pointed out some places where they are not very compatible. Then we talked about some efforts to patch up the structures or the people so that the marriage could continue.

But the remodeling ideas are only partial measures, stopgaps and compromises. They don't really "solve" the problem of designing an organization that is fitted to its industrial job on one side and its people on the other.

The trouble is that no real solution yet exists, probably because no very satisfactory theory of organization or technology of decision making yet exists. Instead we have done a lot of blind flying in our organizational planning, combining rules of thumb with sheer guesswork.

The reader may feel that the preceding sentence is not true, that we do in fact have an elaborate theory of organization to serve us as a guide to organizational planning. Isn't the market flooded with books on organizational theory? Don't we have a whole flock of "principles" of organization? Like the principle that "authority should equal responsibility," the "exception principle," the "span of control principle"? Some of these ideas may not feel right when we try to put them into practice, but aren't they still pretty useful? Aren't they responsible for the existence of the organization chart?

The answer to all these questions is, of course, yes. But the fact remains that we have no *satisfactory* descriptive theory of organization.

We can start this chapter by looking a little at these "traditional" theories of organization to see why they are less than satisfactory. We can then go on, not to a better theory (because we are not yet sure we have one), but to some recent and rapid developments in several diverse fields that promise a better theory a decade from now.

What's Wrong with Traditional
Organization Theory?

If we pick up an older textbook on organization theory, we are likely to find it influenced heavily by the thinking of Frederick Taylor and his "scientific management." Taylor was interested mostly in how operating workers executed specific physical acts efficiently. He experimented with and carefully observed people in organizations, though most other "organization theorists" did not. They based their ideas on personal experience and armchair logic. But though Taylor worried empirically about the layout of jobs and the physiological capacities of individuals, he did not pay much attention to people's psyches. And he did not pay much attention to the unprogramed or semiprogramed problems typically faced by people at managerial levels.

It is true that other theorists did worry about larger managerial problems, but they too (in keeping, perhaps, with the psychological and economic thinking of their time) seem to have ignored the complicated humanness of human beings.

Consequently, traditional organizational theory does not fit our present knowledge of human behavior very well. Its errors are largely of omission. It skips over the complexities of human behavior. But just by skipping over human beings, it automatically and implicitly has to make assumptions about them.

First, it implicitly assumes that people try to satisfy only one kind of needs, physical needs, at work. So Taylor and his followers worried about noise and layout, not about social problems. We talked a good deal about that idea earlier, especially in the chapter on incentives.

Second, it assumes an automatic sharing of goals among members of an organization. We need only tell people exactly what to do to contribute their bit; then they will go right ahead and do it, because there are no conflicts in people's working motives. We talked about that earlier, too.

Third, it assumes that people try "rationally" to maximize their rewards, that they want the *best* solution to a problem. In chapter 6 we tried to show how people, in fact, seem to search for satisfactory rather than optimal solutions to problems and to search through the distorting and simplifying glasses of their own needs.

All these ideas are based on oversimplified (if this book is at all reasonable) models of both human behavior and the industrial environment. For one thing, these theories oversimplify the theory-building process itself. They confuse (although this is not so true of Taylor) what people *should* do with what they *do* do. They propose that authority *should* equal responsibility, without much effort to observe whether it does—which might in turn help define it better. And they assume that people should behave in some standard, simple, rational way, without much concern for whether or not they do behave that way.

They also assume known problems and known alternatives, a kind of static world in which management's job is not to find problems but only to solve given ones.

In some ways these simplified assumptions and propositions have been helpful, especially in dealing with routinized, thoroughly programed tasks—the kinds of tasks that occur at lower organizational levels. There the physiological capacities of people are important; control can be fairly tight; the "human" factors can more easily (still not very easily) be ignored. And the world of problems there *is* likely to stand fairly still or at least to keep on repeating itself.

But when we take these ideas into middle and higher levels, they hit real trouble. They hit the *unprogramed* area of problems for which, by definition, specifications cannot be drawn up. Concurrently, they hit trouble because they ignore the *interdependency* of *complicated* people. Then come the problems we described in the last two chapters, as well as the problems of group operation and influence described in Parts III and II. Authority and responsibility become complicated psychological phenomena. People just don't always *feel* responsible because the book says they *are* responsible. Authority doesn't always work the way it should, and so on.

But these are destructive criticisms, and many people will raise at least two arguments against them. The first is that the "principles" of organization theory should not be treated like the Bible anyway. They were never intended to be taken literally. We should instead use them as a "basis for our thinking," though the meaning of that phrase is not perfectly clear.

The second argument is a better one. What is the alternative? What other theory of organization is there? Right now the answer probably has to be that there isn't any. But that is a misleading answer, for if we do not have a finished theory, we have a great many useful ideas about organizations, ideas with diverse origins and relations to one another that are only now beginning to appear. Many of these ideas are useful right now in thinking about organizations, more useful, in this writer's opinion, than most traditional theory. They will be far more useful after they have been better put together into a descriptive theory and then evolved into an applied one.

Some Ideas That Promise a New Theory of Organization

Some of the ideas that bear on a new theory of organization have been included in earlier sections of this book. Many come from strange places, often from people and disciplines that have no interest or experience in industry. In fact, the reason many of these ideas have failed to show up in industry is not so much their newness (many are not really new) as a failure of communication. For it is only recently that industrial-organization theory has been invaded by the social scientists from other disciplines. Psychologists, sociologists, mathematicians, even economists did not often read books by management people or industrial engineers. And vice versa. In the last decade or so it has happily become considerably more respectable for the longhairs to think about industry and the shorthairs to think about science.

Let's look at some of these ideas, putting them into two rough categories: The first is the critical category that has made people wary about traditional organization theory, without necessarily helping directly to build a new one. The second not really independent category is a set of tools that should help make a new approach possible.

In the first category we have ideas, first, from *individual psychology:*

Man is a *diversely motivated,* complicated animal. Although he has much in common with other men, the pattern of one individual is different from the next. So there is no use expecting all of them to respond in the same way to the same stimulus.

Man is an *irrational* animal, if by irrational we mean that he does not always do what we think is best for him. But though irrational, there is an *internal* logic to behavior. So we can understand it if we look at it from the inside rather than the outside and if we try to deal with it all at once instead of in pieces.

Moreover, man is an *interdependent* animal; so if we treat him as though he operated all by himself, our predictions about him will go pretty far wrong.

Finally, man is *describable in non-value terms.* We do not have to assume him to be "good" or "bad" in order to influence him. We can think about what makes him work.

These ideas are the ones we have hit hardest in this book. As far as organization theory is concerned, they tell us more about what's wrong with it than what to do about it—except in this sense: They tell us that a satisfacory theory of human organization or a satisfactory science of management, for that matter, will have to be more consistent than present ones with these characteristics of human behavior.

Still in the first category, we have ideas from *sociology:* People often affect and are affected by their *social environments.* Social groups and social needs, the Western Electric researchers concluded back in 1927, have as much or more to do with productivity than lighting conditions.

Moreover, organization charts do not tell us much about social groupings. If we use sociometric or other observational tools, we find elaborate *informal organizations* existing within formal ones. All sorts of factors like status and power differentials play large parts in organizational behavior; so predictions that ignore these informal realities are not going to come out right.

Sociology has also tried to tie up the characteristics of people with those of organizations by thinking about *roles* that jobs require people to take. Usually a job description does not say much about the psychological pressures of a job; but if we think of the job as a social role a person has to fill and if we realize that individuals occupy many roles in their lives, we can begin to see how and when a particular role will or will not work out for a particular individual. We can see, for instance, that the several roles required of the industrial scientist may be in conflict. Traditional organization theory writes a job role for him like everyone else's at his level in the hierarchy. It ignores the fact that his training and professional affiliations call for a conflicting, independent, and autonomous professional role. Then both management and the scientist get upset because management assumes motivation to fit the standard job role and the scientist finds that, to continue in his role of scientist, he cannot be what management wants him to be.

From the limbo between individual psychology and sociology, *social psychology* has produced some related but different ideas:

The social psychologist has hit at the idea of *influence* (as has Part II of this book), pointing out that any satisfactory theory of organization or management has to worry about influencing people instead of assuming that people automatically want to do what is best for management. Influencing, in turn, is not simply a matter of wielding authority but a much more complex issue that must take individual perceptions and interdependence into account. "Responsibility" becomes something people have to be influenced to accept and feel, not something that can be passed out like the pay check.

The social psychologist has also been working away at the idea of *group behavior*. Like the sociologist (and the two often are indistinguishable) he has shown that *group* factors affect the way people work. He has gone a couple of steps further, too, showing how conditions of morale and productivity intertwine, sometimes supporting, sometimes conflicting, with one another; and showing how group behavior is different from the sum of individual behaviors. And he has come up with a host of how-to-do-it ideas for group operation.

Finally, he has been pushing at ideas of *communication,* showing, as in the experiments on communication nets, how structural factors like communication channels interlace with human feelings and attitudes on one side and problem-solving effectiveness on the other.

This network emphasis has been influenced heavily by non-social scientists, like engineers and mathematicians. These people, as we shall try to show right now, have begun to provide some new tools and concepts. The promise of a new theory of organization may come to fruition when these tools are successfully coupled with ideas about human behavior like the ones we have just discussed.

These other sets of tool ideas have been developing in the last decade or so. Their sources are harder to identify because in these cases communication among sources has been pretty good. In fact, one healthy result of some of them is precisely that the old lines between what is psychology and what is economics and what is statistics are very rapidly breaking down, at least at this frontier.

Perhaps it isn't fair to classify these ideas before they have jelled more firmly. But for exposition's sake, we consider them here under two headings: Ideas about *information and communication* and ideas about *decision making*. Together with several other ideas, they add up to a concern about *systems* and how they operate. Industrial organizations come into the picture as one kind of system; a computer is another; the human body is still another.

Not very long ago some mathematicians and engineers, along with assorted other people, came up with some theoretical ideas about *information and communication*, ideas about how to measure them and how to relate them to communication systems. These developments were related in their origins to another new field of study: *cybernetics* or *control mechanisms*. In industry, applications of these two sets of ideas showed up very quickly, not in the form of changes in organization theory, but in data (information)-processing machines and in the idea of automation (automatic controls).

But the same ideas hold great promise for organization theory. For isn't an industrial organization in large part an information-processing system? And isn't it also an oversized control system? Certainly if we look at the organization from top management's perspective, we can think of it as an elaborate set of interconnected communication channels designed to collect and collate, analyze, and sort out information; and also as a system for making decisions, acting them out, getting feedback information, and correcting itself, much like the interacting system of thermostat (management decisions) and furnace (the acting, operating people).

Ideas about the *decision-making* process are closely related. *Game theory* is relevant here, though game theory has dealt with situations having one knowable best answer. But game theory has provided ideas about strategies and tactics in interpersonal relations that have already proved useful in making certain classes of industrial decisions.

Ideas about decision making have been coming in from other places, too, from economists and psychologists studying the way people make bets. In a way they are bridging some of the gap between the external and internal points of view about human behavior. They are showing that people may not be "rational" in the traditional sense but their decisions have a kind of personal rationality that is consistent and predictable.

Finally, in this realm of new and useful ideas, we have the development of new *mathematical* and *statistical* tools. Changes in statistical and mathematical techniques are making it possible to deal with the dynamic, changing aspects of organizations. We can think about any event in a chain of changing events more readily now; so we don't have to think only about new organizations. We can deal with ongoing, multivariate organizational problems.

Some Integrating Ideas

The reader can properly ask, How is all this going to change organization or management? What does it all add up to? Most observers of these developments will admit they don't know exactly what it will add up to, but they are also ready to bet that it *will* add up and that it will affect the practice of management considerably in the next decade or two.

As far as organization theory is concerned, we can make some pretty good guesses about what the new baby will look like. For one thing, authority and responsibility will not be the key parts of it; *decision making* will. Organization charts, as we know them, will not be important as a picture of an organization; that picture will have to be drawn on a bigger canvas. It will have to show *systems of intercommunicating roles occupied by people trying to solve changing problems in a changing environment.* Moreover, people will not be thought of as rational or irrational, but as partially, *psychologically rational.* We will also be paying far more attention to *different classes of business problems* as determinants of organization and far less to the development of a general structure supposedly applicable to all classes of problems. The idea of *searching behavior* promises to develop too; so we can think of the business organization *searching* for a *satisfactory* alternative and not assume that all the alternatives are already visible or that only the best need be selected.

More briefly, industrial-organization studies of the future may be noticeably different from today's in two apparently contradictory but really quite consistent ways. They will be more concerned with *people* and more concerned with *numbers.* They will be more *psychological* and at the same time more *analytical*. They will take account of the complex nature of people, and they will take account of science as it applies to groups of people trying to solve problems.

In my own opinion, in fact, much of what I have written here, especially in the two preceding chapters, will be obsolete in a decade. For the technology characterized by decentralization and the committee is right now beginning to back up against another technology, the technology of information processing. We are decentralizing and committeeing now because these are the best techniques we now know for dealing with the ever more complicated unprogramed problems of top and middle management. But the newer technology of information processing, epitomized by the high-speed computer, may allow us to program heretofore unprogramable problems. If that promise is fulfilled, we may see the tide of decentralization stop and reverse in the next decade or two. We may see an "industrial engineering" of middle management far greater than Taylor's industrial engineering of the hourly worker. And we may also see a new elite oligarchy at the top of organizations, where much more rather than much less of the organization's thinking will be concentrated. Should such things come to pass, committees will be of little importance in middle management but perhaps more important than ever at the narrow top. The motivation of middle managers will be of less concern, too, because middle managers will be fewer, and fewer still will really be managers.

In Summary

Traditional organizational theories do not provide very good models for the observable facts of organizations. They make unrealistic implicit assumptions about human motivation, about rationality, about shared goals, and about the nature of managerial problems. The "principles" of traditional organizational theory often do not match observable reality. Where they are based on controlled observation of actual organizational behavior, they are based on observation of low, easily programed levels.

But no better theories are available full blown today. What is available is a series of interrelated ideas developed in diverse fields, many of them distant from industry. Psychology and sociology have contributed ideas about the complexity of human motives, about influence processes, and about group behavior. Mathematicians and engineers have recently come up with some exciting ideas about information and control systems. Economists and others have been working on the way people make decisions, especially in competitive games.

These ideas, along with new, more suitable statistical and mathematical tools, promise to lead to a more accurate descriptive theory of organizational behavior. That descriptive theory, in turn, should be accompanied or followed by a more useful set of applications to real organizations.

The results may be radical and rapid. Though many of these ideas smack a little of pie in the sky, our recent history in other fields suggests that the sky is not very far away.

QUESTIONS AND SUGGESTED READINGS

QUESTIONS

Chapter 1

1. If people behave to satisfy needs, why will some people starve to death before they give away a secret? Are they satisfying needs?
2. We said in this chapter that "People are alike" in their efforts to satisfy needs. Do you think that Eskimos are like us in their efforts? How about the inmates of mental hospitals? Do they all abide by the same rules? Or do the rules apply only to normal people?
3. If all our behavior is "caused" because things in the world stimulate our needs, how can people be held responsible for anything they do? Aren't they just pawns, pushed about by the environment? So why punish the murderer? Why not punish the world that "caused" his murdering behavior?
4. What is a "habit"? Is it behavior that is an exception to the rule that "people behave to satisfy needs"? What needs can the "habit" of biting one's nails satisfy?
5. Is there any such thing as a really free choice? If behavior is caused, isn't the choice always predetermined by the cause?

Chapter 2

1. Most of us would like our children to be independent and ambitious but not hostile or suspicious of the world. How can we get the former qualities without the latter?
2. Suppose I gave you a new-born infant and the following assignment: "Train this child so that at age five he is *badly spoiled.*" What behavior might I mean by "spoiled" behavior? How would you carry out the assignment?

3. Now consider the exactly opposite treatment. Are you sure that it would not spoil the child equally well?

4. Suppose I gave you a new employee and the same assignment. How would you spoil him?

5. Look back fifteen or twenty years. Do you think your personality has changed as much as your body? Or would your mother still recognize your personality even if she couldn't recognize your face or voice? Just how have you changed? New needs? New ways of satisfying needs?

6. We often say that children are dependent on their parents. Are parents *independent* of their children? Are managers less dependent on employees than vice versa?

7. We keep on comparing parents with bosses. Is the comparison fair? How is a boss different from a parent? How is a good boss different from a good parent?

Chapter 3

1. If it is true that each of us sees the world through the rose-colored glasses of his own needs, is it ever possible for people to be *objective*? How about scientists? Are they objective? What if we get the perceptions of several people instead of one? Does the pooling of perceptions make for greater objectivity?

2. Suppose you were an advertiser of automobiles. Suppose you know some people want power more than safety and some want safety and are a little afraid of power. Do you think you could advertise both without scaring off all your customers?

3. Suppose you hold an opinion about something. You find that your boss and all your peers hold the opposite opinion. You don't know why they do, just that they do. Do you think your opinion would be changed? Do you think anybody else's would? Why?

4. We sometimes say that businessmen perceive the whole world in terms of their business. If there's a flood they only think about how it will help or hurt their business, and so on. If that is true, do you think businessmen's perceptions should

be "broadened" so that they would perceive the world as public spirited citizens instead of just as businessmen? Why or why not?

5. Do you and your wife see children, politics, and friends the same way? Do you perceive some things differently? Is it necessary that two people see the world from the same angle in order to get along together? If not, why not?

Chapter 4

1. Suppose you wanted to raise your child to act like the "third man," to treat most adverse experience as a deprivation instead of as a frustration. What kind of experiences would you want to put him through?

2. If you set high standards for junior executives, some of them will experience failure. Does that mean you should not set high standards?

3. Subordinates often frustrate their supervisors by acting stupidly or by making mistakes. A competent supervisor, when frustrated, will want to blow off his aggression at the subordinate. Should he? What does it teach the subordinate? If he doesn't blow off, what should he do with his feelings?

4. Suppose you have an ambitious subordinate. He's pretty good but not so good as somebody else. You appoint the somebody else to a new job. How do you tell the ambitious subordinate that he didn't make it?

5. Suppose you have a man who you feel sure will never go much further than he is now. But he wants to. Would you tell him he isn't going to get far in your organization? Would you tell him to keep trying? What would you do?

Chapter 5

1. If I put two quarters on a table and tell you you may have one, will you be in conflict over the choice? What if you know one of the quarters is burning hot, but you don't know which one? Conflict? What's the difference between the two cases?

2. Is it "right" for parents to try to build *conscience* into their children? Wouldn't we be mentally healthier if we didn't feel guilty over things? What would life be like in a conscience-less society?

3. Does repression serve any purpose? Suppose we didn't deny to ourselves the existence of some of our own needs. Could we get along any better in the real world?

4. Is it possible for people to recognize their own needs and still ignore them? Can someone who knows he's jealous of another person get along with him? Could he get along better if he was not conscious of being jealous?

5. Many people get anxious or even freeze up altogether when they have to make a speech or presentation. Why do you think that happens? What kinds of people would it not happen to? How do people learn to feel scared of an audience? Or is it "just natural"?

Chapter 6

1. We use dollar bills frequently. Do you know how many times the figure "1" appears on one? Can you draw a good facsimile? If you can't, why can't you? Haven't you had a lot of "experience" with dollars? You've also had a lot of experience with the alphabet. Can you say it backward as fast as you can say it forward? Why not?

2. Do you think machines can be designed to replace middle managers? Or is there some quality about *human* problem solving that will always make it superior to machine problem solving?

3. Do people learn better and better under more and more pressure? Do you? Do people learn better when there is no pressure?

4. Suppose your company were trying to decide how much to invest in research. Is there a single best answer to that question? What steps would you go through to find a *satisfactory* answer?

5. Suppose I give you a crossword puzzle to do, and you do it. Does that teach you anything about doing other crossword

puzzles faster? Does it teach you anything about *wanting* to do other crossword puzzles faster? Suppose I put a *very tight deadline* on the first one. Would that help you do later ones better than a loose deadline on the first one?

Chapter 7

1. After reading this chapter, how would you handle the job of selecting a new research director?
2. Suppose you decided that the best man for the job was an outsider but two or three of your present people would be pretty good at it. Would you select the outsider? Why or why not?
3. Suppose a test salesman came to your door. Suppose he claimed he could evaluate your executives, showing you their strengths and weaknesses. How would you decide whether or not to buy?
4. Do you think top management should pick people for promotion who can get along with top management? Or should their ability to get along with present management be irrelevant?
5. Suppose your company were using tests for promotional purposes. Do you think you should know your own results? Should you know other people's results? Do you think the use of tests for this purpose would make you like your company better? Would it make you work harder?

Chapter 8

1. Is it ethical to try to influence your peers? Your subordinates? Your boss? Is advertising ethical? Is it ethical to try to get people to want things they didn't want before? Is it ethical to act as though you like people in order to get along with them, even though you really dislike them?
2. In a research operation, a scientist way down the ladder may know more about an important piece of research than the department head. Is the scientist still the subordinate in the relationship?

3. If there are lots of other jobs around, is a superior in a worse position to influence his subordinates than he is in a tight labor market? Isn't the authority written into his job description unchanged? Then why should the labor market have anything to do with it?
4. Suppose you wanted to get your wife to stop serving a dish you didn't like. How would you do it? Why would you do it that way? Do you think that your actions would have any side effects on your relationship with your wife?
5. Is it always easier to influence unorganized employees than organized ones? Why or why not?

Chapter 9

1. How would you decide whether communication in your organization is "good" or "bad"? What would you look at? How could you test it?
2. Is it possible for people to respect a superior even if they know he makes many mistakes? Does a superior need the respect of his subordinates to function?
3. In general, is two-way communication easier between peers than between superior and subordinate? Why or why not?
4. How is the communication between boy and girl before they are married different from after they are married? When is it more valid? Why?
5. Why are receivers often frustrated by one-way communication? Why do they get emotional about it, even in a game situation like the experiment described here? Why don't they just feel deprived and treat it lightly? What needs are involved?

Chapter 10

1. Sometimes a superior will say: "Go down to the Oshkosh plant and bring their quality control into line, but don't upset people down there." Is it possible to change organizations without upsetting people?

2. When you feel anxious or uncertain about your ability to do a job, can you admit it to your boss? To your wife? Would it help if you could? Why or why not?
3. Have you ever begun to like someone you disliked at first? Why did it happen? Did you ever dislike him *more* as you got to know him better? Why?
4. The supermarket, people say, has depersonalized the old personal relationship between housewife and grocer. Is that, in your opinion, bad or good? Hasn't the large company depersonalized relationships among its members? Is that bad or good?
5. In some companies the threat of firing is kept ever present. In others everybody knows that nobody ever gets fired. What are the pros and cons from the management point of view?

Chapter 11

1. Sometimes we say that children *want* someone to exert authority over them, to require them to do certain things. They cannot decide everything for themselves. Does the same hold true for people in industry? Should a superior use his authority if his subordinates seem to want him to? Would you then say he was using his authority "restrictively" or "rewardingly"?
2. Sometimes a supervisor has to use his authority to enforce a rule he himself does not believe in. Should he claim he believes it? Should he pass the buck by telling his people that he is only doing what top management is forcing him to do?
3. Should top management use its authority to make middle management act as though it believed in all company policies? Or should it allow middle people to tell their subordinates they disagree with a policy?
4. Sometimes bosses worry about using their authority, even when they feel they should. They don't like to fire a man or

bawl people out. Why do they feel this way? Is it only because they don't like to hurt other people?

5. Even if we don't want to use our authority to restrict people, don't we have to? Aren't people restricted just by their awareness of our authority? Can we abdicate our authority?

Chapter 12

1. Is it ever possible for a subordinate to influence his superiors? How would you go about convincing your boss that your idea is better than his? Would you have to go over his head to higher *authority*? Any other alternatives?

2. Suppose you were starting on a new job as office manager of a small plant. On your very first day the manager says: "I know it takes time to change a department, but I want you to do something right away about the people in your group. They've been coming in at all hours of the morning. The old office manager was very lax about it. Do something about it *fast*, because it's hurting morale in other departments." What would you do? Suppose the people you were dealing with were all old-timers and you were young and new.

3. Suppose you were a market-research man reporting to the president. The sales manager thinks market research is nonsense, but to finance any studies you have to get sales department funds. How would you attack the problem?

4. Suppose a friend asks you for advice on a personal problem. You think you have just the right advice to offer. Would you give it? Do you think it would be accepted? Why or why not? What is advice, anyway?

5. A good department head under you comes to you very upset because he can't get his people to accept a methods change, even though other departments are succeeding. How would you handle him? Would you try to make him feel better? Or worse? Would you offer to help him? Or encourage him to go on alone?

Questions

Chapter 13

1. I once had a job in which the incentive rate was based on the productivity of a three-man work group. The foreman used to put one new or unskilled man with two experienced ones and then change the group every few days, arguing that it kept the bonus down and motivated the two good men to train the third. What do you think of his arguments?
2. If you got a big raise in pay, would you work harder? If you were promised a big bonus for completing a particular assignment successfully, would you work harder at it?
3. With taxes what they are, do you think the promise of a money bonus would "motivate" the president of your company to work harder?
4. In some multiple incentive plans, employee committees have a right to full information about sales planning and progress. They also have a right to criticize the sales department and to suggest changes. If you were the sales manager, what would you think of such a policy?
5. If you ran a candy store, how would you keep your stock boy from eating up your profits? What incentives could you set up for him?

Chapter 14

1. Does your boss (or do you) say that his "door is always open?" Is it? Would it be a good idea if it were? Should the president of a company with ten thousand employees try to make himself accessible to any one of them who wants to see him?
2. What is the actual pattern of communication in your department? Does everyone communicate freely with everyone else? Would freer communication help? How would you go about encouraging it?
3. Suppose you are the personnel manager of a small company. The president says: "Our communication is lousy around here. People always claim they didn't get the word. I don't

hear about problems till after someone has fouled them up. You're the personnel manager. Do something about it!" What would you do?

4. How would you go about cutting down the disorderliness and wastefulness of a two-way, equalitarian communication net without destroying its advantages?

5. If you look at your own department, is there only one net that works for all kinds of information, or different ones for different information? Does gossip follow the formal network? Should it?

Chapter 15

1. Suppose you resolved to say exactly what you felt from this moment on. Do you think you could actually do it, even if you wanted to? How do you think the people around you would react to it? Would you make friends or lose them?

2. Have you ever felt one thing in a group meeting and said another? Why? Did this covering up help the group solve its problem? Would it have helped more or less if you had said what you felt?

3. Do most people in a work group or a classroom make the same judgments as you do about other members? Do they all think the way you do about the people who you think talk too much? How do you know whether your opinion is shared? If it is, what ought to happen? If it isn't, how ought you to behave?

4. If you were chairman of a committee and thought people were covering up their real feelings and taking the safe course, just yessing, what would you do about it? How would you do it?

5. Should the senior man on a committee serve as chairman? The junior man? Is seniority irrelevant?

Chapter 16

1. Sometimes we feel that particular people are "bad" committee members. Just what is a bad member? How does one say that a man has talked too much? Or not enough? Is it

"bad" for a committee that one of its members is grumpy or disagreeable?

2. Suppose one member of your committee insists on putting his feet upon the table, or swearing, or doing something else others don't do. Should he be stopped? Why or why not?

3. Should a group chairman not express his own opinions for fear that group members will disagree with him? What if he has useful opinions? Does "permissiveness" exclude the leader?

4. Suppose a supervisor operates his department "democratically." At a meeting his people decide to do something he thinks is wrong. Should he shut up and go along? Should he veto?

5. Suppose the supervisor agrees with his people but knows that *his* boss would disapprove. Should he shut up? Should he say that he knows the people upstairs would disapprove? Should he veto without explanation?

Chapter 17

1. Suppose you were given the carte blanche assignment described at the start of this chapter. What would *you* do.

2. Do you think it's possible for a college to teach people to be managers? Or is "experience" in non-managerial jobs necessary?

3. If you went back to school now, do you think you'd learn more than you did before? Do you think you'd get better grades?

4. Does personal counseling have any proper place in management development? Or should a man's personal life be his own business? Should we involve his wife? What is a man's own business and not the company's? Where should the lines be drawn?

5. Do you think a manager trained in the airplane industry could move to the ladies underwear industry and still be successful? Is "managership" distinct from any *particular* company?

6. How about the transfer from managing a small company to managing a large one? Is that possible? Why or why not? How about the other way, from large industry to small?

Chapter 18

1. What are you trying to teach your children about co-operation and competition? Why?
2. Is "co-operation" the same as "conformity"? Can people be independent and individualistic and yet co-operative? Or does one negate the other?
3. A friend of mine is an executive in a small plant owned by his family. He says that everybody has to know everything, everybody is the boss, everybody countermands everybody else's orders. Though he admits they all say what they think and the business is profitable, he wishes it were "better organized" so that each man would stay in his own area of responsibility. Do you think "better organization" is called for? If so, what would it consist of?
4. Do you think your specific job could be so defined that it would be really independent of other jobs and a good or bad performance would be entirely attributable to your own skill?
5. What is "responsibility" anyway? Can you define it? Do you think "joint responsibility" is realistic?

Chapter 19

1. Suppose you had to write instructions for five thousand people. You couldn't see them all face to face for two-way communication. How could you increase the probability that the instructions would be communicated accurately?
2. If the president today gives the sales manager authority to set prices, is that "decentralization" or "delegation"? What is the difference, if any, between the two?
3. Spot any man in your company. Suppose he wants to communicate something upward and his immediate boss blocks it. Is there any *official* way he can get around his boss? If there is a way, is it safe or risky? Are there other ways that could be set up?

4. Suppose something begins to go wrong in a department. Suppose, for instance, that one supervisor begins to lose control over his people and has the beginning of a revolt on his hands. How does top management learn about it? Does it have any sensory nerves to pick up this sort of thing? Does the personnel manager pick up this sort of information?
5. Does your president have an *assistant?* What is the assistant's job? Is his job as clear in your mind as the sales manager's? Does he serve any special communication purposes? Can he short circuit the formal organization?

Chapter 20

1. Does your "responsibility" equal your "authority"? How do you measure responsibility and authority to see whether they are equal or not?
2. The "exception principle" says that information is only communicated to higher levels about "exceptional" events. Thereby top management keeps from being flooded with routine information. Does this strike you as a good idea?
3. What kind of people does your organization try to select? Does it emphasize loyalty and getting along with other people in the organization? Or does it emphasize independence and imagination? Or both? Are both possible?
4. A lot of business schools these days are hiring longhaired professors of psychology, or anthropology, or mathematics. Do you think it's a good idea, or should they stick to more practical faculties?
5. If you could throw away your present organization chart and start all over from scratch, how would the new one be different? Why?
6. Ten years from now, is the president of your company likely to be somebody who has worked his way up from the bottom? Why or why not?

Some references that I list are non-technical, some quite technical. I have starred [*] the ones that should require no special background for industrial people, though they are not necessarily a lazy man's readings. Although some of the others are difficult, I have included them for readers interested enough in a special problem to want to track it down.

PART I: PEOPLE ONE AT A TIME

The material in chapters 1 through 5 is based on many sources. The design and some of the specific examples came primarily from Douglas McGregor and Irving Knickerbocker. They had laid out this kind of material for an introductory course in psychology for engineering students at the Massachusetts Institute of Technology, and I taught it there for a couple of years.

It should be pointed out that not all psychologists are perfectly satisfied with this conception of motivation. For a good, general critique and some alternatives see:

MASLOW, A. H. *Motivation and Personality.* New York: Harper & Bros., 1954.

Other readable and useful books that cover individual personality are:

* HAIRE, MASON. *Psychology in Management.* New York: McGraw-Hill Book Co., 1956.

* LANGER, WALTER. *Psychology and Human Living.* New York: Appleton-Century, 1943.

* STAGNER, ROSS. *The Psychology of Industrial Conflict.* New York: John Wiley & Sons, Inc., 1956.

CHAPTER 2

I mention some findings about the personalities and backgrounds of executives. Here are some references:

* DOTY, R. A., and WALD, R. "The Top Executive: A First-Hand Profile," *Harvard Business Review,* Vol. XXXII (July–August, 1954).

HENRY, W. E. "The Business Executive: The Psychodynamics of a Social Role," *American Journal of Sociology,* Vol. LIV (January, 1949).

* WARNER, W., and ABBEGGLEN, J. C. *Big Business Leaders in America.* New York: Harper & Bros., 1955.

CHAPTER 3

The reader may be interested in other perceptual illusions and ambiguities. Any introductory psychology text is likely to have half a dozen. Figure 2 is from a German psychology laboratory and was drawn before 1900. For some really impressive perceptual illusions, people willing to do a little carpentry will find the following useful:

ITTLESON, W. H. *The Ames Demonstrations in Perception.* Princeton, N.J.: Princeton University Press, 1952.

For more about "perceptual defense" see:

ERIKSEN, C. W. "The Case for Perceptual Defense," *Psychological Review,* Vol. LXI (May, 1954).

For material on the use of projective devices in marketing see:

* SMITH, G. H. *Motivation Research in Advertising and Marketing.* New York: McGraw-Hill Book Co., 1954.

CHAPTER 5

See the chapters by Liddell, Finger, Miller, and Lewin in

HUNT, J. McV. *Personality and the Behavior Disorders.* New York: Ronald Press Co., 1944.

CHAPTER 6

The reader will get a good picture of current learning theory from:

HILGARD, E. R. *Theories of Learning*. New York: Appleton-Century, 1956.
Two other important books on thinking and problem solving are these:
BRUNER, J. S., GOODNOW, J. J., and AUSTIN, G. A. *A Study of Thinking*. New York: John Wiley & Sons, Inc., 1956.
WERTHEIMER, MAX. *Productive Thinking*. New York: Harper & Bros., 1945.
For the source of the ideas about higher-order problem-solving machines by men whose work is of really major significance see:
NEWALL, ALLEN, and SIMON, HERBERT A. "The Logic Theory Machine," *Transactions on Information Theory* (Institute of Radio Engineers, Vol. II [September, 1956]).
For more general material on computers as problem-solving devices see:
* BERKELEY, E. C. *Giant Brains*. New York: John Wiley & Sons, Inc., 1949.
* BOWDEN, B. U. *Faster Than Thought*. New York: Pitman Publishing Corporation, 1953.

CHAPTER 7

The section on informal assessment comes out of an effort made by the author together with Paul Albrecht and David A. Rodgers to train a group of executives in this area. I have purposely avoided citing the source of the excerpt from a test report.
For a good consideration of the method of pencil and paper tests see:
THORNDIKE, R. L. *Personnel Selection*. New York: John Wiley & Sons, Inc., 1949.
For some ideas about the use of clinical methods see:
* ALBRECHT, P. A. "Projective Methods in Industry," *Journal of Business*, Vol. XXVIII (January, 1955).
STERN, GEORGE, STEIN, MORRIS, and BLOOM, BENJAMIN. *Methods in Personality Assessment*. Glencoe, Ill.: Free Press, 1956.
And for a critique of personnel testing see:
* WHYTE, W. H. JR. "The Fallacies of 'Personality' Testing," *Fortune* (September, 1954).

For sociometric techniques see:

HOLLANDER, E. P. "Buddy Ratings: Military Research and Industrial Implications," *Journal of Applied Psychology*, Vol. VII (August, 1954).

For "non-directive" interviewing methods see:

ROGERS, CARL. *Counselling and Psychotherapy.* Boston: Houghton Mifflin Co., 1942.

PART II: PEOPLE TWO AT A TIME

CHAPTER 8

Some good background material for chapter 8 and this whole part may be found in commentaries on American culture:

* RIESMAN, DAVID *et al. The Lonely Crowd.* New Haven: Yale University Press, 1950.

* WHYTE, W. H. JR. *The Organization Man.* New York: Simon and Schuster, Inc., 1956.

For current research on influence see:

HOVLAND, C. I., JANIS, I., and KELLEY, H. *Communication and Persuasion.* New Haven: Yale University Press, 1953.

CHAPTER 9

More details on the feedback experiments described can be found in:

LEAVITT, H. J., and MUELLER, R. A. H. "Some Effects of Feedback on Communication," *Human Relations*, Vol. IV (1951). Reprinted in HARE, A. PAUL, BORGATTA, EDGAR F., and BALES, ROBERT F. (eds.). *Small Groups.* New York: Alfred A. Knopf, 1955.

CHAPTER 11

Our definition of "authority" is more psychological than many. Traditional organization theorists define it variously:

PETERSON, ELMORE, and PLOWMAN, E. G. (*Business Organization and Management* [Homewood, Ill.: Richard D. Irwin, Inc.,

1946]) call it "the power to make and issue executive decisions." Alvin Brown (*Organization of Industry* [New York: Prentice-Hall, Inc., 1947]) calls it "the aspect of responsibility which represents its power of performance." For a more realistic definition and analysis see:

* SIMON, HERBERT A. *Administrative Behavior*. New York: Macmillan Co., 1957, especially chapter 7.

CHAPTER 12

Material on AA is available from many sources. One is:

* *Alcoholics Anonymous*. New York: Works Publishing Co., 1939.

CHAPTER 13

Surveys of what employees want are reviewed in:

* LINDAHL, L. G. "What Makes a Good Job?" *Personnel,* XXV (January, 1949), 263–66.
For insights into the psychology and sociology of incentives see:
* WHYTE, W. F. *Money and Motivation*. New York: Harper & Bros., 1955.
For reviews of the Scanlon plan see:
* DAVENPORT, RUSSEL. "Enterprise for Everyman," *Fortune* (January, 1950).
* KRULEE, G. K. "The Scanlon Plan: Cooperation through Participation," *Journal of Business,* Vol. XXVIII (April, 1955).

PART III: PEOPLE IN THREES TO TWENTIES

For general background on group behavior in popular form see:

* CHASE, STUART. *Roads to Agreement*. New York: Harper & Bros., 1951.
For the sociological point of view on group and other relationship problems in industry see:
* GARDNER, BURLEIGH B., and MOORE, DAVID G. *Human Relations in Industry*. Homewood, Ill.: Richard D. Irwin, Inc., 1955.

HOMANS, G. C. *The Human Group*. New York: Harcourt, Brace & Co., 1950.

For research on the dynamics of groups and other small group problems, two good books are:

CARTWRIGHT, D. and ZANDER, A. (eds.). *Group Dynamics.* Evanston, Ill.: Row, Peterson & Co., 1953.

HARE, A. PAUL, BALES, R. F., and BORGATTA, E. F. (eds.). *Small Groups.* New York: Alfred A. Knopf, 1955.

CHAPTER 14

The research on communication nets (which was stimulated primarily by Alex Bavelas at the Massachusetts Institute of Technology) can be found in:

BAVELAS, ALEX. "Communication Patterns in Task Oriented Groups," in LASSWELL, H., and LERNER, D., *The Policy Sciences.* Stanford, Calif.: Stanford University Press, 1951.

For a more technical recent summary see:

GLANZER, M., and GLASER, R. *Techniques for the Study of Team Structure and Behavior,* Part II. Pittsburgh, Penn.: American Institute for Research, 1957.

For a recent review of the relationship between attitudes and productivity, one that questions the existence of a necessarily positive relationship, see:

BRAYFIELD, ARTHUR H., and CROCKETT, WALTER H. "Employee Attitudes and Employee Performance," *Psychological Bulletin,* LII (September, 1955), 5.

CHAPTERS 15 AND 16

* BALES, R. F. "How People Interact in Conferences," *Scientific American,* Vol. CXCII (March, 1955).

* HOSLETT, S. D. (ed.). *Human Factors in Management.* New York: Harper & Bros., 1951.

One can also find a great volume of literature on the how-to-do-it phases of meetings and conferences. One good source for such literature is the National Training Laboratory in Group Development, National Education Association, Washington 6, D.C.

CHAPTER 17

* AMERICAN MANAGEMENT ASSOCIATION. *Handbook of Executive Development*. New York: American Management Assoc., Inc. 1952.

PART IV: PEOPLE IN HUNDREDS AND THOUSANDS

Besides some books we have already mentioned, like *The Lonely Crowd, The Organization Man, Human Factors in Management,* and *Administrative Behavior,* some issues raised in these chapters are dealt with in:

* DRUCKER, PETER. *The Practice of Management.* New York: Harper & Bros., 1954.

CHAPTERS 18 AND 19

On size and for the analogy to Jack and the giant see:

* HAIRE, MASON. "Size, Shape and Function in Industrial Organizations," *Human Organization,* Vol. XIV (Spring, 1955). See also:

* MCGREGOR, DOUGLAS. "The Conditions of Effective Leadership in Industrial Organizations," in HOSLETT, S. D. (ed.). *Human Factors in Management.* New York: Harper & Bros., 1951.

Problems of union leadership are described in:

* GOLDEN, C. S., and RUTTENBERG, H. J. *The Dynamics of Industrial Democracy.* New York: Harper & Bros., 1942.

CHAPTER 20

Among the books on "traditional" organization theory are:

* BROWN, ALVIN. *Organization of Industry.* New York: Prentice-Hall, Inc., 1947.

* MOONEY, J. D., and REILY, A. C. *The Principles of Organization.* New York: Harper & Bros., 1939.

* PETERSON, ELMORE, and PLOWMAN, E. G. *Business Organization and Management.* Homewood, Ill.: Richard D. Irwin, Inc., 1946.

For points of view more like the one in this book see:

* BARNARD, CHESTER. *The Functions of the Executive.* Cambridge, Mass.: Harvard University Press, 1948.

* SIMON, HERBERT A. *Administrative Behavior.* New York: Macmillan Co., 1957.

See also the forthcoming:

MARCH, JAMES, and SIMON, HERBERT A. *Organizations.* New York: John Wiley & Sons, Inc., 1958.

For communication theory and control see:

CHERRY, COLIN. *On Human Communication.* New York: John Wiley & Sons, Inc., 1957.

WIENER, NORBERT. *Cybernetics.* Cambridge, Mass.: Technology Press, 1948.

* ———. *The Human Use of Human Beings.* Garden City, N.J.: Doubleday & Co., Inc., 1954.

For mathematics applicable to many organizational problems see:

KEMENY, JOHN G., SNELL, J. L., and THOMPSON, GERALD L. *Introduction to Finite Mathematics.* Englewood Cliffs, N.J.: Prentice-Hall, Inc., 1957.

INDEX

Ability to judge people, 97
Accuracy in communication, 123
Achievement need, 5
Action and feelings, 20
Advertising, 266
Aggression, 39–40
Albrecht, Paul, 322
Alcoholics Anonymous, 156 ff.,
  185, 220; applicability of meth-
  ods of, to management, 160 ff.;
  and management development,
  242
Ambivalence, 20, 112
Anonymity, 270–71
Apprenticeship, 246–47
Aspiration, level of, 45, 77, 163–
  64
Assessment of personality, 81 ff.;
  and atmosphere of an organization, 104; day-to-day, 96 ff.;
  formal methods of, 83 ff.; interviewing for, 99–102; scope of,
  81–83
Atmosphere of an organization,
  284–89; and assessment, 104
Authority, 237; and dependency
  in organizations, 263–66; formal aspects of, 143–44; and responsibility of staff and line,
  279–80; as tool for changing
  behavior, 141 ff.; and two-way
  communication, 237
Autonomy, 56, 98

Barriers to communication, 213
Basic needs, 15
Bavelas, Alex, 325
Behavior, basic assumptions, 7
Behavior change: changee's pow-
  er in, 132; and discomfort, 133,
  167; model of, 167–69; motiva-
  tion and, 129–32; responsibility
  for, 138–39
Behaviorism, 83
Body, the, and personality devel-
  opment, 16
Buddy ratings, 94
Business leaders, characteristics
  of, 234–35
Business schools, 77
Business Week, 131
Businessmen: decisions of, 5; ex-
  plosive, 42

Carnegie, Dale, 101
Categories: of personality charac-
  teristics, 98–99; of relationships,
  116–17; in thinking, 73
Causality, 8 ff.
Child rearing, 23–24, 159
Choice situations, 49 ff.
Classroom training, 76, 245
Coding of information, 127
Committees: attitudes toward,
  190–91; emergence of, in or-
  ganizations, 280; noise and re-
  dundancy in, 207–9; operating
  problems of, 216 ff.